PREFACE

I0427684

1. Scope

This publication provides joint doctrine for the military response to mitigate the effects of a chemical, biological, radiological, or nuclear event or incident.

2. Purpose

This publication has been prepared under the direction of the Chairman of the Joint Chiefs of Staff. It sets forth joint doctrine to govern the activities and performance of the Armed Forces of the United States in operations and provides the doctrinal basis for interagency coordination and for US military involvement in multinational operations. It provides military guidance for the exercise of authority by combatant commanders and other joint force commanders (JFCs) and prescribes joint doctrine for operations and training. It provides military guidance for use by the Armed Forces in preparing their appropriate plans. It is not the intent of this publication to restrict the authority of the JFC from organizing the force and executing the mission in a manner the JFC deems most appropriate to ensure unity of effort in the accomplishment of the overall objective.

3. Application

a. Joint doctrine established in this publication applies to the commanders of combatant commands, subunified commands, joint task forces, subordinate components of these commands, and the Services.

b. The guidance in this publication is authoritative; as such, this doctrine will be followed except when, in the judgment of the commander, exceptional circumstances dictate otherwise. If conflicts arise between the contents of this publication and the contents of Service publications, this publication will take precedence unless the Chairman of the Joint Chiefs of Staff, normally in coordination with the other members of the Joint Chiefs of Staff, has provided more current and specific guidance. Commanders of forces operating as part of a multinational (alliance or coalition) military command should follow multinational doctrine and procedures ratified by the United States. For doctrine and procedures not ratified by the United States, commanders should evaluate and follow the multinational command's doctrine and procedures, where applicable and consistent with US law, regulations, and doctrine.

For the Chairman of the Joint Chiefs of Staff:

WILLIAM E. GORTNEY
VADM, USN
Director, Joint Staff

Intentionally Blank

SUMMARY OF CHANGES
REVISION OF JOINT PUBLICATION 3-41, DATED 2 OCTOBER 2006

- Incorporates a modified title and discussion of high-yield explosives. Does not provide doctrine for explosives incidents because of the lack of a residual hazard.

- Characterizes chemical, biological, radiological, and nuclear (CBRN) consequence management (CM) as an overall United States Government (USG) capability and responsibility.

- Clarifies US military roles as a response to reduce the effects of a CBRN incident, regardless of who is designated the USG lead.

- Highlights the importance of emergency preparedness in CBRN CM.

- Adds a section on limitation and mitigation strategies (risk management).

- Adds or revises 13 definitions and deletes 52 CBRN-related definitions in JP 1-02, *Department of Defense Dictionary of Military and Associated Terminology.*

- Incorporates a new Appendix B, "Planning Considerations for Logistics and Other Services from Domestic Base Support Installations and Foreign Theater Assets."

- Incorporates a new Appendix C, "Department of Defense Domestic Chemical, Biological, Radiological, and Nuclear Response Enterprise Assets."

- Reduces redundancies and improves continuity between JP 3-11, *Operations in Chemical, Biological, Radiological, and Nuclear Environments;* JP 3-27, *Homeland Defense;* JP 3-28, *Defense Support of Civil Authorities;* and JP 3-40, *Combating Weapons of Mass Destruction.*

Intentionally Blank

TABLE OF CONTENTS

EXECUTIVE SUMMARY
COMMANDER'S OVERVIEW

- **Provides an overview of chemical, biological, radiological, and nuclear consequence management**

- **Covers domestic chemical, biological, radiological, and nuclear consequence management**

- **Describes foreign chemical, biological, radiological, and nuclear consequence management**

- **Explains Department of Defense-led chemical, biological, radiological, and nuclear consequence management**

Chemical, Biological, Radiological, and Nuclear Consequence Management Overview

The United States Government (USG) approach to managing the consequences of a Chemical, Biological, Radiological, and Nuclear (CBRN) incident is vested in chemical, biological, radiological, and nuclear consequence management (CBRN CM).

Chemical, biological, radiological, and nuclear consequence management (CBRN CM) can be described as the overarching United States Government (USG) capability and the strategic national direction, to prepare for, respond to, and recover from the effects of a chemical, biological, radiological, and nuclear (CBRN) incident at home or abroad, and whether or not it is attributed to an attack using weapons of mass destruction (WMD). When required, the USG will coordinate its response to a CBRN incident in one of three ways based on the geopolitical situation. The Department of Homeland Security (DHS) is the USG lead agency for incident management that would include a domestic CBRN incident. Overseas, excluding homeland areas, the Department of State (DOS) is the USG lead for what is termed foreign consequence management (FCM).

Domestic, Foreign, and Military Situations

The geographic scope of the domestic CBRN response is associated with the US homeland. Generally, when tasked, Department of Defense (DOD) is a supporting agency, coordinating agency, or cooperating agency in support of DHS within the National Response Framework (NRF) and National Incident Management System

Both the geographic location and the political or diplomatic context factor into the selection of USG lead for a CBRN incident response.

(NIMS). A response could take place in a permissive or uncertain foreign operational environment. Requests for FCM originate from an affected nation through DOS. The military situation is when CBRN incidents occur requiring DOD to lead the USG response effort due to the lack of DOS and/or sufficient affected nation 'federal' presence as a result of military operations or for a CBRN incident on a DOD installation.

Emergency Preparedness for CBRN CM

CBRN CM provides the operational framework for those authorized measures DOD takes in preparation for anticipated CBRN incidents to mitigate the loss of life and property and to assist with the response and short-term recovery that may be required. This includes having plans, policies, procedures, training, and equipment necessary to effectively respond to CBRN incidents

CBRN Response

Domestic CBRN response (with DOD and/or National Guard [NG] in Title 10 or Title 32, United States Code (USC), status or state active duty) is a form of civil support (CS)/defense support of civil authorities (DSCA) (with DHS as the lead for coordinating the USG response). **FCM** encompasses the overall USG effort to prepare for and respond to a CBRN incident on foreign territory in which an impacted nation has primary responsibility, and DOS is the lead USG agency responsible for coordinating the USG response. **DOD-led CBRN CM** would typically occur during military operations (e.g., WMD offensive operations), or in other situations in which DOS lacks sufficient local authority or presence to lead the USG effort.

General Planning Considerations for CBRN Response

Planning considerations for responding to CBRN incidents and requests for assistance are influenced by a variety of factors, including USG policy decisions, lessons learned from responses to previous incidents, capability limitations, time, current military operations, studies and analyses, modeling and simulation, live-agent tests and experiments, as well as analysis and exercise of national planning scenarios. CBRN materials present hazards that can be both immediate and delayed. In some instances the delayed effects can cause significant problems for joint forces and may alter planned operations. Operational planning considerations for a CBRN response include: assessment, coordination planning, logistics planning, health services support planning, populace care planning, decontamination planning, site management support planning, religious affairs, and biometric and identity assurance.

Limitation and Mitigation Strategies

Any CBRN response must be rapid in order to save lives and minimize the overall impact of the incident.

In conducting risk management, the joint force commander (JFC) should employ risk assessment procedures to help identify hazards and then assess those hazards to determine risk. Risk management entails developing controls and making risk decisions, implementing those controls, and then supervising and evaluating. JFCs providing CBRN incident response need to have viable plans and be prepared to make rapid decisions with minimal knowledge of the scope and magnitude of the incident.

Domestic Chemical, Biological, Radiological, and Nuclear Consequence Management

CBRN CM conducted by department of defense (DOD) in the homeland in support of civil authorities is conducted as a defense support of civil authorities operation.

In conducting DSCA to include CBRN response, a distinction is made between the different chains of command for active DOD, Title 10, USC, federal forces providing support to civil authorities and for NG forces commanded by the state governor under Title 32, USC, and state active duty. State and local governments are closest to those affected by incidents, and have a lead role in response and recovery. For a federal response to a CBRN incident, DOD support is tailored to the scope and magnitude of the incident.

Roles, Responsibilities, Authorities, and Assets

When conducting CBRN response in accordance with (IAW) the NRF, DOD is in support of an NRF emergency support function (ESF) primary agency or NRF incident annex coordinating agency. Domestic CBRN CM is managed at the lowest possible level, with DOD providing support as directed. Commanders and their staffs at all levels should be knowledgeable about the NRF and NIMS and how their commands fit in to the overall national response framework. The NRF is a guide to how the US conducts all-hazard responses.

Commander, United States Northern Command and Commander, United States Pacific Command

When Secretary of Defense (SecDef) approves a request for DSCA during a CBRN incident, **Commander, United States Northern Command and Commander, United States Pacific Command** are the supported geographic combatant commanders (GCCs) for CBRN responses within their respective areas of responsibility (AORs) as designated in the Unified Command Plan for a federal response. The operational chain of command for federal forces remains with the GCC; the operational chain of command for state controlled NG forces remains with the governor.

Secretary of Defense

SecDef retains approval authority for the use of forces, personnel, units, and equipment for DSCA, to include support to CBRN CM.

Assistant Secretary of Defense (Homeland Defense and Americas' Security Affairs)

Assistant Secretary of Defense (Homeland Defense and Americas' Security Affairs) (ASD[HD&ASA]) serves as the DOD Domestic Crisis Manager and provides policy oversight for all domestic CBRN incident support.

Chairman of the Joint Chiefs of Staff

Chairman of the Joint Chiefs of Staff (CJCS) serves as the principal military advisor to SecDef and the President in preparing for and responding to CBRN incidents, and ensures that military planning is accomplished to support the lead or other primary agency for CBRN CM, and provides strategic guidance to the combatant commanders (CCDRs) for the conduct of operations.

Joint Director of Military Support

Joint Director of Military Support (JDOMS), located within the operations directorate of a joint staff, works closely with ASD(HD&ASA) and the Services, CCDRs, and National Guard Bureau to produce military orders pertaining to domestic emergencies for the CJCS. JDOMS forwards these orders to SecDef for approval, and then to the appropriate military commander for execution.

Military Services

Each Service has some capability (based on its available assets and doctrine) to conduct or support CBRN CM. These capabilities may be called upon, when approved by SecDef, to provide forces, facilities, and assets to the supported CCDR as part of the DOD response to a CBRN incident.

National Guard (NG)

Because forces in Title 32, United States Code, status remain under the command of the governor, NG units may conduct law enforcement missions and are not subject to the restriction of the Posse Comitatus Act

NG forces, unless federalized, operate under the command and control (C2) of the governor and the adjutant general (TAG) in state active duty and Title 32, USC, status. National Guard coordination centers, NG joint force headquarters, joint task forces-state, weapons of mass destruction-civil support teams, chemical, biological, radiological, nuclear, and high-yield explosives enhanced response force package, homeland response forces, Joint Continental United States Communications Support Environment, and Joint Interagency Training Capability form the keystone of NG CBRN response capabilities.

United States Coast Guard (USCG)

The USCG is a military Service, a branch of the Armed Forces, and a law enforcement agency at all times.

The United States Coast Guard (USCG) provides unique authorities, surge capacities, and capabilities for CBRN CM. During CBRN CM operations, the USCG may be supported by DOD forces or may support DOD forces. The National Strike Force deploys specialized capabilities and incident command expertise to support lead agency, incident commander, and federal on-scene coordinator preparation and response to CBRN incidents, hazardous substance releases, oil discharges, and other emergencies.

Combat Support Agencies

Combat support agencies provide direct support to CCDRs during emergency situations and are subject to evaluation by CJCS. Defense Threat Reduction Agency (DTRA) provides operational and technical advice and support to DOD components and other USG departments and agencies, as requested and approved, regarding CBRN CM operations.

Command Relationships

Domestic CBRN CM may engage the full spectrum of government, nongovernmental organizations, and the private sector.

Unity of effort can be achieved without unity of command and is the predominant solution in domestic CBRN response operations. Success requires unity of effort, which respects the chain of command of each participating organization while harnessing seamless coordination across jurisdictions in support of common objectives.

Military forces always remain under the control of the chain of command as established by Title 10, USC, Title 14, USC, Title 32, USC, or state active duty. NG Soldiers and Airmen may serve either in a federal status like other reserve soldiers, or in a state status (state active duty or Title 32, USC), under the command of the governor. The state governors, through TAGs, control NG forces when those forces are performing active duty in their state role and when performing active duty under Title 32, USC. Legislation allows for a dual-status commander to have command authority over both federal and state forces. A dual-status commander provides a means for providing unity of effort for military forces operating in Title 32, USC, and Title 10, USC. A dual-status commander must be duly appointed and can be an active duty officer who accepts an additional state commission or can be a federalized state NG officer. At the operational level, the joint field office ensures unity of effort by identifying agencies that have the requisite capabilities to reach the common objectives or the ability to adapt their wide-area operations in light of the response by bringing their core competencies to the interagency forum. The JFC can facilitate unity of effort with civil authorities at the tactical level by recognizing the incident commander's need to integrate the JFC's resources into his incident action plan, while remaining cognizant that US law prevents direct tasking by any entity outside the military chain of command.

Considerations for Domestic CBRN CM

Considerations for domestic CBRN CM include:

The joint force in a CBRN environment. The joint force is also responsible for protecting each member of DOD in support of civil authorities. The CBRN environment causes joint forces to plan in a unique way and recognize the primary reason for employment of the joint force is to support civil authorities and mitigate the consequences of a CBRN incident.

Layered CBRN response. The NRF describes a tiered response and emphasizes that response to incidents should be handled at the lowest jurisdictional level capable of handling the work. The response to a CBRN incident requires the integration and synchronization of capabilities from the local, state, tribal, and federal level.

Integrated CBRN CM framework. During a CBRN incident, DHS coordinates the federal government's incident management efforts in support of the civil authorities. However, it is likely that the major elements of operational framework will have already been established IAW strategic decisions made by state and local responders in the initial hours of the response effort.

Organizing considerations. A joint task force (JTF) established in support of CBRN CM is organized in a manner similar to a conventional JTF.

CBRN response options. The Joint Publication (JP) 5-0, *Joint Operation Planning,* phasing model is adapted for domestic CBRN response operations with the following phases:

Phase 0—Shape - interagency coordination, planning, identification of gaps, exercises, and public affairs outreach;

Phase I—Anticipate - alerting and preparing the joint force may be directed through a CJCS warning order, planning order, or alert order;

Phase II—Respond - executes deployment of forces to key theater nodes and to the joint operations area (JOA) to save lives, minimize human suffering, and maintain public confidence;

Phase III—Operate - planning and execution efforts are synchronized and integrated with the efforts of the supported civil authorities, as well as other military operations that may be occurring simultaneously within the same operational area;

Phase IV—Stabilize - scaling down of operations as DOD Title 10, USC, forces, Title 32, USC, NG, and/or state active duty utilization diminishes with the associated completion of a majority of incident site mission assignments; and

Phase V—Transition - consequences of the CBRN incident have been mitigated and adequate support of civil authorities has been provided such that further support is no longer required.

Unique Planning Considerations in the Domestic Operational Environment

Unique planning considerations may include the following:

Base Support Installation (BSI). A BSI is a military installation within the US or its territories controlled by any military Service or agency, in or near an actual or projected domestic emergency operational area, designated by DOD to provide military support for DOD and federal agency disaster response operation efforts.

United States Army Corps of Engineers (USACE) Services. USACE can provide water, ice, construction materials, and engineer services when activated under ESF#3 and ESF#6 (Mass Care, Emergency Assistance, Housing, and Human Services).

Mortuary Affairs. The joint force may aid federal and state agencies by providing mortuary affairs assistance.

Decontamination Planning. The Environmental Protection Agency is the ESF coordinator and primary agency responsible for hazardous waste.

Control Zones. In CBRN response, control zones are established to ensure the safety of all responders and control access into and out of a contaminated area. The three zones established at a chemical, radiological, nuclear, and some biological incident sites are often referred to as the hot zone, the warm zone, and the cold zone.

Applicable Laws and Agreements in the Domestic Operational Environment

Key **executive and legislative guidance** documents include: Homeland Security Presidential Directive-5, *Management of Domestic Incidents;* The Robert T. Stafford Disaster Relief and Emergency Assistance Act; The National Strategy for Homeland Security; the National Strategy to Combat Weapons of Mass Destruction; and the National Strategy for Countering Biological Threats. Some key **DOD guidance** documents include: The Strategy for Homeland Defense and Civil Support; the Department of Defense Directive 3025 series of directives that provide policy on and responsibilities for CS activities; and Chairman of the Joint Chiefs of Staff Instruction (CJCSI) 3125.01, *Defense Support of Civil Authorities (DSCA) for Domestic Consequence Management Operations in Response to a Chemical, Biological, Radiological, Nuclear, or High-Yield Explosive (CBRNE) Incident.* The NRF is a guide to how the nation conducts all-hazards response.

Foreign Chemical, Biological, Radiological, and Nuclear Consequence Management

Foreign consequence management is assistance provided by the USG to an impacted nation to mitigate the effects of a deliberate or inadvertent CBRN incident.

From the national level, FCM encompasses USG efforts to assist partner nations to respond to incidents involving CBRN contaminants and the coordination of the US interagency response to a request from a partner nation following an incident involving CBRN contaminants. DOD's CBRN response includes efforts to protect its citizens and its Armed Forces abroad, as well as those of its friends and allies, in order to mitigate human casualties and to provide temporary associated essential services. When requested by DOS and directed by SecDef, DOD supports FCM operations by performing CBRN response activities to the extent allowed by law and subject to the availability of forces.

Roles and Responsibilities

Impacted Nation. Primary responsibility for responding to, managing, and mitigating the consequences of a foreign CBRN incident resides with the affected nation's government. When overwhelmed, the impacted nation is responsible for requesting foreign assistance and sharing all relevant information about the CBRN incident with international partners.

The Department of State. Unless directed otherwise by the President, DOS coordinates all USG support to an affected nation. After such an FCM support request by DOS is approved by SecDef, DOD commences its support to the affected nation as part of the overall USG response.

The US Embassy/Chief of Mission (COM). Normally, all USG support to the affected nation will be coordinated by the responsible COM and country team.

Geographic Combatant Commanders. Each GCC has the inherent responsibility to provide support to DOS, the lead for FCM, unless otherwise directed by the President. Each GCC develops plans for FCM within their assigned AOR and is prepared to deploy a liaison element to the vicinity of the incident site to liaise with the US embassy and to provide situational awareness to the supported CCDR.

Service Chiefs. When directed by SecDef, provide forces (to include forces from the Reserve Component) as part of the supported GCC's response during a CBRN incident.

Installation Commanders. As in the US, if a CBRN incident occurs, US commanders on foreign territory may, when requested by the impacted nation, exercise their immediate response authority; however, it is more restrictive (limited to saving lives) than within the homeland.

Authorities and Assets

In the event of a CBRN incident affecting foreign territory, various authorities exist to govern the response. The two major laws which govern US responses to foreign CBRN incidents are the International Disaster Assistance section of the Foreign Assistance Act (Title 22, USC), and the military humanitarian response authorities set forth in Title 10, USC. Organizations that could respond to an FCM incident include: foreign emergency support team; consequence management support team; DTRA consequence management advisory team; US Armed Forces Radiobiology Research Institute; United States Air Force Radiation Assessment Team; US Marine Corps Chemical-Biological Incident Response Force; and United States Army 20th Support Command (CBRNE).

Command Relationships

SecDef designates the supported and supporting combatant command relationships, and the supported CCDR establishes the command relationships of assigned forces for each specific CBRN response. The DOD supports the lead federal agency during USG FCM operations unless otherwise directed by the President. DOD forces remain under the C2 of the supported CCDR. DOS retains responsibility for coordination among USG entities

Affected Nation Considerations

The affected nation has primary responsibility for responding to, managing, coordinating other nations' augmenting support, and mitigating the consequences of a CBRN incident within its borders. A major part of any FCM operation is augmenting affected nation operations, not replacing them. In order to avoid duplication of effort, affected nation capabilities need to be determined.

Joint and Multinational Force Considerations

CJCSI 3121.01, *Standing Rules of Engagement/Standing Rules for the Use of Force for US Forces (U),* outlines the DOD standing rules of engagement (SROE) and standing rules of force for US forces. In general, when conducting FCM, SROE should be applied. However, CCDRs may augment SROE with supplemental measures or by submitting supplemental measures to SecDef for approval. The US has standing agreements with some foreign governments that allow for the sharing of high-level intelligence (e.g., special category), but in all cases, the release of classified information to multinational partners is made IAW the national disclosure policy. The ability of the JTF to work with all organizations and groups is essential to mission accomplishment. Conceptually, the civil-military operations center is the meeting place of these elements, represented by US Service liaisons, military liaisons from participating countries, Office of Foreign Disaster Assistance representatives, DOS personnel, affected nation representatives, and representatives from the United Nations, nongovernmental organizations (NGOs), and intergovernmental organizations.

Unique Planning Considerations in a Foreign Operational Environment

As in the domestic operational environment, CBRN response is based on a six phase construct; however, phase names and associated activities differ from the JP 5-0, *Joint Operation Planning,* model. The six phases are:

Phase 0—Shape - ensure DOD is organized, trained, equipped, and prepared to support USG efforts to minimize the effects of CBRN incidents on foreign soil;

Phase I—Situation Assessment and Preparation - actions required to conduct situation assessment and preparation, including the timely and accurate assessment of the CBRN situation, preparation for deployment, and deployment of selected advance elements;

Phase II—Deployment - SecDef-approved CJCS deployment and/or execute order designating the intermediate and/or forward staging bases and establishing formal command relationships (i.e., supported and supporting commanders). The order serves as the formal authority for the deployment of forces;

Phase III—Assistance to Affected Nation Authorities - begins with the arrival of required military assistance at the incident location and supporting locations and ends with the determination that DOD support is no longer required or appropriate;

Phase IV—Transition to Affected Nation and/or Other Agencies - begins with the formal implementation of the transition plan for those tasks and responsibilities being accomplished by DOD and ends when directed by SecDef or the affected nation has assumed full responsibility for response activities; and

Phase V—Redeployment - redeployment of US military forces involved in CBRN CM operations or the formal transition of those forces to a purely disaster relief or humanitarian assistance mission.

Applicable International Laws and Agreements

The complexity of FCM policies, treaties, and agreements requires continuous involvement of the staff judge advocate or appropriate legal advisor with the planning, control, and assessment of operations. Because of the international nature of FCM efforts, this will also include continuous interorganizational coordination to establish the legal authorities, capabilities, and limitations associated with engaged organizations. International law, policies, treaties, and agreements to which the US is a signatory identify certain rights and obligations that may affect joint operations. These legal requirements may pose constraints and restraints. They shape the design of operations and campaigns that deal with support to an FCM mission.

Department of Defense-Led Chemical, Biological, Radiological, and Nuclear Consequence Management

DOD conducts CBRN CM to mitigate hazards in support of operations or to support others in response/recovery (when required/as directed).

All DOD CBRN CM capabilities are designed to be used in support of military operations. Like any other DOD capability, these military assets may be used in support of civilian operations or joint or multinational forces, as directed. Mitigating the hazard reduces the threat to personnel, facilitates freedom of action, and supports mission completion.

Roles and Responsibilities

Office of the Secretary of Defense (OSD) coordinates JFC requests for support and forces with other USG departments and agencies and coordinates through DOS for support from partner nations and NGOs. OSD coordinates with the interagency for the transition or transfer of responsibility of CBRN CM operations to other USG departments and agencies, international agencies, or other countries, as appropriate. OSD coordinates with both DOS and the Joint Staff to obtain international legal authorities, protocols, standards, and agreements and multinational support for operations.

CJCS through the Joint Staff coordinates with combatant commands and Services to make sure that DOD-led CBRN CM operations are executed in compliance with domestic, international, and foreign laws, policies, treaties, and agreements. They assist with interagency support for operations and assist in planning and exercising activities within the interagency process. They also coordinate and provide intelligence support to the CCDRs for threat identification and prioritization.

GCCs plan and execute DOD-led CBRN CM operations within their AORs. They incorporate DOD-led CBRN CM operations into their operational plans. GCCs also provide for intratheater movement of specialized personnel and equipment and coordinate transportation of suspect or confirmed CBRN related material, to include weapons, agents, delivery systems, and infrastructure for short- to long-term storage, protection, dismantlement, destruction, or disposal.

DTRA provides operational and technical advice and support to DOD components and other USG departments and agencies, as requested and approved regarding CBRN CM operations.

Command Relationships

The JFC coordinates the response to a CBRN incident in the assigned JOA. The JFC requests additional support through the appropriate GCC. The GCC coordinates with DOS for support from other USG departments and agencies or foreign countries. For DOD-led CBRN CM, the JFC is the supported commander.

Joint Force Considerations

In the context of DOD-led CBRN CM operations, the appropriate JFC assumes responsibility for the execution of operations within the JOA when a CBRN incident requiring a response occurs, mission permitting. The GCC approves end states for these operations by phase within the JOA. One major objective is to conduct DOD-led CBRN CM operations without jeopardizing critical military operations and objectives; however, commanders should plan for the diversion of combat forces and possible changes to overall end states and objectives due to the significance of a CBRN incident.

Planning Considerations During Military Operations

DOD-led CBRN CM operations may be required to facilitate combat operations, and depending on the nature and purpose of the activities, may require coordination with response operations of multiple countries, partners, and a wide variety of international organizations and other NGOs. DOD-led CBRN CM operations can occur at any point in a campaign; therefore, these operations should be considered as a branch to contingency operations.

General Planning Considerations

Many important DOD-led CBRN CM activities take place as shaping (phase 0) activities and are included in theater campaign plans, regional combating WMD plans, and contingency plans. International law, policies, treaties, and agreements to which the US is a signatory identify certain rights and obligations that may affect DOD-led CBRN CM operations. These legal requirements may pose constraints and restraints and shape the planning and execution of operations. To protect both DOD forces and civilian populations, DOD-led CBRN CM mission planning should address both immediate and long-term effects of dispersed CBRN hazards. Planning should include the capability for CBRN hazard identification and assessment, protection, avoidance, and decontamination.

CONCLUSION

This publication provides joint doctrine for the military response to mitigate the effects of a chemical, biological, radiological, or nuclear event or incident.

CHAPTER I
OVERVIEW

"You can't improvise consequence management."

Honorable Paul McHale
Assistant Secretary of Defense for Homeland Defense
Visit to Joint Task Force Civil Support
29 October 2004

1. General

a. This publication focuses on the US military response to reduce the effects of a chemical, biological, radiological, and nuclear (CBRN) incident, regardless of who is designated the Unite States Government (USG) lead. This includes the response to both deliberate and inadvertent releases of CBRN threats and hazards. As preparation is a requirement for effective response, emergency preparedness (EP) activities are discussed as well. A US military response is not automatically triggered by a CBRN incident.

b. **USG Approach to a CBRN Incident.** The USG approach to managing the consequences of a CBRN incident is vested in chemical, biological, radiological, and nuclear consequence management (CBRN CM). CBRN CM can be described as the overarching USG capability and the strategic national direction, to prepare for, respond to, and recover from the effects of a CBRN incident at home or abroad, and whether or not it is attributed to an attack using weapons of mass destruction (WMD). When required, the USG will coordinate its response to a CBRN incident in one of three ways based on the geopolitical situation. The Department of Homeland Security (DHS) is the USG lead agency for incident management that would include a domestic CBRN incident. Overseas, excluding homeland areas, the Department of State (DOS) is the USG lead for what is termed foreign consequence management (FCM). In either of those situations, and when directed, Department of Defense (DOD) typically supports the USG lead. A third scenario could require DOD to lead the USG effort during military operations when the host nation (HN) is unable to respond properly, or DOS is unable to lead the USG response. Also, a USG response is not necessarily triggered by recognition of a CBRN hazard or environment.

(1) **CBRN Hazards.** CBRN hazards are CBRN materials that, if released, could create an adverse effect within the environment. If the size and scope of a CBRN hazard and/or environment exceeds established parameters, civil authorities may declare an emergency and the situation may be deemed a CBRN incident. However, only when local, tribal, or state authorities are overwhelmed by the situation would a USG response normally be required. Subsequently, if there are shortfalls in federal and state CBRN capabilities, the USG approach would likely require a request for DOD assistance in the form of CBRN CM.

(2) **CBRN Incidents.** A CBRN incident is any occurrence resulting from the use of CBRN weapons or devices, or the release of CBRN hazards, to include toxic industrial materials (TIMs) from any source. This may include the emergence of CBRN hazards arising from counterforce targeting during military operations. Domestically, an incident

may result in the President declaring an emergency or a major disaster. For CBRN incidents occurring on foreign soil, either an HN or intergovernmental organization (IGO) could request a USG response, or if it is likely to create a deleterious domestic effect, such as the spread of infectious disease or radioactivity across borders into the US, that may require the President to declare an emergency under the National Emergencies Act. Outside of certain response requirements discussed in DOD issuances, an order from the President/Secretary of Defense (SecDef) is typically required for DOD CBRN response.

(3) **CBRN CM.** CBRN CM considers the capabilities and limitations of the affected civil authorities, from the local first responders, up through the state response, to the federal (national) level. When the civil authorities up to and including the federal level lack necessary capabilities to mitigate the situation, or they anticipate being overwhelmed, military support typically is requested. For all domestic incidents (including a CBRN incident), the *National Response Framework* (NRF) and the *National Disaster Recovery Framework* provide national guidance for incident management and acknowledges the DOD as a full partner in the federal response when tasked. DOD and Chairman of the Joint Chiefs of Staff (CJCS) issuances frame US military support of a USG response for foreign and domestic CBRN incidents.

(4) **CBRN Response.** DOD installation commanders develop CBRN responses for the installation as part of their installation emergency action plan in accordance with (IAW) Department of Defense Instruction (DODI) 2000.18, *Department of Defense Installation Chemical, Biological, Radiological, Nuclear, and High-Yield Explosive Emergency Response Guidelines,* and DODI 6055.17, *DOD Installation Emergency Management (IEM) Program.* Note: "CBRN response" is captured in the NRF and in Presidential Policy Directive (PPD)-8, *National Preparedness.* Domestically, DOD conducts CBRN response in support of the broader USG activities to prepare for, respond to, and provide a foundation to recover from CBRN effects as a result of natural or man-made disasters. The term FCM still applies to foreign support through DOS to an HN and is a valid term when used accordingly.

c. **DOD Perspective of CBRN CM.** The strategic national direction outlined above leads to the characterization of CBRN CM as DOD support of the overarching USG response to a CBRN incident at home or abroad. As such, a CBRN incident may be managed at the national level (USG or HN government), with DOD providing support as directed. During military operations, the USG would typically have DOD lead the response. Examples of CBRN incidents related to military operations include those that result from the execution of US military operations (e.g., offensive operations against WMD facilities); and a CBRN attack or inadvertent release affecting civilians in areas in which the US military is responsible for civilian security, safety, public health, etc., as determined by the President.

(1) Ideally, each CBRN response may (see Figure I-1) include a whole-of-government approach as required by the President or lawful directives. While NRF incident management includes operations to "prevent, protect, prepare, respond, and recover" from an incident, and FCM includes operations to "prepare US forces to provide requested assistance," CBRN CM addresses only the common areas of "prepare" and "respond" within the USG overarching response to reduce the effects of a CBRN incident.

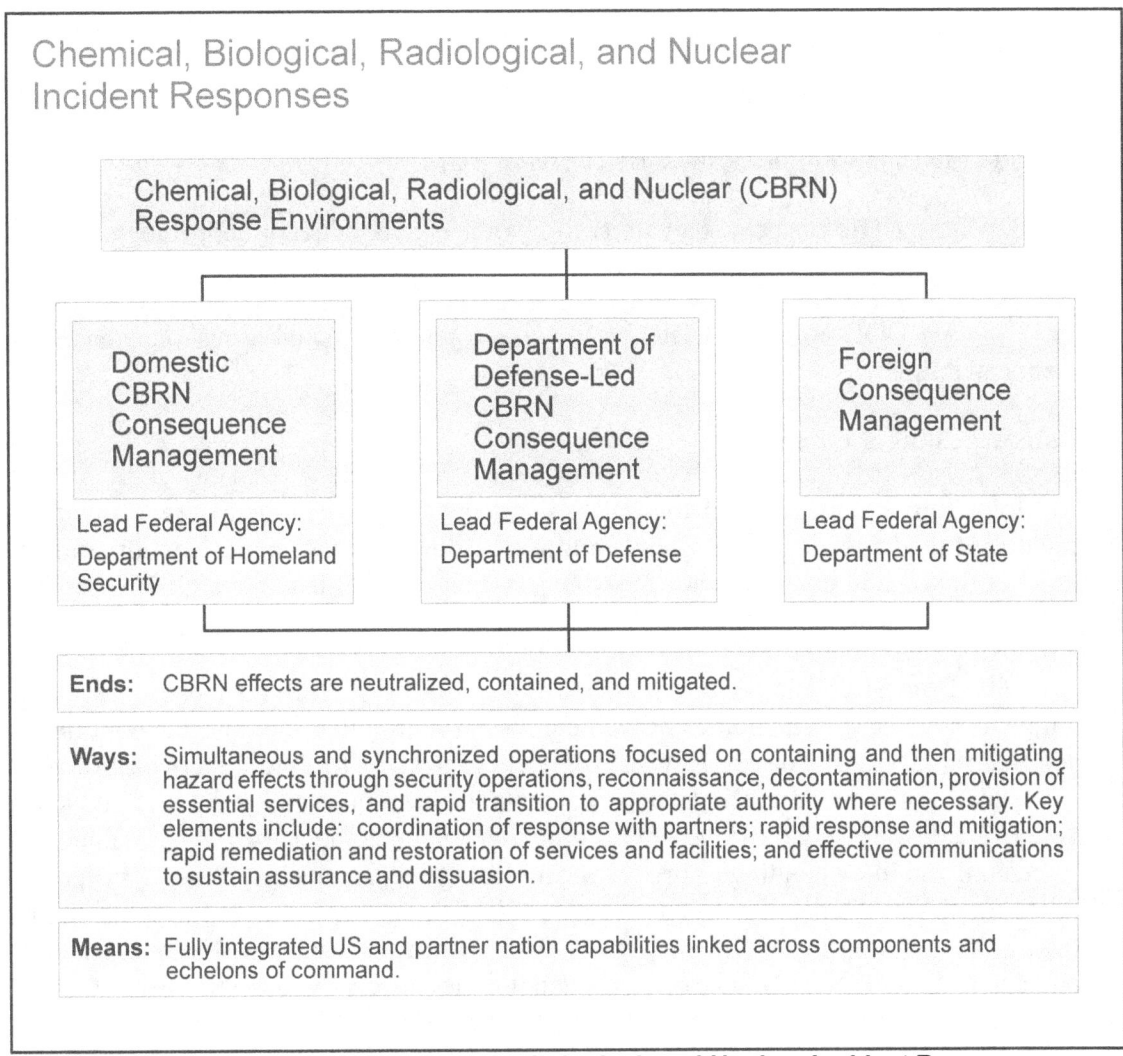

Figure I-1. Chemical, Biological, Radiological, and Nuclear Incident Responses

(2) CBRN CM operations typically include four activities: planning, preparation, execution, and assessment. Within the CBRN CM process, the execution activity is further expanded into two subordinate activities: response and short-term recovery. Assessment begins with planning and is continuous from before an incident through post-incident activities.

(3) No single concept of operations exists that covers the entire range of DOD CBRN CM activities. The following guidelines or principles should be considered:

(a) DOD conducts CBRN CM to mitigate hazards in support of operations or to support others in response/recovery when directed/requested.

(b) For DOD, the CBRN environment is hazard-focused and may involve deliberate, prolonged actions in and around the hazard area to support response and recovery efforts.

(c) When required/directed, DOD conducts CBRN CM as soon as possible to support mission completion.

(d) DOD can conduct CBRN CM wherever the hazard may be: on the battlefield or in support of domestic CBRN CM or FCM.

(e) DOD can access a variety of resources to conduct or contribute to CBRN CM.

(f) DOD conducts CBRN CM using a tailored, scalable response based on inherent capabilities.

2. Domestic, Foreign, and Military Situations

a. Joint forces may respond to CBRN incidents under several different situations characterized as domestic, foreign, and military. Both the geographic location and the political or diplomatic context factor into the selection of USG lead for a CBRN incident response.

(1) **Domestic.** The geographic scope of the domestic CBRN response is associated with the US homeland. The homeland is the physical region that includes the continental United States (CONUS), Alaska, Hawaii, US territories, and surrounding territorial waters and airspace. For most domestic CBRN incidents, when requested by the affected state, DHS coordinates the federal government's incident management efforts to include the resources utilized in responding to or recovering from terrorist attacks, major disasters, or other emergencies. Generally, when tasked, DOD is a supporting agency, coordinating agency, or cooperating agency in support of DHS within the NRF and National Incident Management System (NIMS). The complex and unique aspects of domestic CBRN CM are detailed in Chapter II, "Domestic Chemical, Biological, Radiological, and Nuclear Consequence Management."

(2) **Foreign.** A response could take place in a permissive or uncertain foreign operational environment. Requests for FCM originate from an affected nation through DOS. Chapter III, "Foreign Consequence Management," outlines the specific details of DOD CBRN response under FCM.

(3) **DOD-Led.** The military situation is when CBRN incidents occur requiring DOD to lead the USG response effort due to the lack of DOS and/or sufficient affected nation 'federal' presence as a result of military operations or for a CBRN incident on a DOD installation. On-scene commanders may take appropriate action in responding to life-threatening situations while awaiting DOD/DOS tasking (see information on immediate response in subsequent chapters). More information on CBRN CM and how the DOD CBRN response effort associates with the USG effort is provided in Chapter IV, "Department of Defense-Led Chemical, Biological, Radiological, and Nuclear Consequence Management."

b. DOD has an associated preparation and CBRN response framework for specific employment of military forces in the USG effort in each of the three designated situations.

3. Emergency Preparedness for Chemical, Biological, Radiological, and Nuclear Consequence Management

CBRN CM provides the operational framework for those authorized measures DOD takes in preparation for anticipated CBRN incidents to mitigate the loss of life and property and to assist with the response and short-term recovery that may be required. This includes having plans, policies, procedures, training, and equipment necessary to effectively respond to CBRN incidents.

a. **Planning and Policies.** All geographic combatant commanders (GCCs) are responsible for planning effective coordinated responses to CBRN incidents in their areas of responsibility (AORs) IAW DOD policies and law. United States Northern Command (USNORTHCOM) and United States Pacific Command (USPACOM) plan to respond to domestic and foreign incidents. Guidance documents are listed in Appendix A, "Key Legal, Strategy, and Policy Documents and International Protocols."

b. **Training and Equipment.** Responding to a CBRN incident requires specialized training and equipment, especially in warm (decontamination) and hot (contamination) zones. However, CBRN response forces receive required training and equipment to mitigate CBRN effects under a variety of conditions. Procedures for employing forces to effectively respond to the CBRN incidents are detailed in subsequent chapters.

4. Chemical, Biological, Radiological, and Nuclear Response

a. Domestic CBRN CM is the USG effort to prepare for and respond to a CBRN incident within the US and its territories IAW the NRF. Domestic CBRN response (with DOD and/or National Guard [NG] in Title 10 or Title 32, United States Code (USC), status or state active duty) is a form of civil support (CS)/defense support of civil authorities (DSCA) (with DHS as the lead for coordinating the USG response). Domestic CBRN response leverages the total force capabilities of the Active Component (AC) and Reserve Component (RC) (NG, and reserves) in the homeland. The DOD CBRN Response Enterprise is an integrated AC and RC approach to CBRN response. As such, different elements of the DOD CBRN Response Enterprise may be in direct support of different entities at any given time. For example, NG forces may be under the command and control (C2) of a state governor while Title 10, USC, forces are under the C2 of Commander, United States Northern Command (CDRUSNORTHCOM) in support of the lead federal agency (LFA).

b. FCM encompasses the overall USG effort to prepare for and respond to a CBRN incident on foreign territory in which an impacted nation has primary responsibility, and DOS is the lead USG agency responsible for coordinating the USG response. DOD provides support as requested by the impacted nation, coordinated through DOS, and approved by SecDef. The USG may provide FCM to an affected nation either at the request of the affected nation or upon affected nation acceptance of a USG offer of assistance.

c. Domestic and FCM responses formally begin when support is requested by either domestic or foreign civilian authorities, and continues until either those civilian authorities have determined that DOD support is no longer required or otherwise directed by SecDef. The final phase of USG operations will almost always be addressed and coordinated by civilian authorities in both the domestic and foreign situations. This final recovery phase may or may not require continued DOD assistance, depending upon the hazard and the circumstances.

d. In DOD-led CBRN CM, DOD serves as the lead USG agency, although it may be supported by other organizations. DOD-led CBRN CM would typically occur during military operations (e.g., WMD offensive operations), or in other situations in which DOS lacks sufficient local authority or presence to lead the USG effort.

e. **The Joint Force in CBRN Response**

(1) Due to the potentially catastrophic nature of a CBRN incident, a DOD joint force may be called upon to assist with a civilian CBRN incident prior to civilian resources being overwhelmed or depleted. Even prior to being formally tasked to assist, the joint force commander (JFC) should strive to develop full situational awareness with respect to the incident's cause to better understand the impact and to prevent further injury or harm to the civilian populace or the responding joint force. Situational awareness is especially important in suspected or known adversary attacks for force protection considerations.

(2) SecDef designated supported JFC is ultimately responsible for the DOD CBRN response and its role in providing resources to mitigate the consequences of the CBRN incident.

f. Many DOD strategies, activities, and programs support preparation for a CBRN response. Examples include unit training, local, regional, and national and international level planning, and national and command exercises in both the domestic and foreign environments. Security cooperation and partner activities (e.g., multinational exercises, exchanges, experimentation, and counterproliferation and nonproliferation activities), while not a part of FCM, still serve to foster positive working relationships and build partner capacity to prepare for and respond to CBRN incidents, which may reduce the need for US forces in FCM operations.

g. **Notional Joint Task Force-Consequence Management (JTF-CM) Structure.** A joint task force (JTF) may be established, or an existing one tasked, to provide or facilitate the provision of a variety of response capabilities to mitigate the incident. These capabilities may be located within the current force or they may have to be requested from other DOD sources and attached temporarily to the JTF. The capabilities may be CBRN specific (e.g., CBRN reconnaissance, decontamination) or general (e.g., security, transportation) capable of functioning in CBRN environment. For example, some tasks, associated with CBRN CM technical rescue, require the rescuers to function in personal protective equipment (PPE), a specific capability that all rescue units may not possess. Possible capabilities the JTF might be tasked to provide or facilitate are included in Appendix C, "Department of Defense Domestic Chemical, Biological, Radiological, and Nuclear Response Enterprise Assets." The exact composition of each element will be based on incident type and severity.

(1) **CBRN CM Command and Control Element.** This element focuses on the overall management of the incident as well as the intra-team communications, interagency communications, and ability to provide situational awareness to adjacent agencies and supported higher headquarters. The CBRN CM C2 element should provide:

(a) Secure encrypted digital voice and data communications via Nonsecure Internet Protocol Router Network (NIPRNET)/ SECRET Internet Protocol Router Network (SIPRNET)/Global Command and Control System.

(b) High-speed secure multimedia communications with reachback capability.

(c) Warning reporting services.

(d) Functionality to conduct incident simulation and projection exercises.

(e) Assistance in dealing with displaced civilians (civil affairs).

(f) Assistance in transitioning support to civilian authority.

(2) **CBRN Reconnaissance and Surveillance Element.** This element provides capabilities to locate, detect, identify, quantify, collect samples, survey, observe, monitor, report, and mark contaminated areas.

(3) **CBRN CM Decontamination Element.** This element supports methods and technologies required to neutralize or remove hazardous materials (HAZMAT) including chemical warfare (CW) agents, TIMs, biological warfare agents, and radiological contamination. The capabilities needed for decontamination include:

(a) Rapid assembly and dissemination of the decontamination capability at multiple sites.

(b) Decontamination of personnel, ambulatory and non-ambulatory.

(4) **CBRN CM Medical Element.** This element supports force health protection and all capabilities required for the transport, tracking, diagnosis, and treatment of casualties involved in a CBRN incident.

(5) **CBRN CM Force Protection Element.** This element supports the protection of DOD personnel attending to a CBRN CM incident. Separate security elements may be required to provide convoy, airport, military aircraft, seaport, and ship security, as appropriate to the mission being performed. Additionally, coordination with USG crime scene investigators may be necessary. The force protection element may be called upon for:

(a) Implementing appropriate antiterrorism (AT) measures.

(b) Establishing early warning systems within the JTF operational area.

(c) Providing convoy and patient transport security.

(d) Incident site control, to include entry and exit management.

(6) **Search and Rescue Element.** This element supports all capabilities necessary to search for and rescue casualties from a contaminated or hazardous environment. Casualties are usually decontaminated prior to transit from the incident site. This element requires specialized technical rescue training to support the rescue of personnel and equipment from a CBRN environment using unique equipment for structural collapse (urban) search and rescue.

(7) **General Support Element.** This element supports all capabilities necessary to provide the general support to all the other mission areas and maintain force readiness. This includes providing the transportation, maintenance, engineering, and personnel support services to enable the effective employment of the other mission areas.

Guidelines for establishing a JTF and standing JTF headquarters can be found in Joint Publication (JP) 3-33, Joint Task Force Headquarters.

h. **Doctrinal Publication Relationships.** Several joint doctrine publications relate to CBRN response and provide critical information on employment of forces in a CBRN environment. JP 3-41, *Chemical, Biological, Radiological, and Nuclear Consequence Management,* shares a relationship with several publications within the joint doctrine hierarchy, specifically: JP 3-11, *Operations in Chemical, Biological, Radiological, and Nuclear (CBRN) Environments;* JP 3-28, *Defense Support of Civil Authorities;* JP 3-29, *Foreign Humanitarian Assistance;* JP 3-40, *Combating Weapons of Mass Destruction;* and JP 4-02, *Health Service Support.* However, each publication stands alone, as each has a particular focus and scope. The National Strategy to Combat Weapons of Mass Destruction identifies the three pillars of combating WMD as: nonproliferation, counterproliferation, and weapons of mass destruction consequence management (WMD CM). The National Military Strategy to Combat Weapons of Mass Destruction also identifies WMD CM as one of the eight military mission areas to combat WMD. As such, it will include capabilities to perform CBRN CM. As a mission area for DOD, WMD CM is action authorized by SecDef to mitigate the effects of a WMD attack or incident and, if necessary, provide temporary essential operations and services at home and abroad (JP 3-40, *Combating Weapons of Mass Destruction*).

i. **Global Considerations.** Whether in WMD form or occurring due to natural events, disasters, or accidents, CBRN threats and any resulting incidents and accidents may require coordinated international action. The US partners with other nations to encourage nonproliferation and counterproliferation of WMD, promote increased security for storage of all hazardous CBRN materials, and also build capacity to respond to global CBRN related incidents.

j. **Pandemic Influenza (PI) and Other Infectious Diseases.** A pandemic is an outbreak of an infectious disease that may be of natural, accidental, or deliberate origin, occurring over a wide geographic area. It is unique in that it is not a discrete event but a prolonged environment in which military operations, including any CBRN response, may continue. The National Strategy for Pandemic Influenza (NSPI) uses a three-pillar construct

Joint Publication (JP) 3-11, *Operations in Chemical, Biological, Radiological, and Nuclear (CBRN) Environments,* focuses on maintaining the joint forces' ability to continue military operations in a CBRN environment. This is done by describing the CBRN environment in a strategic context, providing a CBRN defense framework, discussing planning and operational considerations, and highlighting the complexities of sustainment. It expands the discussion of CBRN passive defense actions in JP 3-40, *Combating Weapons of Mass Destruction,* to include those plans and activities intended to mitigate or neutralize adverse effects on operations and personnel resulting from the use or threatened use of CBRN weapons and devices, and the release, or risk of release, of toxic industrial materials into the environment. Furthermore, this publication carefully considers how logistics, personnel services, and health service support (HSS) are critical components of military operations in a CBRN environment.

JP 3-28, *Defense Support of Civil Authorities,* shares a close relationship with JP 3-41, *Chemical, Biological, Radiological, and Nuclear Consequence Management,* as the Department of Defense (DOD) response activities to mitigate the effects of a CBRN incident within a domestic scenario are provided as defense support of civil authorities operations. Both publications address emergency preparedness and response, rely on the National Response Framework, and refer the user to the associated National Incident Management System for additional guidance on incident management.

JP 3-29, *Foreign Humanitarian Assistance,* provides joint doctrine for foreign humanitarian assistance (FHA) operations. It characterizes foreign consequence management (FCM) as a mission that is common with FHA operations. FCM operations may be conducted concurrently with foreign disaster relief and humanitarian assistance operations. DOD supports United States Government (USG) FCM operations as part of the USG response to CBRN incidents abroad to relieve suffering and avoid further loss of life.

JP 3-40, *Combating Weapons of Mass Destruction,* forms the foundation for all other joint and Service doctrine for combating weapons of mass destruction (WMD) and provides overarching guidelines and principles to assist in planning and conducting operations to combat WMD. JP 3-40 describes WMD consequence management which is one of the eight military mission areas of combating WMD.

JP 4-02, *Health Service Support,* accepts that the joint force commander (JFC), at all levels, is faced with the possibility that any operation may have to be conducted in a CBRN environment. Therefore, the component command surgeons, working with the appointed joint force surgeon/joint task force surgeon, have a critical role in guiding and integrating all HSS capabilities available to the JFC toward mission accomplishment in that CBRN environment.

for preparation and response that can be extended to other pandemics as well. These three pillars are: EP, surveillance and detection, and response and containment. DOD plays a major role in the USG effort to contain, mitigate, and reduce the spread of PI or infectious diseases. Such actions also help preserve US combat capabilities and readiness, support USG efforts to save lives, reduce human suffering, and mitigate the spread of infection.

(1) **EP Within DOD for PI and Infectious Diseases.** Throughout a PI or infectious disease outbreak, US military forces strive to preserve combat capabilities, accomplish assigned missions, and achieve strategic objectives. Implementation of force health protection measures is the primary focus throughout the entire spectrum of PI and infectious disease preparation, planning, and operations regardless of whether the virus was natural, accidental, or of deliberate origin.

(2) **Health Surveillance.** Detecting and tracking the spread of an infectious disease is key to its containment. The same assets used to detect and track a biological threat or hazard are used to detect a PI or infectious disease outbreak.

(3) **Response and Containment.** CBRN forces should be prepared to respond to CBRN incidents during a pandemic.

For further doctrinal guidance on epidemics and medical procedures, refer to JP 4-02, Health Service Support.

5. General Planning Considerations for Chemical, Biological, Radiological, and Nuclear Response

a. **Planning Considerations Regarding Hazard Effects.** Planning considerations for responding to CBRN incidents and requests for assistance (RFAs) are influenced by a variety of factors, including USG policy decisions, lessons learned from responses to previous incidents, capability limitations, time, current military operations, studies and analyses, modeling and simulation, live-agent tests and experiments, as well as analysis and exercise of national planning scenarios. Military planners need to be able to translate military analysis capabilities for use in a CBRN CM response. For more information on possible scenarios, see the *National Preparedness Guidelines*.

(1) The planning process begins with determining and assessing potential CBRN responses with respect to the end state the supported combatant commander (CCDR) plans to achieve. The developed response includes standing contingency plans and procedures to determine what forces and capabilities are required in support of RFAs. Accidents may occur at chemical plants, nuclear power plants, or other facilities (to include those on DOD installations) that have the potential for release of CBRN material, or they may occur during the transportation of TIMs. Intentional acts include use of CBRN materials by adversaries, sabotage, and acts of terrorism. CBRN materials present hazards that can be both immediate and delayed. In some instances the delayed effects can cause significant problems for joint forces and may alter planned operations. In all cases, the setting and managing of operational exposure guide (OEG) by the operational commander is a key requirement in protecting forces.

(2) **Chemical Agents, Industrial Chemicals, and Their Effects**

(a) The JFC may be required to manage the consequences of a deliberate or accidental release of chemical agents (chemical substances intended for use in military operations to kill, seriously injure, or incapacitate mainly through their physiological effects) or toxic industrial chemicals (TICs) (chemicals developed or manufactured for use in industrial operations or research).

(b) The risks associated with TIC release vary. Such risks include inhalation, absorption, or ingestion of a lethal or incapacitating dose as well as secondary complications such as asphyxiation, smoke inhalation, and fire. The use of appropriately certified PPE is critically important during responses to CBRN incidents involving TICs.

(c) The scope of these environmental and industrial hazards may be quite extensive in an industrialized area. Any site that stores or uses TICs may pose a threat to personnel even if the site is operating under normal conditions. Industrial accidents or sabotage, such as destruction of a large industrial complex, may release these potentially toxic substances. For information on TIC hazards, see the current edition of the *National Institute for Occupational Safety and Health Pocket Guide to Chemical Hazards,* http://www.cdc.gov/niosh/npg, and the US Department of Transportation's *Emergency Response Guidebook,* http://phmsa.dot.gov/hazmat/library/erg.

For further doctrinal guidance on chemical agents and TICs, their effects, operational considerations, and force protection, refer to JP 3-11, Operations in Chemical, Biological, Radiological, and Nuclear (CBRN) Environments, *and Field Manual (FM) 4-02.283/Marine Corps Reference Publication (MCRP) 4-11.1B/Navy Tactical Reference Publication (NTRP) 4.02.21/Air Force Manual (AFMAN) 44-161(I),* Treatment of Nuclear and Radiological Casualties.

(3) **Biological Hazards and Their Effects**

(a) Biological agents are microorganisms and/or biologically derived compounds or molecules that cause disease in personnel, plants, or animals; and/or cause the deterioration of material. Biological agents are divided into two broad categories: pathogens and toxins. Biological hazards from industrial, medical, or commercial toxic industrial biologicals can also cause a potential infectious or toxic threat.

(b) Infectious diseases represent one of the greatest potential threats due to their reproductive ability and incubation period, the time delay from infection to the onset of symptom(s). An infectious biological incident anywhere in the world may remain undetected for several days to weeks after release due to the incubation periods. Diagnosis may be slow as many infectious agents have a slow onset and nonspecific symptoms that rapidly escalate in severity. Another compounding problem is that infectious casualties may be contagious without showing symptoms specific to the disease as they move from one geographic location to another, spreading the range of infection. Additionally, doctors often find difficulty in differentiating biological diagnoses as many initial symptoms often resemble those of the common cold. Depending on the pathogen, preventive measures and treatment are difficult to implement due to factors such as large numbers of casualties, ease of travel, and challenges of quarantining. Finally, first responders may be among the first casualties, rapidly overwhelming local and government support systems.

(c) When people are infected, medical facilities may be the first source to notice an increase in specific symptoms. Alternatively, the first signs of an attack may be unusually high and widespread purchase of over-the-counter medicines by civilians within a region. Domestically, hospitals report to their state departments of health and to the Centers for Disease Control and Prevention (CDC). The CDC and National Institutes of Health can then recommend steps for containment and treatment. GCCs with foreign AORs encounter similar reporting processes that serve as warning and information sources.

(d) Terrorists and other enemy elements may also attempt to use biological agents to infect agricultural plants and animals or to contaminate infrastructure, industry, and the environment.

<u>1</u>. Agriculture can be attacked through animals or crops. This type of attack can affect a nation's food supply, economics, and international trade.

<u>2</u>. Bacteria, fungi, and viruses can be genetically engineered for specific functions. An example is an oil-eating bacterium. This technology could be used to deteriorate or contaminate industrial supplies or materials. A bacterial pathogen can be modified to be resistant to a variety of antibiotics and, thus, could be difficult to treat.

For further guidance on biological agents, their effects, operational considerations, and force protection against biological hazards, refer to JP 3-11, Operations in Chemical, Biological, Radiological, and Nuclear (CBRN) Environments.

(4) **Sources of Radiation and Their Effects**

(a) Radiological Sources. Radioactive materials cause damage by ionizing effects of neutron, gamma, x-ray, beta, and/or alpha radiation. A population may be exposed to radiation intentionally through two primary methods (other than a nuclear detonation): radiological dispersal devices (RDDs) or radiological exposure devices (REDs). RDDs and REDs require limited technical knowledge to build and deploy as compared with a nuclear device. Also, the radioactive materials used in RDDs and REDs are widely used in medicine, agriculture, industry, and research, and thus are far easier to obtain than weapons-grade uranium or plutonium. Alternatively, any population can be unintentionally exposed to radiation released during an industrial accident or natural disaster involving a nuclear facility such as a nuclear power plant.

<u>1</u>. RDDs is an improvised assembly or process, other than a nuclear explosive device, designed to disseminate radioactive material in order to cause destruction, damage, or injury. Adversary use of an RDD—often called "dirty bomb"—is considered far more likely than employment of a nuclear explosive device. An RDD typically combines a conventional explosive device (such as a bomb) with radioactive material. RDDs are not designed to produce a nuclear detonation; rather, they produce a small area of acute immediate and residual hazard, and larger areas of delayed residual hazards. The immediate

dispersion incident produces radioactive aerosols that can be inhaled and particles that can be embedded in open cuts and sores or incorporated into food products growing in nearby agricultural areas. Inhaled materials can be dispersed throughout the body, captured by different organs and tissues, and remain internal hazards for a long time. Due to the unpredictability associated with radiation material dispersion over surfaces, the immediate surroundings may be littered with fragments of hazardous radiological source material.

2. REDs are covertly placed radioactive sources intended to expose people to significant doses of ionizing radiation without their immediate knowledge. Constructed from partially or fully unshielded radioactive material, a RED could be hidden from sight in a public place, exposing those who pass by. A RED does not distribute physical contamination (however, if the seal around the source is broken, radiological contamination may occur). The ability of a RED to cause injuries depends on several factors: the size of the source, type of isotope, distance and shielding materials between the source and personnel, and the length and/or frequency of exposure. Unless an installation routinely employs radiation detection devices and/or dosimeters, patients presenting to a medical facility with acute radiation syndrome (ARS) or radiation sickness will likely be the first indication of a RED's employment.

(b) When responding to a radiological incident, the commander's priorities are to keep critical missions operating while keeping exposure of all personnel as low as reasonably achievable (ALARA). ALARA guidance or parameters should be utilized to establish acceptable levels of contamination as prescribed by policy or the appropriate authority based on the CBRN incident. Unique post-radiological-incident challenges include determining personnel exposure (dose) rates; decontamination challenges; hazard duration that measures in months to years; and lifelong health concerns for personnel with even low-level radiological exposure. The setting and managing of OEG by the operational commander is a key requirement in protecting forces.

For further guidance on the sources of radiation, their effects, and force protection against radiological hazards (to include setting and managing OEG), refer to JP 3-11, Operations in Chemical, Biological, Radiological, and Nuclear (CBRN) Environments, FM 3-11.3/*Marine Corps Warfighting Publication (MCWP) 3-37.2A/Navy Tactics, Techniques, and Procedures (NTTP) 3-11.25/Air Force Tactics, Techniques, and Procedures (Instruction) (AFTTP[I]) 3-2.56,* Multi-Service Tactics, Techniques, and Procedures for CBRN Contamination Avoidance, *and FM 4-02.283/MCRP 4.11.1B/NTRP 4-02.21/AFMAN 44-161(1),* Treatment of Nuclear and Radiological Casualties. *DOD forces conducting CBRN response operations in support of a primary federal agency (Federal Emergency Management Agency [FEMA] or DOS) should comply with OEG set by the primary agency.*

For additional information on radiation injuries and ARS, see both Medical Management of Radiological Casualties Handbook, *Armed Forces Radiobiology Research Institute,* http://www.afrri.usuhs.mil, *and FM 4-02.283/MCRP 4-11.1B/NTRP 4-02.21/AFMAN 44-161(I),* Treatment of Nuclear and Radiological Casualties. *The latter document is the Services' consensus reference for medically qualified personnel on the recognition and treatment of nuclear and radiological casualties.*

(5) **Nuclear Environment, Nuclear Detonations, and Their Effects.** Nuclear detonations cause three types of injuries: blast, thermal, and radiation; as well as electromagnetic pulse (EMP) effects. The type and distribution of casualties depends on the weapon (e.g., yield, height of burst), environmental conditions (e.g., weather conditions), physical environment (e.g., structure types), and personnel conditions (e.g., age, health, skin tone, clothing).

(a) Blast (pressure) injuries are caused by the overpressure wave traveling outwards from the center of the nuclear detonation. The types of injuries are much the same as occur with conventional explosives. The human body is remarkably resistant to overpressure, particularly when compared with rigid structures such as buildings. Although many would survive the blast overpressure itself, they will not easily survive the crushing injuries incurred during the collapse of buildings from the blast overpressure or the impact of shrapnel (e.g., flying debris and glass). The majority of casualties from blast effects will result from wind generated from the blast overpressure. For a 10 kiloton (KT) yield, the velocity of the wind within 1.0–1.6 kilometers of ground zero will lift and throw people, causing serious injuries. It will also turn lighter objects into flying shrapnel, resulting in impalement injuries (probability of injury increases with velocity). Heavier objects may present crushing hazards.

(b) Thermal (heat) injuries present as flash burns (burns from direct exposure to the thermal radiation pulse, typically ultraviolet, visible, and infrared waves) or flame burns (burns from materials set afire by the infrared energy wave igniting flammable materials). Close to the fireball, the thermal energy is so intense that infrastructure and humans are incinerated. Immediate lethality would be 100 percent in close proximity. The distance of lethality will vary with nuclear yield, position of the burst relative to the Earth's surface, weather, environment, and how soon casualties can receive medical care. People within line of sight of the burst may be subject to burn injuries up to two miles away for a 10 KT device. The farther away from ground zero a person is, the less severe the burn injury will be. Early treatment can reduce mortality rates among the severely burned victims.

(c) Radiation injuries from a nuclear blast occur from two sources: initial and residual. Initial radiation effects occur due to the neutrons and high-energy gamma rays emitted within the first minute after detonation of the weapon. Severity of exposure depends on the weapon's yield, emissions, shielding, and distance from the explosion. Residual radiation effects result from either fallout or neutron-induced activity. The amount of residual radiation will depend on whether the detonation is an air or surface burst (air burst, the fireball does not touch the ground; surface burst, the fireball does). A surface burst will cause a tremendous amount of residual radiation. The hazards from surface bursts are more prevalent due to the presence of emissions (typically alphas, betas, and low-energy gammas) generated when unused-fissile material mixes with vaporized dirt, debris, and other materials, drawn back into the fireball and subsequently deposited downwind. In contrast, neutron-induced activity (when specific materials are bombarded by neutrons and become radioactive themselves) occurs more prevalently as a result of airbursts. Collectively, these sources are called fallout. The extent of fallout depends on the weapon's yield, type, and height of burst, while the area affected depends heavily on the wind. The hazard to personnel depends on the level of radiation present and the duration of exposure.

(d) **Electromagnetic Pulse.** EMP is unlikely to have a direct health threat; however, personnel with pacemakers or other implanted devices may be affected. EMP can also be very damaging to electronic equipment.

For further information on EMP effects with graphical representation, refer to the 2008, Critical National Infrastructures, Report of the Commission to Assess the Threat to the United States from Electromagnetic Pulse (EMP) Attack, www.empcommission.org/docs/A2473-EMP_Commission-7MB.pdf. *For further guidance on the nuclear weapon effects and hazard considerations, refer to JP 3-11,* Operations in Chemical, Biological, Radiological, and Nuclear (CBRN) Environments.

(6) **Explosives Effects and Role in CBRN Incidents.** Even though this publication does not provide doctrine for explosives incidents because explosives do not leave a residual hazard, explosives are addressed here based on their role in CBRN incidents.

(a) According to Technical Manual 9-1300-200, *Ammunition, General* (Chapter 2-11 to 2-15), explosives are categorized as high explosives (HE) and low-order explosives (LE). HE detonate and produce a defining supersonic overpressurization shock wave. Examples of HE include TNT (trinitrotoluene), nitroglycerin, dynamite, and ammonium nitrate fuel oil. LE deflagrate (rapidly burn rather than detonate), create a subsonic explosion, and lack HE's overpressurization wave. Examples of LE include gunpowder and most pure petroleum-based bombs such as Molotov cocktails or aircraft improvised as guided missiles. The differing injury patterns caused by HE and LE should also be factored in when mitigating the consequences of a chemical or radiological incident involving an explosive.

(b) Explosives can generate casualties in several ways depending on the type of explosion, secondary effects of the explosion (e.g., building collapse, fire), and the surrounding environment of the explosion (e.g., confined spaces, availability of debris or materials to generate an expanding area of potential injuries). Some chemical compounds are unstable. When shocked or burned they react, possibly to the point of deflagration or even detonation, thereby adding to the potential hazards when dealing with a chemical incident.

(c) An RDD may use explosives (e.g., bulk HE) or nonexplosive means (e.g., a crop duster spraying finely ground radioactive material) to disperse radioactive material. Explosives may be used to release chemical agents from ordnance or release a chemical agent from its container. The explosion itself and its effect on vehicles and structures will be a contributing factor in many of the injuries or add to the difficulty of getting to casualties trapped in rubble and collapsed structures, leaving them at further risk from the agent. Estimating CBRN response requirements only on the casualties with agent injuries will significantly underestimate the magnitude of the problem. Those injured who get radiation particles into their wounds will have significantly greater recovery problems and reduced life expectancy than those who have uncompromised skin surface that can be decontaminated. Conditions similar to this exist for chemical incidents. Secondary explosions, due to fires, can cause their own injuries and make the response more dangerous, particularly in a nuclear incident. Due to the negative effect of heat on most biological agents, explosives do not generally play a role in biological incidents. Finally, a secondary attack using improvised explosive devices should always be considered during any CBRN CM response planning.

(7) **Consequences of CBRN Incidents on Infrastructure**

(a) A CBRN incident can disrupt production and delivery of essential goods and services. Water supplies may be contaminated or unable to flow to incident area populace. Public health and emergency services will likely be affected by the CBRN incident either directly by their proximity to the incident or indirectly by the overwhelming need for the emergency response. EMP can destroy or cause transitory disruption of the power grid and damage or destroy portable/mobile electronic devices or equipment. EMP may further complicate immediate response operations by damaging/destroying the electronics in equipment first responders require. The transportation and communication infrastructure may be stressed through evacuations, providing relief supplies, or as a direct result of the CBRN incident. The response required by a joint force could potentially span the range of these effects.

(b) Support to civilian authorities may also include specific public health support to government health departments, hospitals, health clinics, mortuaries, and pharmacies, to include distribution of pharmaceutical stockpiles. Joint forces supporting civilian authorities may assist in responding to the needs of affected communities. A primary concern to all response efforts is restoration of government functions to the affected area. Effects to public safety and security may result directly from CBRN attacks on government institutions or indirectly from cascading disruption of the institutions. Indirect effects include cascading disruption and financial consequences to government, society, and the economy through public and private sector reactions to an incident. Joint forces have the capability to assist in this area by supporting civilian authorities in restoration of essential goods and services.

(c) Another consequence of CBRN incidents is contamination of infrastructure and terrain. Contamination can be concentrated or be spread over a significant area depending on the means of delivery and the agent used. These areas are of operational concern during the recovery phase of the incident. For larger areas of contamination, specialized forces may be requested to assist governmental authorities logistically by providing transportation for the affected population, assisting with decontamination efforts, assisting with infrastructure restoration, and monitoring operations.

b. **General Planning Strategy for Decontamination**

(1) Considering the scope of the emergency and determining proper decontamination procedures for different scenarios can help this process run more efficiently. Different forms of decontamination can be worked into response plans for different scenarios.

(2) Decontamination operations should be set up in the warm zone, which is sometimes also referred to as the "contamination reduction corridor." It should be far enough away from the hazard that decontamination workers are not in immediate danger.

(3) If the decontamination line or area is established outdoors, it should be in an area that is upwind of the hazard.

(4) Locate decontamination lines in areas easily accessible to ambulances or other emergency transport vehicles if at all possible.

(5) Determining the number of decontamination lines necessary is also a factor to consider. For a small incident, one line may be sufficient. If casualties are being taken from the area by one group of responders while another group of responders stops or cleans up a spill, it might be advantageous to have multiple lines: one for ambulatory casualties, a second for responders and equipment or non-ambulatory casualties.

(6) Everyone and everything that comes out of the hot zone must be checked for contamination and decontaminated as necessary. Critical medical treatment should not be delayed for thorough radiological decontamination. However, contaminated clothing from the casualty should be removed, and initial skin decontamination should be completed if possible because a contaminated individual can easily pass contamination on to emergency medical personnel, ambulances or response vehicles, and hospital emergency rooms— potentially putting these resources out of service until they can be properly decontaminated. In a large-scale emergency, this can be very problematic.

See FM 3-11.5/MCWP 3-37.3/NTTP 3-11.26/AFTTP(I) 3-2.60, Multi-Service Tactics, Techniques, and Procedures for Chemical, Biological, Radiological, and Nuclear Decontamination.

c. **Operational Planning Considerations for a Chemical, Biological, Radiological, or Nuclear Response**

(1) **Assessment.** A thorough assessment of the employed CBRN material and/or its effects provides feedback such as protection requirements, hazard levels, areas of contamination, expected duration of hazards, etc. This information contributes to the commander's situational awareness and technical assessment capability throughout any response. Objectives may include providing temporary critical life support; protecting critical infrastructure, preventing great property damage, protecting the environment; containing the incident and enabling community recovery. In addition, it is advantageous to respond in such a manner that the effects of the incident are minimal and serve as a deterrent for future domestic and international terrorist attacks. Every incident will be different, but the underlying concepts remain constant.

(a) Immediately after a CBRN incident, initial assessments determine the scope and magnitude of the incident and ultimately determine the need for DOD and joint force participation. Assessments should be done as quickly as possible to avoid additional lives being lost.

(b) The CCDR, at the request of federal and state/territory or supported nation authorities, sends a site assessment team to conduct assessments to gain early situational awareness in response to a CBRN incident. Common assessment requirements are provided below:

1. **Damage and Injury Reports.** Examine initial damage and injury reports for information on specific CBRN effects. Reports should be scanned for details including contamination control measures initiated and the number of contaminated casualties. Each CBRN incident has unique characteristics requiring appropriate follow-on response measures.

2. **Nature of the Incident.** Examine the effect on the population and infrastructure to identify response capabilities required to address the incident. This includes assessing risk to responders in order to determine force protection requirements.

3. **Force Protection.** Plan for and implement force protection measures. Force protection considerations are a top priority during any CBRN response operation and include providing proper protective equipment to personnel, planning for site safety, security, individual awareness of hazards and dangers, protection from contamination through proper marking and avoidance of contaminated areas, air monitoring, and health service support (HSS). Force protection efforts must include consideration of secondary incidents/devices that may target first responders or be designed to intentionally spread contamination. While these factors are primarily CBRN-oriented, the force may also be vulnerable to multiple types of opportunistic threats by adversaries, so the threat assessment must not be focused solely on CBRN.

4. **Duration and Geographical Extent of the Incident.** Assess the number of jurisdictions affected by the incident and the likelihood of the scope expanding significantly due to population migration and weather/terrain.

5. **Weather and Terrain.** Examine the effects weather and terrain may have on the CBRN material to include dispersion of chemical, biological, or radiological agents or toxic material by wind or water (e.g., stream/river flows).

6. **Public Reaction.** Gauge public reaction to the incident as it can affect response requirements, particularly if the level of fear is high or likely to grow, or if massive population movement is under way or expected.

7. **Mission Duration.** Assess mission duration, as it drives sustainment requirements. Extenuating circumstances may prolong CBRN response in the event civilian capability is lacking or inadequate. However, transition back to local responders should occur as soon as practical.

8. **CBRN Reconnaissance and Surveillance Tasks.** Plan for the conduct of locating, detecting, identifying, quantifying, sample collecting, surveying, observing, monitoring, reporting, and marking contaminated areas. Military forces generally have only basic sampling and detection capabilities, so specialized military units may be required.

9. **Identification of Supporting DOD Forces.** Local authorities may have some DOD forces assisting within their area under immediate response authority. The GCC should coordinate through the Services to identify Title 10, USC, units that are providing support either under immediate response or under local authority prior to the execute order (EXORD) and JTF establishment. Understanding the capabilities of forces

currently operating within the joint operations area (JOA), and leveraging their communications and logistics capabilities will accelerate JTF force arrival and employment. Locally available forces may be able to continue response operations or be committed to emerging requirements, thereby eliminating duplication of capabilities required for the CBRN response.

(2) **Coordination Planning**

(a) **Interorganizational Coordination.** DOD will liaise and coordinate with other agencies and civilian authorities. Interorganizational coordination is a continuous process that should be established and emphasized prior to an incident, as well as during and after an incident. Coordination takes place at the strategic, operational, and tactical levels. Whether coordination is conducted through the CCDR's joint interagency coordination group or other means such as an interagency planning cell or group at the combatant command or JTF levels, the importance of interorganizational coordination in the planning process cannot be overstated. Of particular concern is information management and public affairs (PA). These activities are done in concert with DHS or the chief of mission (COM) and impacted nation, depending upon the operational environment. The NRF provides additional guidance for domestic situations. JFCs should be prepared to coordinate operational activities with technical nuclear forensics sample collection task force (TF) in the event of a response to a radiological or nuclear incident. The CCDR and staff will coordinate with the collection TF through DHS to the Department of Justice/Federal Bureau of Investigation (FBI) for national incidents and via DOS in response to a foreign RFA.

Refer to JP 3-08, Interorganizational Coordination During Joint Operations, *for a detailed discussion on interagency, IGO, and nongovernmental organization (NGO) coordination during joint operations.*

(b) **State and Local Coordination.** Determine if specialized national, international, or local assets are responding to the incident. Chemical, biological, radiological, nuclear, and high-yield explosives (CBRNE) enhanced response force packages (CERFPs) and homeland response forces (HRFs) coordinate through NG joint force headquarters-state (NG JFHQ-State) with state and local civilian response planners and responders to verify that the DOD CBRN Response Enterprise is synchronized with civil authorities. The state NG weapons of mass destruction-civil support team (WMD-CST) and the state HAZMAT coordinator also synchronize with state organizations and advise on specialized response assets and private resources (such as industrial resources) available for use during a response. Attempt to determine response capability gaps and seams that will require filling by DOD resources or capabilities, i.e., equipment, material, or personnel. These processes should be practiced during training events and exercises.

(c) **Federal Coordination.** The CCDR and staff coordinate through DHS for national incidents and DOS for incidents involving foreign nations. These contacts should be verified with every training event.

(d) **Communications.** Determine if communications infrastructure is intact. If not, or if it is overwhelmed, joint forces may need to augment or replace the communications infrastructure in the affected areas using organic equipment. This is particularly important in a nuclear incident with resulting EMP. It should be anticipated that normal civilian communications means (i.e., land-line, cell phone, Internet) will be greatly affected and should not be considered as primary means of communications during a catastrophic incident.

(e) **Explosive Ordnance Disposal (EOD) and Technical Support.** EOD personnel should be part of any response to a possible CBRN incident. Consider the potential for secondary devices designed to explode or release a CBRN hazard after EOD or CBRN hazard response personnel have arrived. Ensure reachback is possible for CBRN hazard disposition or other technical expertise.

(f) **Occupational and Public Health.** Identify a lead medical/health DOD point of contact/liaison to provide support and recommendations regarding personnel and public health and safety including cleanup levels and risk assessments. Environmental Protection Agency (EPA), CDC, and Occupational Safety and Health Administration may provide recommendations to the DOD regarding health and safety.

(g) **Biometric and Forensic Requirements.** Where exclusive federal jurisdiction applies, coordinate with the appropriate military legal advisor to determine evidence collection procedures in case the incident is a criminal or terrorist act. Ensure that biometric evidence is vetted with the Biometrics Identity Management Agency and queried against authoritative federal biometrics databases: DOD Automated Biometric Identification System, DHS Automated Biometric Identification System, and the FBI Integrated Automated Fingerprint Identification System.

(h) **Transition and Disengagement.** Plan for the termination of military support. This is a politically sensitive phase requiring detailed planning. DOD typically disengages from operations when the local authorities are capable of assuming the responsibilities for the response operations. This is generally when the immediate danger from the CBRN incident is eliminated, the capabilities to save lives are in place, and critical services are restored. DOD generally does not remain to conduct site recovery operations.

(i) **Legal Requirements.** In both domestic and FCM, unique legal requirements may exist. Legal review by the assigned judge advocate should occur as the incident unfolds to ensure compliance with any such requirements.

(j) **Strategic Communication.** Accurate and timely communication with the public is crucial. Themes, messages, images, and actions should be synchronized across jurisdictions, agencies, and organizations. Planning must include anticipated outages of civilian mass media capabilities for communicating evacuation and quarantine information.

For further guidance on applicable laws and agreements refer to the operational environment chapters and Appendix A, "Key Legal, Strategy, and Policy Documents and International Protocols."

(3) **Logistics Planning**

(a) **Conduct Logistic Support.** Providing logistic support for a CBRN response produces numerous challenges. The force may need to deploy with unique assets and specialized equipment depending upon the mission, situation, and the designated response force. Examples of such equipment include decontamination systems, mobile laboratories, field hospitals, medical equipment, and facilities for temporary accommodation of persons. Forces may also be required to operate and/or maintain unfamiliar equipment that will impact maintenance requirements and repair parts management. It is also likely that much of the most critical equipment will require decontamination or hazard mitigation procedures during daily checks, refueling, and maintenance. These additional requirements illustrate that the nature of such deployments require unique planning and significant joint reception, staging, onward movement, and integration (JRSOI) support to receive, organize, and stage the forces for follow-on operations. Plans should allow forces to rapidly deploy, conduct JRSOI, and successfully execute their mission immediately after a CBRN incident. Contamination mitigation needs to be inherent in all CBRN logistics response planning in order to contain the spread of CBRN contamination and to prevent the unnecessary loss of valuable US assets. The responsiveness of support forces influences the success of the mission and the trust of the population affected by the CBRN incident. Logistical planning should address the integration of logistical support for Title 10 and Title 32, USC, and state active duty forces. Logistical planning should also address support United States Coast Guard (USCG) forces if they are to be a part of the support operations. While the DOD CBRN Response Enterprise contains significant tactical-level logistics/support forces, it requires a responsive theater opening and theater sustainment capability to support it.

See Appendix B, "Planning Considerations for Logistics and Other Services from Domestic Base Support Installations and Foreign Theater Assets."

(b) **Deployment and JRSOI.** DOD response units, with direction from the parent unit and Service, are responsible for coordinating and executing predeployment activities, movement to and activities at ports of embarkation, and arrival at ports of debarkation (PODs). The designated JTF, in coordination with the designated base support installation (BSI) commander and joint field office (JFO), coordinates activities for JRSOI activities. Depending on the situation, JRSOI of incoming Title 10, USC, forces may not be tied to a designated installation. It may have to be conducted through an abbreviated method of capturing personnel and equipment status without requiring the traditional deliberate JRSOI model.

For other deployment and redeployment operations, see JP 3-35, Deployment and Redeployment Operations.

(c) **Transportation.** Planners must anticipate/plan that critical transportation routes and infrastructure may be disrupted by the incident itself or by secondary effects such as populace movement and emergency response efforts. Both primary and alternate transportation routes and staging areas need to be identified. The joint force headquarters staff coordinates movement restrictions and transportation safety and determines accessibility and status of the road network, aerial ports of debarkation (APODs), and seaports of debarkation (SPODs) within the operational area. The CJCS, by the authority of and at the direction of the President or SecDef, issues a deployment order (DEPORD) to deploy US forces supporting CBRN CM.

1. All transportation modes should be considered for providing support to the CBRN response including organic assets. The deployment of unit personnel, supplies, and equipment should be phased so as to not overwhelm throughput of PODs, road networks, and on-site reception and support capabilities. For those units that cannot deploy with organic assets, United States Transportation Command (USTRANSCOM) can provide deployment, employment, and redeployment common-user air, land, and sea transportation for forces engaged in domestic CBRN response operations. Due to the detrimental effects of aircraft contamination and the difficulties of decontaminating aircraft, operational commanders should consider all measures consistent with mission priorities and operational risks to debark uncontaminated or packaged decontaminated cargo, equipment, and personnel at uncontaminated or clean airfields.

For more information on air mobility operations in a CBRN-contaminated environment, refer to Military Committee Memorandum (Memorandum in the Name of the Chairman) 0026-02, Chemical Warfare (CW) Agent Exposure Planning Guidance, *and JP 3-17,* Air Mobility Operations.

2. USTRANSCOM also provides aeromedical evacuation, air refueling, and aerial port services to support CBRN response. However, in a contaminated environment, USTRANSCOM will not transport contagious and contaminated casualties within the aeromedical patient movement system. In extreme circumstances, there may be a requirement to move contagious index cases (approximately two) for evaluation or critical medical care. If patient movement is required, the involved GCCs, Commander, United States Transportation Command, and SecDef in consultation with medical authorities provide necessary prior approval. Logistic planners need to be cognizant of the potential issues pertaining to requirements for the staging, reuse, transportation of, and/or disposition of decontaminated or residually contaminated equipment used during the CBRN response. These issues could significantly slow the normal redeployment process. Planners also need to consider the impact of cleanliness policy initiatives involving the transport of contaminated patients/cargo.

For more information on current cleanliness policy, refer to JP 4-02, Health Service Support, *Air Force Instruction (AFI) 41-307 (Attachment 12),* Aeromedical Evacuation Patient Considerations and Standards of Care, *and USTRANSCOM policy documents titled* Policy on Patient Movement of Contaminated Contagious or Potentially Exposed Casualties.

(d) **Contracting Services.** Critical contracting administration support is essential to expedite the procurement of services and material in support of any CBRN response. Logisticians should be familiar with the services provided by the Defense Contract Management Agency that support the CCDR. When contracting for supply, transportation, and services, logisticians should consider existing contracts already supporting military installations and other federal agencies in the operational area and contracts available through the state's United States Property and Fiscal Office (the primary National Guard

Bureau [NGB] focal point in each state for federal funds and property allotted to the state) when applicable.

(e) **Mortuary Affairs.** When authorized by SecDef, DOD mortuary affairs assets can help mitigate the potential health risks posed by mass fatalities and assist in incident response and recovery operations. The primary mortuary affairs missions in a CBRN environment are mortuary affairs identification tasks and contamination mitigation. When responding to a domestic incident the mortuary affairs assets perform mission assignments in support of the lead agency.

For more information on joint mortuary affairs operations, refer to JP 4-06, Mortuary Affairs, *and Technical Guide 195,* Safety and Health Guidance for Mortuary Affairs Operations: Infectious Materials and CBRN Handling.

(f) **Resupply.** Ensure that critical resupply items are identified and addressed (e.g., self-contained breathing apparatus refills and other CBRN related consumables).

(g) **Response Times.** Time sensitivity for DOD response may vary depending upon the severity and type of incident and may determine the need for a particular mode of transportation. Another factor that may influence response time is whether other high priority operational missions (e.g., technical nuclear forensics) are occurring simultaneously and compete for limited transportation. Some logistics assets may be pre-positioned forward into theater to facilitate a more effective response.

For more information on general logistic planning and support, refer to JP 4-0, Joint Logistics.

(4) **Health Services Support Planning.** Civil authorities consistently require assistance in Emergency Support Function (ESF) 8 (Framework Public Health and Medical) of the NRF. Providing initial essential stabilizing medical care and forward resuscitative/surgical care are the two essential capabilities that are required in the first hours following any CBRN incident. DOD may also be required to provide medical augmentation to local hospitals, community health (vaccinations, disease investigation, prophylaxis dispensing, preventive medicine, and veterinary support), patient movement. It may also be asked to assist with distribution/redistribution of patients, medical logistics distribution, and behavioral health, as well as direct medical treatment and patient decontamination. DOD coordinates HSS with the state health officer through the state's office of EP.

(a) **Health Facilities.** DOD health facilities have important roles in the National Disaster Medical System, local medical response organizations, and the Laboratory Response Network. Local health facilities should identify their capabilities to support and sustain patient movement, patient treatment, ancillary services, and medical sheltering. DOD health facilities should plan to work in concert with operational medical units in CBRN CM responses.

(b) **At-Risk Population.** Identify the demographics of population at-risk (elderly, young, pregnant, etc.).

(c) **Medical.** Augment the analysis of available information on epidemiological and diagnostic patterns resulting from the incident to address preventive medicine requirements, laboratory services, and casualty evacuation and treatment conducted by local, state, and federal public health authorities. If foreign medical support is provided, ensure that operating procedures are provided. Recognize that there are unique issues relating to military medical support to include personnel and supplies.

(5) **Populace Care Planning.** During a CBRN catastrophic incident, large numbers of people may be left temporarily or permanently homeless and may require prolonged temporary housing. The JFC may be requested to support short-term mass care in meeting basic human needs of food, water, shelter, hygiene, and medical care. DOD may also be requested to provide cots and tents or assist with construction of temporary shelters. Key to planning populace care is determining the transition of responsibilities from DOD to civilian authorities in the event that temporary shelters and camps become more permanent. DOD forces will ensure attention to property accountability so that transfers/disposals are properly documented for eventual reimbursement when it is authorized.

(6) **Decontamination Planning.** Tasks may include decontamination of civilian and military personnel as well as civilian and military equipment and critical infrastructure. Additionally, contamination mitigation of remains is a viable mission. Local hospital decontamination tasks are also required. Contaminated waste disposal is a key requirement, and important in the context of interagency coordination. A DOD medical/health representative, with appropriate technical expertise, should be made available to civilian authorities to provide health-based recommendations concerning worker health and safety as well as environmental cleanup aspects related to military unique hazards (such as CW agents). If expertise is not available within the AOR, there are a number of technical reachback agencies/capabilities that can be contacted (such as the US Army Medical Research Institute of Chemical Defense) and US Army Public Health Command to assist the JFC.

For the most current clearance criteria and policy guidance for materiel returning to the United States, refer to the Office of the Secretary of Defense (OSD) (Policy) Revised Radiological Clearance Criteria Guidelines for Platforms and Materiel. For more guidance on decontamination operations, refer to FM 3-11.5/MCWP 3-37.3/NTTP 3-11.26/AFTTP(I) 3-2.60, Multi-Service Tactics, Techniques, and Procedures for Chemical, Biological, Radiological, and Nuclear Decontamination.

(7) **Site Management Support Planning**

(a) **Containment.** Joint force CBRN response forces can provide the capability to mitigate or reduce further risk or damage to persons, materiel, facilities, and the environment. Contamination-control measures include leaving equipment in a potentially contaminated area until it is tested for contamination by qualified personnel. Other measures include encapsulating contaminated items by covering the equipment with plastic bags or tarps.

(b) **Detection/Identification.** DOD forces may be tasked to detect and identify the specific hazard(s) and set hazard boundaries. Military CBRN surveillance and reconnaissance units may also be tasked to survey the contaminated area to determine extent and level/degree of contamination. Survey elements might need to consider the incident site as a crime scene by setting boundaries and cordoning the site to safeguard responders and onlookers and prevent further contamination or environmental damage. Hazard areas may need to be marked and isolated to warn and protect the response personnel working in the area. Setting boundaries facilitates strict control into and out of the incident site.

(c) **Security.** The JFC may provide Title 10, USC, forces in support of nonmilitary law enforcement agencies. This support may include, but is not limited to, providing information concerning a violation of state or federal laws, loaning military equipment and facilities, providing personnel to operate and/or maintain the loaned equipment, and providing basic training or expert advice.

(d) **Evidence.** Evidence collected for forensic analysis on-site or at a different location and time.

(e) **Zone Control.** In a response role, joint forces may assist with verification and management of containment boundaries set by civilian (or affected nation) authorities. Control zones are operational areas established by civilian authorities at an incident site within which only specific types of operations are conducted. Personnel working in these areas must adhere to strict procedures to ensure the safety of those working in the zones. Control zones are established to ensure the safety of all responders and control access into and out of a contaminated area. See Chapter II, "Domestic Chemical, Biological, Radiological, and Nuclear Consequence Management," for domestic zone operations as a guide when local authorities have not established controls.

(f) **Movement.** Consider requirements to decontaminate personnel, vehicles, and equipment in support of evacuation, redeployment, or any movement from a contaminated site. The intent to retrograde residually contaminated equipment/cargo will require special approval through CJCS due to potential risks and political and environmental sensitivities.

(g) **Disposal.** Consider requirements to dispose of unsalvageable equipment and vehicles. Also plan for disposal/disposition of contaminated materials that cannot be feasibly decontaminated.

(h) **Monitoring.** Consider requirements to monitor personnel, vehicles, and equipment entering or exiting a contaminated zone.

(8) **Safety Planning.** Emphasis should be placed on safety during any CBRN response because response forces may be directed with little warning and preparation time. Forces may move immediately into employment with little rest and under extremely stressful conditions. Military issue protective equipment may not protect against all CBRN hazards. While Service safety programs are generally run by Service components, guidelines,

standards, and instructions should be set by the JFC. Tracking of exposure and force health protection compliance should be captured, analyzed, and acted upon as a joint safety issue.

(9) **Religious Affairs**

(a) Guidance in this section pertains to domestic, foreign, and DOD-led CBRN CM. The primary role for DOD chaplains during CBRN incidents will be to support authorized DOD personnel. Only during rare and exceptional emergencies may DOD chaplains provide religious support (RS) to non-DOD civilians or first responders, and then only strictly in compliance with command direction, legal guidance, and supervisory chaplain oversight.

1. As part of the DOD CBRN response, military chaplains and their assistants deliver RS and advisement to the commander and authorized recipients according to applicable policies and standard operating procedures. They can work cooperatively and collaboratively to build partnerships with faith-based organizations and civilian clergy in order to facilitate the delivery of humanitarian care to the affected population. Emergency spiritual care, traumatic incident management, respecting and honoring the dead, and other religious activities are critical to sustaining DOD personnel and supporting the restoration of a stable society. Additionally, military chaplains are trained in counseling and, as such, may be able to augment medical forces in the provision of some level of psychological care, when necessary.

2. Many DOD CBRN units do not contain embedded religious support teams (RSTs). States will likely establish a NG JTF for C2 of NG forces. The NGB Office of the Chaplain will provide additional qualified RSTs as needed to support the NG JTF.

(b) RST roles differ according to control zones. (See Chapter II, "Domestic Chemical, Biological, Radiological, and Nuclear Consequence Management," for full descriptions of each control zone.) Most RST activities including those pertaining to casualty care, counseling, worship opportunities, memorial services, and stress management occur in the cold zone. Selected RSTs with proper training and certification, equipment, and command direction may also be tasked to provide limited RS in the warm zone. RST warm zone activities could include hot zone casualty reception and support to medical triage, mass casualty decontamination, and mortuary affairs operations. It is not recommended that RSTs enter the hot zone, but be prepared to provide RS to those personnel operating within the hot zone.

(c) The following specific key locations at the incident site normally require the presence of properly trained, equipped, and authorized RSTs: the decontamination line, casualty collection point, medical treatment facilities, mortuary affairs collection points, and evacuation centers/emergency family assistance centers. At these locations, RSTs normally focus on RS to casualties and care givers. They also ensure honor and respect for the deceased.

For more information on legal guidance and supervisory chaplain oversight, see JP 1-05, Religious Affairs in Joint Operations, *and JP 3-28,* Defense Support of Civil Authorities.

(10) **Biometric and Identity Assurance.** When the US conducts foreign humanitarian and disaster relief (DR) operations in support of other nations, the employment of biometric capabilities is a mission enabler. Working by, with, and through the partner nations, employment of biometric capabilities can assist in the management of local populations, force protection, initial accountability, access to relief sites, and the management of aid (including food and medicine).

6. Limitation and Mitigation Strategies

a. Risk Management

(1) **Risk Assessment.** In conducting risk management, the JFC should employ risk assessment procedures to help identify hazards and then assess those hazards to determine risk. Assessment is usually a mechanical process of assessing the probability of the incident or occurrence, estimating the expected result or severity of an incident or occurrence, and then determining specified level of risk for a given probability and severity. Matrixes and tables are often used to assist in this process. The joint force may have an established standard operating procedure for risk assessment.

For further doctrinal guidance on force employment risk management during a CBRN incident, refer to JP 3-11, Operations in Chemical, Biological, Radiological, and Nuclear (CBRN) Environments. *For further guidance on the risk management process and useful examples of matrixes and tables, refer to FM 5-19*, Composite Risk Management.

For further guidance on force protection posture vulnerability analysis and risk reduction, refer to Army Tactics, Techniques, and Procedures (ATTP) 3-11.36/MCRP 3-37B/NTTP 3-11.34/AFTTP(I) 3-20.70, Multi-Service Tactics, Techniques, and Procedures for CBRN Aspects of Command and Control.

(2) **Risk Control.** Risk management entails developing controls and making risk decisions, implementing those controls, and then supervising and evaluating. Maintaining safety discipline is extremely important during CBRN response operations. The heightened sense of urgency in working to help parents, children, and the elderly who have been contaminated may impact on decisions and cause Service members to want to take more personal risk. Other examples of long-term hazards requiring leaders to establish controls that consider the reason for the hazard and not just the hazard itself include climatic extremes, CBRN and hazardous waste contamination, or disease threats within the particular operational area or indigenous population.

b. **Operational and Strategic Risk.** Any CBRN response must be rapid in order to save lives and minimize the overall impact of the incident. JFCs providing CBRN incident response need to have viable plans and be prepared to make rapid decisions with minimal knowledge of the scope and magnitude of the incident. Self-confidence and high competency are necessary to execute effectively in a hazardous environment. Those forces committed by DOD to this mission as part of national preparedness need to be trained and ready when the nation calls. When these conditions are met, the risk of strategic and operational failure has been minimized.

Intentionally Blank

CHAPTER II
DOMESTIC CHEMICAL, BIOLOGICAL, RADIOLOGICAL, AND NUCLEAR CONSEQUENCE MANAGEMENT

"We are building our capability to prepare for disasters to reduce or eliminate long-term effects to people and their property from hazards and to respond to and recover from major incidents. To improve our preparedness, we are integrating domestic all hazards planning at all levels of government and building key capabilities to respond to emergencies."

National Security Strategy 2010

1. General

a. **Overview.** CBRN CM (Figure II-1) conducted by DOD in the homeland in support of civil authorities is conducted as a DSCA operation. See JP 3-28, *Defense Support of Civil Authorities,* for a complete discussion of DSCA operations. The capability and capacity to effectively respond to domestic CBRN incidents and sustain operations in CBRN environments require properly trained and equipped forces that follow the parameters set forth in this chapter. A description of DOD's participation in the whole-of-government response to a domestic CBRN incident is provided in the NRF. It further details the authorities that delineate the roles and limits for DOD in a domestic response. In conducting DSCA to include CBRN response, a distinction is made between the different chains of command for active DOD, Title 10, USC, federal forces providing support to civil authorities and for NG forces commanded by the state governor under Title 32, USC, and state active duty. State and local governments are closest to those affected by incidents, and have a lead role in response and recovery. For a federal response to a CBRN incident, DOD support is tailored to the scope and magnitude of the incident. DOD assets are employed with a focus on response requirements beyond the resources of state and federal civil authorities. The DOD CBRN response is typically conducted via a JTF that provides C2 of forces trained and equipped for this mission, as well as contingency sourced conventional forces. Using a six-phased approach, the JFC leads the response forces from steady state through CBRN response operations. During phase 0, the CCDR sustains subordinate response force readiness through exercises, training, and rehearsal activities.

b. **Defense Support of Civil Authorities.** DSCA policy and procedures guide DOD support provided by federal military forces, NG forces performing duty IAW Title 10 and Title 32, USC, DOD civilian, military contract personnel, and DOD component assets in a domestic response. It includes immediate response and response to approved RFAs during domestic CBRN incidents. This DSCA response includes support to federal departments and agencies that assist local, state, and tribal authorities within the US territories for CBRN CM operations. Figure II-1 illustrates the basic relationships of CBRN CM. It includes support provided by NG forces performing duty conducted as state-directed actions when approved by SecDef IAW Title 10 and Title 32, USC, or when NG forces are in state active duty status. SecDef policy and Joint Staff instructions provide guidance for the operational framework that serves as the foundation for a joint force's relationship with local, state, tribal, other federal, or nongovernmental entities.

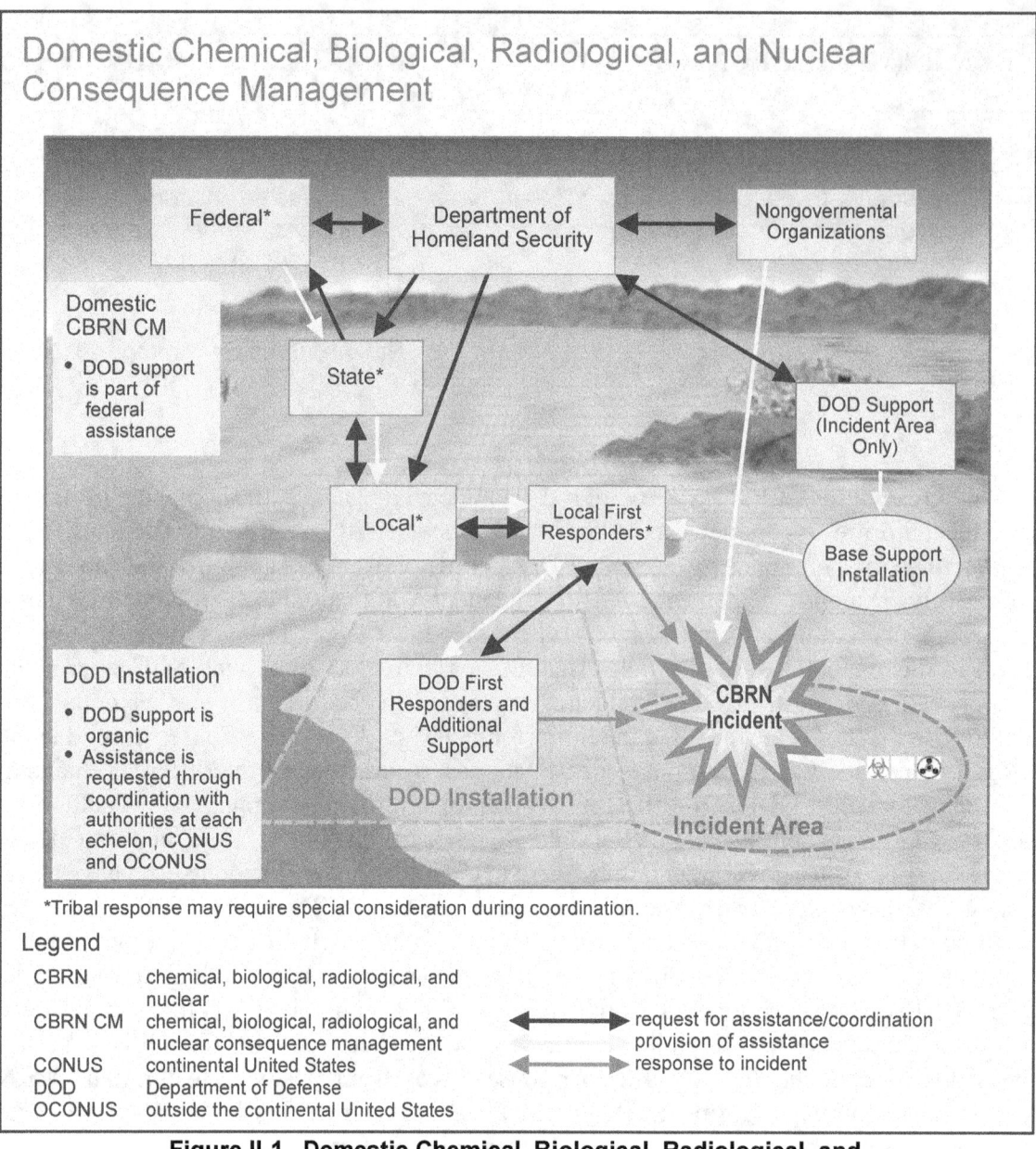

Figure II-1. Domestic Chemical, Biological, Radiological, and Nuclear Consequence Management

2. Roles, Responsibilities, Authorities, and Assets

    a. **Department of Defense and the National Response Framework.** DOD provides assistance upon request by an appropriate authority and after approval of SecDef. When conducting CBRN response IAW the NRF, DOD is in support of an NRF ESF primary agency or NRF incident annex coordinating agency. As a practical matter, DOD prefers a single source for mission assignments and generally identifies DHS FEMA as the primary agency in its EXORD, operation plan, or operation order (OPORD) authorizing federal military assistance. In any case, DOD may provide assistance that has been approved by the appropriate authorities.

For more information on ESFs, see the NRF and JP 3-28, Defense Support of Civil Authorities.

b. The domestic environment for DSCA presents many challenges to the JFC and more so when responding to a CBRN incident. It is imperative that commanders and staffs at all levels understand the statutory and operational relationships among all federal departments and agencies involved in the operation. NIMS provides a consistent nationwide template to enable federal, state, tribal, and local governments, the private sector, and NGOs to work together to prepare for, prevent, respond to, recover from, and mitigate the effects of incidents regardless of cause, size, location, or complexity. NIMS can be utilized for all incidents, ranging from daily occurrences to incidents requiring a coordinated federal response.

c. Commanders and their staffs at all levels should be knowledgeable about the NRF and NIMS and how their commands fit in to the overall national response framework. The NRF is a guide to how the US conducts all-hazard responses. It is built upon scalable, flexible, and adaptable coordinating structures to align key roles and responsibilities across the Nation. It describes specific authorities and best practices for managing domestic incidents that range from the serious but purely local, to large-scale terrorist attacks or catastrophic natural disasters. The NRF contains a number of incident annexes that apply to CBRN incidents. Each annex lists the coordinating agency or agencies and cooperating agencies involved in the response and provides information on applicable policies, authorities, planning assumptions, concept of operations, actions, and responsibilities of cooperating agencies for the particular incident described.

For more information on the NRF and NIMS, refer to the NRF Resource Center: http://www.fema.gov/NRF *and the* NIMS Resource Center: www.fema.gov/NIMS. *These online resources are routinely updated and evolving.*

d. **DOD Roles and Responsibilities.** Domestic CBRN CM is managed at the lowest possible level, with DOD providing support as directed. When SecDef approves a request for DSCA during a CBRN incident, CDRUSNORTHCOM and Commander, United States Pacific Command (CDRUSPACOM) are the supported GCCs for CBRN responses within their respective AORs as designated in the Unified Command Plan (UCP) for a federal response. DOD supports the NRF primary and coordinating agencies during domestic CBRN CM operations. The operational chain of command for federal forces remains with the GCC; the operational chain of command for state controlled NG forces remains with the governor. A brief synopsis of specific DOD roles and responsibilities for CBRN response in the domestic operational environment is provided below:

(1) **Secretary of Defense.** SecDef retains approval authority for the use of forces, personnel, units, and equipment for DSCA, to include support to CBRN CM. SecDef has the primary responsibility to provide the overall policy and oversight for DOD in the event of a domestic incident.

(2) **Assistant Secretary of Defense (Homeland Defense and Americas' Security Affairs) (ASD[HD&ASA]).** The Office of ASD(HD&ASA) is within the office of the

Under Secretary of Defense for Policy (USD[P]). ASD(HD&ASA) serves as the DOD Domestic Crisis Manager and provides policy oversight for all domestic CBRN incident support. ASD(HD&ASA) coordinates with the heads of the DOD components, the Under Secretary of Defense for Personnel and Readiness, and the Under Secretary of Defense for Acquisition, Technology, and Logistics on matters regarding the readiness posture of forces, to include critical infrastructure protection and CBRN nuclear response enterprise assets. See Appendix C, "Department of Defense Domestic Chemical, Biological, Radiological, and Nuclear Response Enterprise Assets," for a description of these assets.

(3) **Assistant Secretary of Defense (Health Affairs) (ASD[HA]).** ASD(HA) is within the Office of the Under Secretary of Defense for Personnel and Readiness. This office is responsible for interactions with the Department of Health and Human Services in the National Disaster Medical System. Each Service maintains federal coordinating centers, which are medical facilities responsible for locating all civilian beds in their geographic location, arranging the transport of patients from arriving aircraft, and all logistics in support of receiving mass casualties from a disaster area.

(4) **Office of the Deputy Assistant Secretary of Defense for Countering Weapons of Mass Destruction** supports the USD(P) and Assistant Secretary of Defense for Global Strategic Affairs (ASD[GSA]), by developing strategies and policies and overseeing the execution of approved policies and programs regarding CBRN defense, WMD missile proliferation, and global threats.

(5) **Assistant Secretary of Defense (Reserve Affairs) (ASD[RA]).** ASD(RA) is responsible for monitoring RC readiness. ASD(RA) provides policy regarding the appropriate integration of RC forces into response efforts.

(6) **Chairman of the Joint Chiefs of Staff.** CJCS serves as the principal military advisor to SecDef and the President in preparing for and responding to CBRN incidents, and ensures that military planning is accomplished to support the lead or other primary agency for CBRN CM, and provides strategic guidance to the CCDRs for the conduct of operations.

(7) **Joint Director of Military Support (JDOMS).** JDOMS, located within the operations directorate of a joint staff (J-3), works closely with ASD(HD&ASA) and the Services, CCDRs, and NGB to produce military orders pertaining to domestic emergencies for the CJCS. JDOMS forwards these orders to SecDef for approval, and then to the appropriate military commander for execution. The initial request enters through the DOD Executive Secretary and is forwarded to the Office of ASD(HD&ASA) and JDOMS, who evaluates the request against six criteria: legality (compliance with laws); lethality (potential use of lethal force by or against DOD forces); risk (safety of DOD forces); readiness (impact on the DOD ability to perform its primary mission); appropriateness (whether the requested mission is in the interest of DOD to conduct); and cost (who pays, impact on DOD budget).

(8) **Combatant Commands**

(a) **Commander, US Northern Command, and Commander, US Pacific Command.** When directed by the President or SecDef, these GCCs provide Title 10, USC,

CS/DSCA support to domestic CBRN CM and are the supported commanders in a CBRN response. CDRUSNORTHCOM is responsible for providing CBRN CM assistance to US and Allied authorities, as directed, within the USNORTHCOM AOR, to include US territories and protectorates in that AOR. Other geographic and functional commands support CDRUSNORTHCOM and CDRUSPACOM in their DSCA efforts.

(b) **Commander, United States Special Operations Command (CDRUSSOCOM).** When directed by the President or SecDef, CDRUSSOCOM conducts special operations in support of national CBRN CM activities. CDRUSSOCOM may provide liaison officers (LNOs) and other assistance to the supported CCDR, as required.

(c) **Commander, United States Transportation Command,** is a joint force provider and provides deployment, distribution, sustainment, and redeployment of common-user air, land, and sea transportation for forces supporting CBRN CM and provides aeromedical evacuation as required, IAW current guidance.

(d) **Commander, United States Strategic Command (CDRUSSTRATCOM).** CDRUSSTRATCOM is responsible for synchronizing planning for DOD combating weapons of mass destruction (CWMD) efforts in coordination with other combatant commands, the Services, and as directed, appropriate USG departments and agencies.

(9) **USNORTHCOM Subordinate Commands.** In USNORTHCOM AOR, five JTFs or TFs are identified to provide C2 for DOD Title 10, USC, response efforts with AORs that coincide with the NRF for PI regional construct.

(a) **United States Army Forces North (USARNORTH).** When approved by SecDef and directed by CDRUSNORTHCOM, Commander, United States Army Forces North (CDRUSARNORTH) deploys a mission-specific TF or JTF, and conducts CBRN response operations to support federal, state, local, and tribal authorities. CDRUSARNORTH serves as the USNORTHCOM standing joint force land component commander (JFLCC) and has operational control (OPCON) of Joint Task Force-Civil Support (JTF-CS). It is also prepared to deploy additional JTF-level mission-specific headquarters for multiple CBRN incidents to provide appropriate C2 based on the magnitude of the response. USARNORTH can be augmented by other services to establish a JFC over subordinate JTFs and/or functional components when required by the scope and magnitude of the incident. It supports single or multiple incidents with communication zone coordination and logistics operations.

(b) **Joint Task Force-Civil Support.** JTF-CS is a standing joint operational headquarters dedicated to DOD planning and response to domestic CBRN and other HE incidents in support of civil authorities. CDRUSNORTHCOM has combatant command (command authority) over JTF-CS, and the JFLCC has OPCON of the unit. JTF-CS forms the command headquarters of defense chemical, biological, radiological, and nuclear response force (DCRF). Routine day-to-day functions include providing advice in doctrine development, requirements identification, training and exercise management, and the promotion of domestic interoperability for DOD CBRN CM capable assets in the AC and

RC. When approved by SecDef, and directed by the USNORTHCOM chain of command, JTF-CS deploys to take C2 of Title 10, USC, resources and forces, and conducts military support operations to assist civil authorities in responding to a CBRN or other HE incident within the homeland. When CBRN or bulk HE incidents occur in the USPACOM AOR, CDRUSPACOM is the supported commander, and JTF-CS may deploy in their support.

(c) The **DOD CBRN Response Enterprise** includes:

<u>1.</u> NG units from the NG of their respective states:

<u>a.</u> WMD-CSTs.

<u>b.</u> CERFPs.

<u>c.</u> HRFs.

<u>2.</u> Title 10, USC, units allocated to USNORTHCOM for this mission:

<u>a.</u> DCRF.

<u>b.</u> Command and control chemical, biological, radiological, and nuclear response elements (C2CREs).

<u>3.</u> In addition, a catastrophic incident may require significant contingency-sourced follow-on forces.

See Appendix C, "Department of Defense Domestic Chemical, Biological, Radiological, and Nuclear Response Enterprise Assets," for additional information on CBRN response forces.

(d) **Joint Task Force-Alaska (JTF-AK).** When established, JTF-AK is responsible to USNORTHCOM for the conduct of homeland defense (HD) and CS within its assigned JOA. JTF-AK is responsible for deterring, detecting, preventing, and defeating national security threats within the Alaska JOA to protect US territory, citizens, and interests, and as directed, conduct CS.

(e) **Joint Force Headquarters National Capital Region (JFHQ-NCR).** As a standing subordinate organization of USNORTHCOM, JFHQ-NCR plans, coordinates, and maintains situational awareness within its assigned JOA to accomplish assigned HD and CS missions. When approved by SecDef and directed by CDRUSNORTHCOM, Joint Task Force National Capital Region is established and provides C2 of military support operations to help federal, state, and local authorities respond to a CBRN incident within the National Capital Region.

(10) **Defense Coordinating Officer (DCO), USARNORTH.** CDRUSARNORTH appoints a DCO to each of the 10 FEMA regions to serve as DOD's single point of contact at a JFO. A DCO may be the first DOD representative on-site and acts as the single DOD point of contact. The DCO is the designated DOD on-scene member of the FEMA-led JFO, the multiagency coordination center established locally for federal response-related prevention,

preparedness, response, and recovery actions. The DCO, supported by a defense coordinating element (DCE), coordinates all RFAs and approved mission assignments with the principal federal official (PFO), federal coordinating officer (FCO), or designated representative from the NRF primary and coordinating agencies. If a JTF is established and colocated with the PFO at the JFO, this colocation does not replace the requirement for a DCO and DCE as part of the JFO coordination staff. The DCO continues to exercise the JFO staff function of mission assignment coordination and validation and acts as a liaison between the JFO staff and the JTF staff.

(11) **USPACOM Subordinate Units.** Joint Task Force-Homeland Defense (JTF-HD) is CDRUSPACOM's HD and DSCA headquarters. The Commander, US Army Pacific, serves as the Commander, JTF-HD. JTF-HD, when directed, conducts CBRN response in support of civil authorities to mitigate the effects of deliberate and inadvertent CBRN and bulk HE incidents in Hawaii, Guam, American Samoa, and US territories and insular areas within its JOA. The JTF-HD establishes C2 of designated DOD forces within the JOA and provides DSCA to save lives, prevent injury, and provide temporary critical life support. Although it may require augmentation, many of the JTF capabilities, subject matter experts, and resources are already within US Army Pacific. JTF-HD works with state, territorial, and military organizations to ensure response across a large AOR. Because of the vast geographical distances within the Pacific, each territory and base has plans to respond to a variety of threats with forces in place, since any external forces have to come by air or sealift. The USPACOM CBRN CM plan includes flexible task organizations of multiple services, components, and capabilities.

(12) **Military Services.** Department of Defense Directive (DODD) 2060.02, *Department of Defense (DOD) Combating WMD Policy,* directs the Services to organize, train, and equip to support the CWMD mission areas. Each Service has some capability (based on its available assets and doctrine) to conduct or support CBRN CM. These capabilities may be called upon, when approved by SecDef, to provide forces, facilities, and assets to the supported CCDR as part of the DOD response to a CBRN incident. Specifically, the Service Chief responsibilities are as follows:

(a) Provide the Joint Staff J-3 with information on assigned CBRN response capabilities, assets, units, and research or support facilities that are capable of providing reachback or on-scene support to CBRN CM operations.

(b) Identify units available to the supported CCDR consistent with Title 10, USC.

(c) Provide designated forces, to include RC forces, in order to prepare for and respond to a CBRN situation and assistance to the supported CCDR through the appropriate Service component commanders.

(13) **US Marine Corps Chemical-Biological Incident Response Force (CBIRF).** CBIRF is a unit that was created to deploy on short notice in response to CBRN incidents. CBIRF consists of specially trained personnel and specialized equipment suited for operations in a wide range of contingencies. CBIRF is designed to minimize the effects of a

CBRN incident through detection, identification, extraction, mass decontamination, medical triage, and emergency medical support.

(14) **RC Forces.** NG and reserve forces are known collectively as RC forces. RC forces consist of the Army National Guard (ARNG), Air National Guard (ANG), United States Air Force Reserve (USAFR), United States Army Reserve (USAR), United States Navy Reserve (USNR), United States Marine Corps Reserve (USMCR), and United States Coast Guard Reserve (USCGR). Guidelines for utilization of RC forces can be found in Title 10, USC, and Title 32, USC. Guidelines for utilization of NG forces under state active duty will be found in their respective state codes. The Chief, National Guard Bureau (CNGB) facilitates and resources ANG and ARNG forces and assets through the states adjutants general to conduct CBRN response operations to assist federal, state, local, and tribal authorities in responding to a domestic CBRN incident. When directed by SecDef, the CNGB supports transition of state active duty or Title 32, USC, NG forces to federalized Title 10, USC, status for DSCA in coordination with individual states, and the ANG and ARNG.

(a) **National Guard.** The NG primarily operates under two chains of command, state or federal. However, NG forces may be operationally employed under three different legal statuses: Title 10, USC (federalized and federally funded); Title 32, USC (non-federalized and federally funded); and state active duty (non-federalized and state funded). NG forces, unless federalized, operate under the C2 of the governor and the adjutant general (TAG) in state active duty and Title 32, USC, status.

For more information, see JP 3-28, Defense Support of Civil Authorities.

1. Under certain circumstances, a governor may request that the USG pay for the costs associated with a state call up of the NG for emergency response. When SecDef approves, NG forces change from state active duty status to Title 32, USC status. Even though the NG forces are on active duty and funded by the USG, in Title 32, USC status, the governor retains command of the NG. Although the distinction between funding lines is important to the respective state and federal treasuries, tactical employment of forces remains the same. For the JFC, the important distinction is that NG units in Title 32, USC, status remain under state control; and, as a result, have authority for some missions that Title 10, USC, units do not. Because forces in Title 32, USC, status remain under the command of the governor, NG units may conduct law enforcement missions and are not subject to the restriction of the Posse Comitatus Act (PCA).

2. Additionally, the NG of one state can assist other states responding to a disaster through formal agreements, such as the emergency management assistance compact (EMAC). Typically, this occurs in state active duty (non-federalized and state funded). When requested by the supported state's governor and authorized by the supporting state's governor under a separate memorandum of agreement (MOA), NG elements deploy to the supported state. The supporting NG forces operate under operational command of the supported state's TAG as granted by the supporting state's governor. Typically, deployments under a state-to-state MOA are limited to a specific period, such as 30 days.

(b) **NG Capabilities and Contribution.** National Guard coordination centers (NGCCs), NG JFHQs-State, joint task forces-state (JTFs-State), WMD-CSTs, CERFPs, HRFs, Joint Continental United States Communications Support Environment (JCCSE), and Joint Interagency Training Capability form the keystone of NG CBRN response capabilities.

1. **NG Coordination Center.** The NGCC provides mutual, shared situational awareness among the NG JFHQs-State, NGB, and USNORTHCOM during a CBRN incident or other major or catastrophic incidents. The NGCC synchronizes alert notification and deployment of designated WMD-CSTs, CERFPs, and HRFs and synchronizes notification of deployment of other NG capabilities when requested by a state or agency. The JCCSE enables the NGCC to maintain situational awareness and share information with NG commanders at all levels throughout the 50 states and four territories. Additionally, it provides a deployable, interoperable communications capability to the JTF-State commander.

2. **NG Joint Force Headquarters-State.** The NG JFHQ-State provides the governor C2 capability for all NG forces in their state or territory, or in the case of the District of Columbia, the C2 of the District of Columbia NG has been delegated to the Secretary of the Army by SecDef and therefore the Joint Force Headquarters-District of Columbia currently operates on behalf of the Secretary of the Army. During a CBRN or bulk HE incident, the NG JFHQ-State assumes control of additional WMD-CSTs and CERFPs deployed into the supported state and provides JRSOI and logistical support.

3. **Joint Task Force-State.** The JTF-State controls all subordinate state NG assets deployed in support of a CBRN or bulk HE incident. The JTF-State commander works closely with the incident commander to verify that NG resources are effectively, safely, and legally employed.

4. **Weapons of Mass Destruction-Civil Support Teams.** WMD-CSTs are NG units designed to support civil authorities at a domestic CBRNE incident site by identifying CBRNE agents/substances, assessing current and projected consequences, advising on response measures, and assisting with requests for additional support. The WMD-CST mission is accomplished primarily in a Title 32, USC, operational status within the US and its territories, as established by Title 10, USC, Section 12310.

For more information on WMD-CSTs, see FM 3-11.22, Weapons of Mass Destruction Civil Support Operations.

See Appendix C, "Department of Defense Domestic Chemical, Biological, Radiological, and Nuclear Response Enterprise Assets," for additional information on CBRN response forces.

5. **Chemical, Biological, Radiological, Nuclear, and High-Yield Explosive Enhanced Response Force Package.** CERFPs are designed and trained to provide search, extraction, medical triage, emergency medical treatment, decontamination of casualties, and recovery of remains during CBRN and non-CBRN incidents, as well as advice and assistance to the incident commander, state emergency management, the NG JFHQ-State, TAG, the governor, other key officials, and representatives of federal agencies.

For more information on CERFPs, see ATTP 3-11.47, Chemical, Biological, Radiological, Nuclear, and High-Yield Explosive Enhanced Response Force Package Operations.

See Appendix C, "Department of Defense Domestic Chemical, Biological, Radiological, and Nuclear Response Enterprise Assets," for additional information on CBRN response forces.

6. **NG Homeland Response Force.** The HRF is part of the support to improve DOD's CBRN response capability through reorganization of CBRN response forces. Designed to be employed primarily with forces in state active duty or Title 32, USC, status, the HRF leverages the current WMD-CSTs and CERFPs force structure and capabilities through augmentation by force packages that include a brigade level C2 element and a battalion sized CBRN response security element in each of the 10 FEMA regions. Designated NG JFHQs-State establish HRFs and maintain current NG HRFs with essential CBRN response capabilities.

See Appendix C, "Department of Defense Domestic Chemical, Biological, Radiological, and Nuclear Response Enterprise Assets," for additional information on CBRN response forces.

7. **Reserve Forces.** The RC forces are structured and operated to mirror their respective AC counterparts. Unlike the ANG and ARNG, the USAR, USNR, USAFR, USMCR, and USCGR C2 relationships remain intact in both peacetime and wartime. These RC forces do not have state-specific relationships. When called to active duty, RC forces conduct CS missions under Title 10, USC, guidelines exactly as AC forces; USCGR is recalled pursuant to Title 14, USC. While on federal active duty, members of the ARNG of the United States, ANG of the United States, USAR, USNR, USAFR, USMCR, and USCGR are subject to the provisions of the Uniform Code of Military Justice. RC forces are called to active duty through the mobilization and demobilization processes.

For more information on the RC mobilization and demobilization processes, see JP 4.05, Joint Mobilization Planning.

(15) **Combat Support Agencies (CSAs).** CSAs provide direct support to CCDRs during emergency situations and are subject to evaluation by CJCS. The seven CSAs are the Defense Information Systems Agency, Defense Intelligence Agency, Defense Logistics Agency (DLA), National Security Agency, Defense Contract Management Agency, National Geospatial-Intelligence Agency, and Defense Threat Reduction Agency (DTRA). Each plays a critical role in supporting CBRN response operations by ensuring the supported commander has the technical CBRN information, situational awareness, technical support, 24/7 reachback capability, logistics, and contracting support necessary to carry out the mission. DTRA provides operational and technical advice and support to DOD components and other USG departments and agencies, as requested and approved, regarding CBRN CM operations. This is accomplished through training and exercises, the deployment of CBRN CM advisory teams, and operational planning assistance. DTRA also provides modeling, predictions, assessments, publications, training, lessons learned, analysis, and other support as required. DTRA provides technical reachback through the DTRA Operations Center, a 24/7 WMD and CBRN national reachback and situational awareness facility, for all technical support. During CBRN CM, DTRA liaises with other technical

support providers and the intelligence community to meet support requests. DTRA provides operational and technical advice and support to DOD components and other USG departments and agencies, as requested and approved, regarding CBRN CM operations. This is accomplished through training and exercises, the deployment of CBRN CM advisory teams, and operational planning assistance. DTRA also provides modeling, predictions, assessments, publications, training, lessons learned, analysis, and other support as required. DTRA provides technical reachback through the DTRA Operations Center, a 24/7 WMD and CBRN national reachback and situational awareness facility, for all technical support. During CBRN CM, DTRA liaises with other technical support providers and the intelligence community to meet support requests.

e. **US Coast Guard**

(1) The USCG is a military Service, a branch of the Armed Forces, and a law enforcement agency at all times. When directed by the President, or by a congressional declaration of war, the USCG may be transferred from DHS to the Department of the Navy. The USCG is not constrained by the PCA and has jurisdiction on US waters, the high seas, and at selected land-based maritime transportation and industrial facilities.

(a) USCG's homeland security (HS) mission is to protect the US maritime domain and the US marine transportation system and deny their use and exploitation as a means for attacks on US territory, population, and critical infrastructure. Additionally, USCG prepares for and, in the event of attack, conducts hazard response operations.

(b) The USCG is the LFA for maritime security. CCDRs may assign forces to USCG area commanders under tactical control (TACON) to support short notice HS operations without a formal request for forces (RFF) for up to 48 hours. Longer duration operations require an RFF.

(c) USCG CBRN Capabilities. The USCG provides unique authorities, surge capacities, and capabilities for CBRN CM. During CBRN CM operations, the USCG may be supported by DOD forces or may support DOD forces.

(2) **USCG National Strike Force (NSF).** The NSF deploys specialized capabilities and incident command expertise to support lead agency, incident commander, and federal on-scene coordinator preparation and response to CBRN incidents, hazardous substance releases, oil discharges, and other emergencies. NSF assets include the NSF Coordination Center in Elizabeth City, North Carolina, and three strike teams: the Atlantic Strike Team in Joint Base McGuire-Dix-Lakehurst, New Jersey; the Gulf Strike Team in Mobile, Alabama; and the Pacific Strike Team in Novato, California. NSF equipment includes CBRN detection; air, water, and soil sampling; Level A, B, and C personnel protection; self-decontamination equipment; hazardous material packaging; mobile command posts; boats; pumps, generators, and weather stations. NSF equipment is palletized for immediate deployment by truck or aircraft. The NSF supports domestic response and may deploy detachments to support overseas military environmental response operations.

(3) **Domestic USCG Search and Rescue and Security Forces.** The USCG maintains widely distributed search and rescue and security forces. Selected units are trained to operate in a maritime CBRN environment and may support limited CBRN CM operations. These include the maritime security response force and maritime safety and security teams.

(4) **USCG expeditionary forces** include USCG ships, aircraft, port security units, security teams, NSF detachments, and law enforcement detachments assigned to overseas GCCs. These forces are trained and equipped to DOD CBRN defense standards and may support limited FCM operations.

3. Command Relationships

a. **Domestic CBRN Response Command and Control.** Domestic CBRN CM may engage the full spectrum of government, NGOs, and the private sector. The efficient coordination of military and civil capabilities and activities within a stricken operating environment requires a unifying command structure to achieve unity of effort. Military forces always remain under the control of the chain of command as established by Title 10, USC, Title 14, USC, Title 32, USC, or state active duty.

b. NG Soldiers and Airmen may serve either in a federal status like other reserve soldiers, or in a state status (state active duty or Title 32, USC), under the command of the governor. The state governors, through TAGs, control NG forces when those forces are performing active duty in their state role and when performing active duty under Title 32, USC. Figure II-2 depicts these command relationships. Two crucial principles clarify the duty status of NG personnel:

(1) Unless ordered into federal service, NG Soldiers and Airmen serve in state active duty or Title 32, USC, status under a state chain of command under the governor.

(2) The duty status of these NG Soldiers or Airmen is not determined by who funds an operation; rather, it depends upon their legal status and associated chain of authority.

c. **Dual-Status Command.** Legislation allows for a dual-status commander to have command authority over both federal and state forces. A dual-status commander provides a means for providing unity of effort for military forces operating in Title 32, USC, and Title 10, USC. A dual-status commander must be duly appointed and can be an active duty officer who accepts an additional state commission or can be a federalized state NG officer. Dual-status command can leverage military leadership that has local situational awareness and existing relationships with local civil agencies; provide continuity as federal forces are integrated into the response effort; and provide for continuity in response (same JTF C2 prior to and after federal response). Dual-status authority is vested in an individual commander, not the organization. Therefore, a dual-status commander should have a Title 10, USC, deputy and a Title 32, USC, deputy, as well as a joint staff manned by Title 10, USC, and state active duty/Title 32, USC, personnel. This augmented staff is particularly important should a dual-status JTF-State have to control naval forces since few states have naval militias from which to draw maritime expertise. The primary shared DOD and state interests are unity of effort and effective execution.

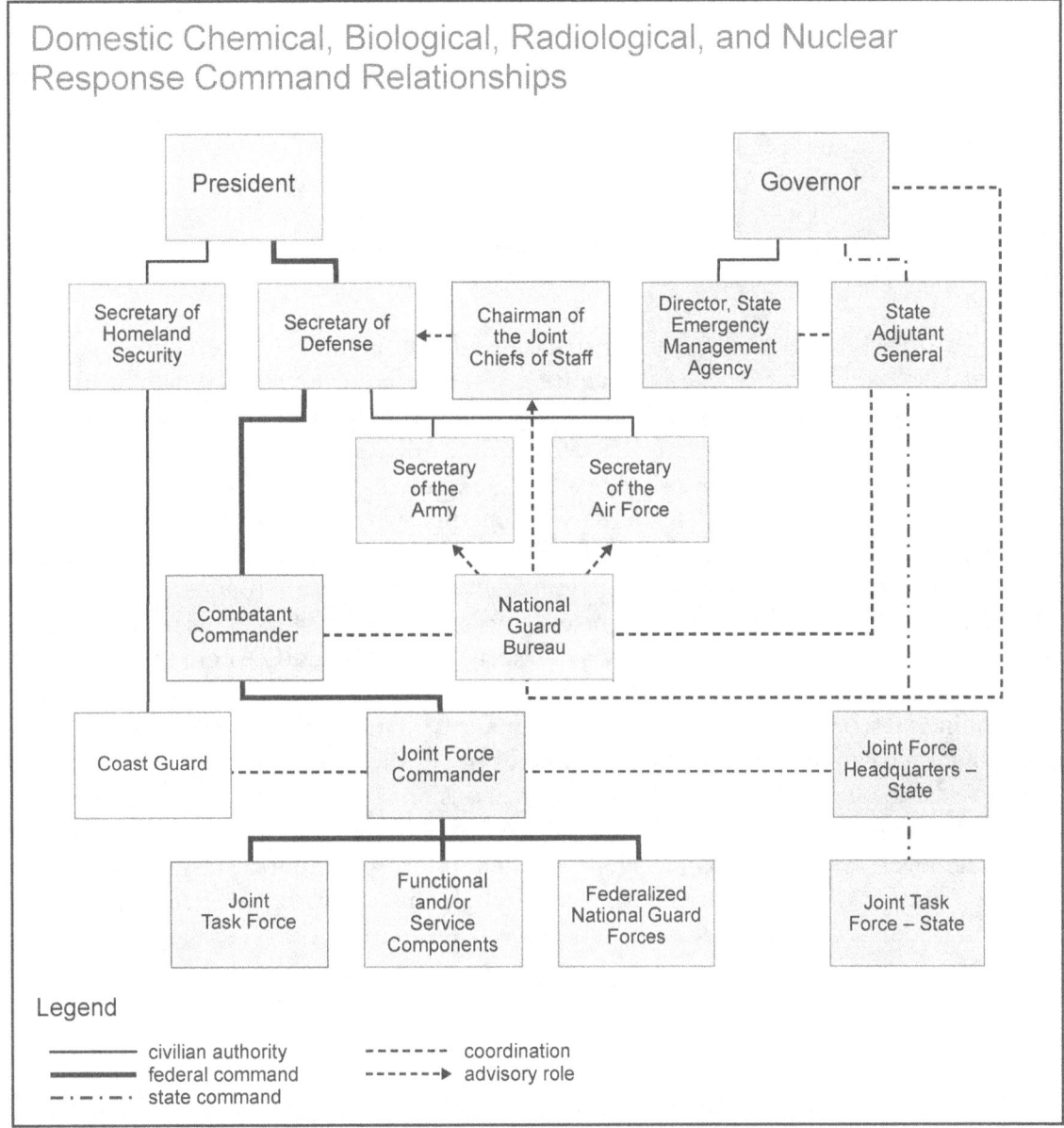

**Figure II-2. Domestic Chemical, Biological, Radiological, and
Nuclear Response Command Relationships**

*For more information on dual authority under Title 10, USC, and Title 32, USC, see
JP 3-27*, Homeland Defense, *and JP 3-28*, Defense Support of Civil Authorities.

d. **Achieving Unity of Effort Without Unity of Command.** When the US undertakes
military operations, the Armed Forces of the United States are only one component of a
national-level effort involving all instruments of national power. Unity of effort can be
achieved without unity of command and is the predominant solution in domestic CBRN
response operations. Unity of effort does not depend on "what" capabilities are employed;
rather, it depends on "how" they are employed.

(1) Joint doctrine focuses on multinational and interagency coordination employing the broad term of "unified action" in referring to the synchronization, coordination, and/or integration of the activities of governmental and nongovernmental entities with military operations to achieve unity of effort. Instilling unity of effort at the national level is, of necessity, a cooperative endeavor involving a number of federal departments and agencies. A similar unity of effort will be necessary at the state and local levels.

For more information on interagency coordination and unity of effort, see JP 3-08, Interorganizational Coordination During Joint Operations.

(2) National response doctrine in the NRF identifies unity of effort through unified command as one of its five key principles for the federal interagency/state/local/tribal response. Effective unified command is indispensable to response activities and requires a clear understanding of the roles and responsibilities of each participating organization. Success requires unity of effort, which respects the chain of command of each participating organization while harnessing seamless coordination across jurisdictions in support of common objectives. Use of the incident command system (ICS) is an important element across multi-jurisdictional or multiagency incident management activities. It provides a structure to enable agencies with different legal, jurisdictional, and functional responsibilities to coordinate, plan, and interact effectively on scene. The ICS "unified command" concept is distinct from the military chain of command construct of "unity of command" and, as such, military forces do not operate under the authority of the incident commander or under the ICS unified command structure. As a team effort, unified command allows all agencies with jurisdictional authority and/or functional responsibility for the incident to provide joint support through mutually developed incident objectives and strategies established at the command level. Each participating agency maintains its own authority, responsibility, and accountability. NIMS supports response through the following elements of unified command: developing a single set of objectives; using a collective, strategic approach; improving information flow and coordination; creating common understanding of joint priorities and restrictions; ensuring that no agency's legal authorities are compromised or neglected; and optimizing the combined efforts of all agencies under a single plan.

For more information on unified command and unity of effort in the NRF, NIMS, and ICS, refer to the NRF Resource Center, www.fema.gov/NRF, *and the* NIMS Resource Center, www.fema.gov/NIMS. *These online resources are routinely updated and evolving.*

(3) At the operational level, the JFO ensures unity of effort by identifying agencies that have the requisite capabilities to reach the common objectives or the ability to adapt their wide-area operations in light of the response by bringing their core competencies to the interagency forum. When all participants in the interagency process understand what needs to be done, agree upon the means to accomplish it, and identify who will accomplish specific activities through coordination, a common sense of ownership and commitment toward resolution helps achieve unity of effort.

(a) To facilitate unity of effort outside the interagency, the unified coordination group may include a limited number of principal state (represented by an appropriate state official or state coordinating officer, as under a Stafford Act declaration), local, and tribal officials, as well as NGO and private-sector representatives. The unified coordination group functions as a multiagency coordination entity (as defined by the NIMS) and works to establish coordinated priorities (single or multiple incidents) and allocate resources, resolve agency policy issues, and provide strategic guidance to support federal incident management activities. Because the principles of unified command apply to the unified coordination group, the objectives are a reflection of the agencies' collective approach rather than "tasking" from a senior commander. JFO standard operating procedures ensure consideration to departmental/agency timelines and requirements to ensure a coordinated federal response.

(b) Based on the magnitude, type of incident, and anticipated level of resource involvement, the supported CCDR may utilize a JTF to command federal (Title 10, USC) military activities in support of the incident. If a JTF is established, consistent with operational requirements, its C2 element is colocated at the JFO and included within the unified coordination group to ensure coordination and unity of effort. NIMS standardized structures and tools enable a unified approach to be effective both on scene and at the emergency operations centers (EOCs).

For more information on unity of effort within the JFO, refer to the NRF Resource Center section on JFO job aides and the JFO Standard Operating Procedures and JFO Field Operations Guide, www.fema.gov/emergency/nrf/jobaids.htm. *These online resources are routinely updated and evolving.*

(4) Unity of effort is expected at the tactical level. This is because the designated incident commander develops the incident objectives on which subsequent incident action planning is based and integrates all capabilities into the response. The incident commander approves the incident action plan (IAP) pertaining to ordering and releasing of incident resources.

(a) Almost all tasks given to DOD are tasks that someone in a civil position normally does, but the disaster conditions have overwhelmed their capacity. The technical knowledge and expertise is still resident with the activity or organization that needs the support (initial state requestor) but they are limited in their ability to cover the sheer magnitude of requirements on their own. Regardless of agency affiliation, newly reporting emergency management and response personnel check in at the designated staging area, base, camp, or location with the incident commander to receive their assignment IAW the established procedures. This direct control of resources at the local/tactical level is sometimes at odds with DOD procedures which require funded mission assignments in support of the federal response. The JFC can facilitate unity of effort with civil authorities at the tactical level by recognizing the incident commander's need to integrate the JFC's resources into his IAP, while remaining cognizant that US law prevents direct tasking by any entity outside the military chain of command.

(b) The JFC shapes tactical unity of effort by having a common operating picture with all levels of the local, state, tribal, and federal response where DOD capabilities are being employed. Unity of effort in CBRN response is improved by interoperability with common methods of operation and common training using compatible or comparable equipment. Finally, common control measures reflected in shared and common plans, concepts of execution, and IAPs can provide for civil authority oversight and direction in incident management, coordination of actions, and supervision of tactical effort without requiring a unity of command construct to get unity of effort. The JFC tasked with integrating DOD capabilities at the tactical level into domestic operations improves unity of effort when there is clarity at the tactical level in these four areas:

1. **Certainty as to Requirement(s).** DSCA policy imposes strict controls for staying within the scope of the FEMA mission assignment process, leaving little latitude for tactical nimbleness in adjusting to quickly changing situations. The JFC should put controls into place to ensure that actual requirements are being met to the satisfaction of the entities closest to the situation.

2. **Clarification of Expectations.** Ground truth at the work site can often change from the initial situation described in the federal response IAP and mission assignment. Thereafter, adjustments are made by first line leaders during execution to achieve the incident commander's objectives. Direct coordination with the initial in-state requestor closest to the point of execution facilitates measured and reasonable adjustments while staying within the operational and fiscal constraints of the mission assignment.

3. **Efficient Resolution of Performance Issues.** Even with the best intentions, support efforts sometimes don't satisfy the expectations of the requestor who initially articulated the requirement. During a catastrophic incident, lost productivity or additional rework because of incomplete or improper performance can have a devastating impact on meeting goals and objectives. The JFC should encourage subordinate leaders to request routine checks and oversight by the initial state requestor to permit quick and efficient resolution of issues among requestors and responders closest to the point of performance.

4. **Risk Management.** Just as in contracting, management of performance risk is allocated by the control measures agreed to by the parties within the contract, with the drafter (in this case the state requestor) initially setting the standards. The JFC should ensure that the initial requestor is part of the controls that are in place to identify and manage performance risk and not rely completely on the ESF coordinator in the JFO. Safety risks can be mitigated by the initial requestor, who routinely does the task, providing oversight over the DOD forces, perhaps even conducting on-site training for nontechnical forces.

e. **Achieving Unity of Effort Between Initial DOD Response Forces.** Effective employment of federal and NG forces simultaneously is never easy, even with common doctrine and organizational design. Presidential directives and DOD regulatory guidance mandate that DOD civilian personnel and Service members meet minimum federal compliance standards for emergency responders and command and staff personnel. Law and circumstance often impede unity of command; leaders at every level depend on their experience, flexible initiative, and understanding of CS operations to ensure integrated and synchronized military CBRN response. Initial DOD response forces, consisting of both NG in Title 32, USC, status and federal forces in Title 10, USC, status, consult, coordinate with, and respond to state authorities or federal civil authorities in the tactical-level execution of assigned tasks, pursuant to an order by SecDef or the President to provide support to those authorities. The DOD CBRN Response Enterprise is structured to achieve an early unity of effort and integration of capabilities for responding to CBRN incidents. Key to achieving unity of effort is the integration of the enterprise through sourcing, training, exercising, readiness reporting, planning, and coordination in phase 0 prior to an incident.

See Appendix C, "Department of Defense Domestic Chemical, Biological, Radiological, and Nuclear Response Enterprise Assets," for additional information on response forces.

4. Considerations

a. **The Joint Force in a CBRN CM Environment.** Overarching requirements for a joint force in a CBRN environment are two-fold: the joint force shapes the composition of the response through proactive planning and interagency, intergovernmental, and nongovernmental coordination. The joint force is also responsible for protecting each member of DOD in support of civil authorities. The CBRN environment causes joint forces to plan in a unique way and recognize the primary reason for employment of the joint force is to support civil authorities and mitigate the consequences of a CBRN incident. Planning considerations are significantly different for the joint force conducting CBRN response as the primary mission than for the joint force conducting other missions. Requirements for protecting joint forces remain a constant priority for the JFC, especially when operating in a contaminated environment. Supporting civil authorities also may entail unique legal implications that need to be considered through all phases of planning and operations.

b. **Layered CBRN Response.** The NRF describes a tiered response and emphasizes that response to incidents should be handled at the lowest jurisdictional level capable of handling the work. The response to a CBRN incident requires the integration and synchronization of capabilities from the local, state, tribal, and federal level. Federal agency teams respond on their agency's authority, if the problem exceeds the capabilities of lower tiers. From the DOD perspective, the layered response will likely begin within hours with employment of NG WMD-CSTs, HRFs, and CERFPs in Title 32, USC, or state active duty in addition to local Title 10, USC, commanders providing assistance under immediate response authority. When directed by SecDef, USNORTHCOM responds within hours with JTF-CS and the first DCRF and C2CRE echelons. These layered capabilities build quickly as depicted in Figure II-3.

c. **Integrated CBRN CM Framework**

(1) **Strategic.** During a CBRN incident, DHS coordinates the federal government's incident management efforts in support of the civil authorities. However, it is likely that the major elements of operational framework will have already been established IAW strategic decisions made by state and local responders in the initial hours of the response effort. A major decision is the determination of controls for the employment of first responders (police, fire, and emergency medical services) into the incident area to ensure that significant portions of the first responder community do not themselves become casualties. Another major decision concerns the ability of local civil government to control

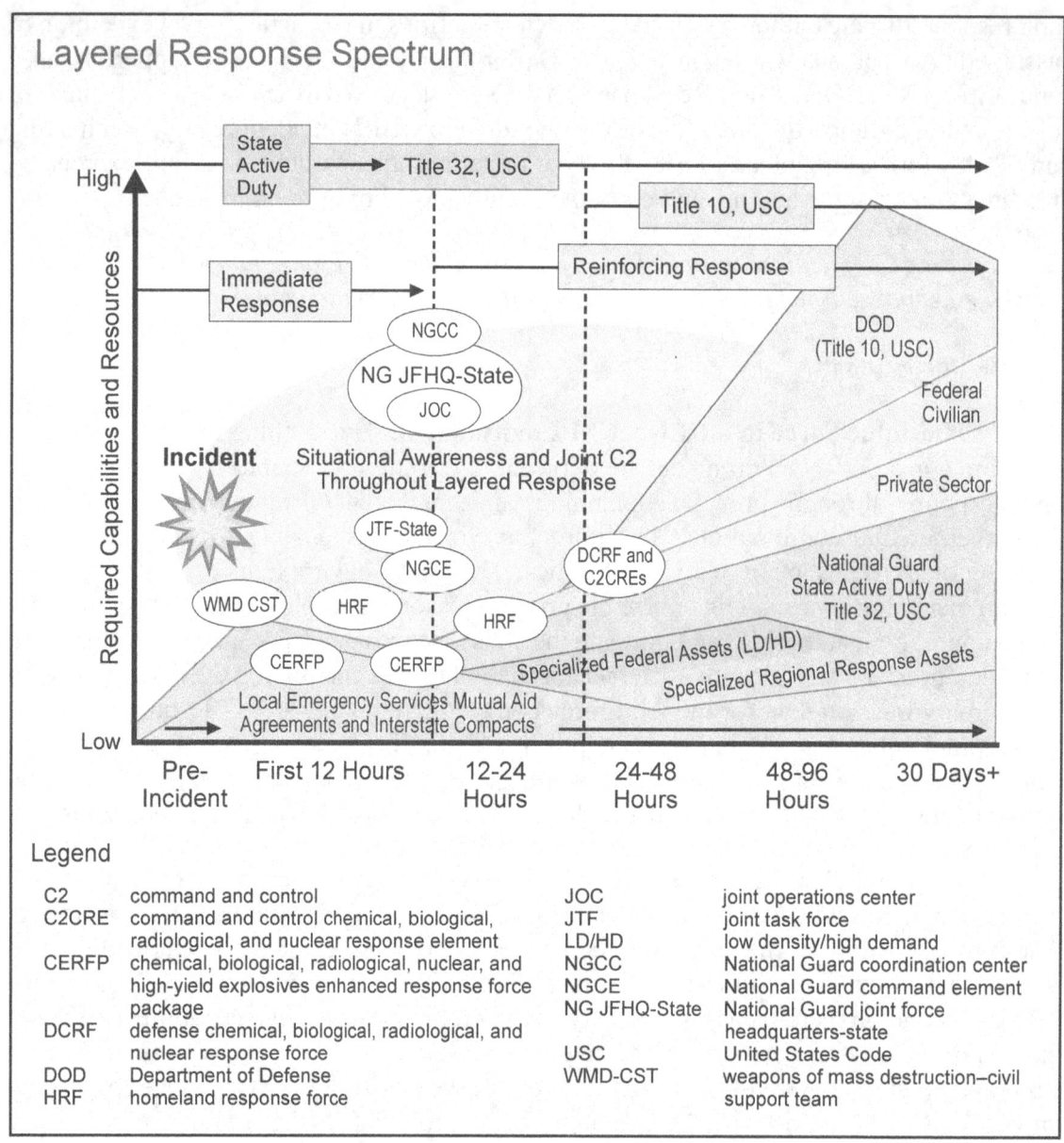

Figure II-3. Layered Response Spectrum

the evacuation out of the incident area. If the local government can control the evacuation through public information and rapid establishment of traffic control points, then operational conditions are favorable for the deliberate application of local, state, and federal resources at designated evacuee processing centers and urban search and rescue, decontamination, and medical triage and emergency medical sites at points upwind or crosswind from the incident area. If the local civil government is unable to control the evacuation of the civil population, then evacuation centers are established at resulting choke points either on major roads or near hospitals and will result in a less deliberate approach to application of local, state, and federal resources. Both these decisions have significant impact on the operational environment that CBRN response forces will find when they are employed into the incident area. Therefore, the initial assessments conducted by NG WMD-CSTs or other federal assessment teams are critical in providing DHS and other federal departments and agencies the necessary situational awareness to make quick decisions regarding resource sharing and coordination.

(2) **Operational.** The WMD-CST arrives in the vicinity of the incident site within the first 6 hours. The WMD-CST is able to provide the initial assessment to the NG JFHQ-State, JTF-State, and the incident commander, which forward the assessment to the NGCC and to USNORTHCOM. It is important the NGCC and USNORTHCOM joint operations center (JOC) forward the initial assessment and characterization of the threat to follow-on deploying NG WMD-CSTs, CERFPs, HRFs, and DCRF and C2CRE units, respectively, so these units can be better prepared for conditions they will face in the incident area. However, as discussed previously, much of the operational environment for CBRN response will be set based on early strategic decisions of the local authorities. If the evacuation of the population is controlled, CBRN response forces deploy to staging areas where they link up with local responders and are integrated into an existing network of evacuation processing centers. If the evacuation is uncontrolled, CBRN response forces may be required to establish evacuation centers at designated choke points or vicinity hospitals. For CBRN response forces, the most critical operational decision in the first 24 hours will be determination of how and where to employ life-saving (search and extraction, decontamination, and medical triage and emergency medical) capabilities. The most likely employment of forces is at the upwind or crosswind points either reinforcing local responders or establishing additional search and extraction, decontamination, and medical triage and emergency medical sites at upwind and crosswind points that local responders do not have the capability to cover.

(3) **Tactical.** At the tactical level, the critical effort is rapid, and effective employment of reconnaissance capabilities is necessary to provide assessments on the effects in terms of casualties and medical treatment (detect and monitor). These assessments provide the necessary information to assist the incident commander in determining upwind and crosswind points and best locations for search and extraction, decontamination, medical triage and emergency medical services, and other sites. The next major effort is to increase the capability and capacity of local responders to perform search and extraction, decontamination, and medical triage and emergency medical care of casualties. DOD forces can reinforce evacuation centers to increase capacity and throughput or establish search and extraction, decontamination, medical triage and emergency medical—expanding the geographic distribution of response capability. An important force multiplier is DOD's ability to assist with decontamination of local fire, police, and emergency medical services personnel and equipment, thus helping these immediate responders to stay safely engaged in the response.

d. **Organizing Considerations**

(1) A JTF established in support of CBRN CM is organized in a manner similar to a conventional JTF. The CCDR normally establishes a JTF to plan and conduct CBRN response. However, a JTF may be established subordinate to a geographic combatant command or subunified command. For example, a GCC may elect to form a JTF to conduct CBRN response in a specific region of the theater. In establishing a JTF for CBRN response,

the CCDR experiences significant organizational, operational, and training challenges as he fuses a diverse group of key personnel, with varying degrees of understanding and experience in joint operations, CBRN response, and interagency cooperation, into a functioning JTF that can conduct a CBRN response. To be effective in such a response, key personnel need to fully understand both interagency and CBRN response techniques and procedures. JTF-CS can function as the core JTF headquarters element. Guidelines for establishing a JTF can be found in JP 3-33, *Joint Task Force Headquarters*.

(2) **Augmentation.** The JTF staff conducts crisis action planning (CAP) and determines whether mission requirements will exceed the JTF staff's capabilities (e.g., qualified personnel, facilities, or equipment). The commander, joint task force (CJTF) requests assistance from the supported CCDR. The supported CCDR prepares in advance to identify or request possible resources from both AC and RC forces to meet critical needs. Additionally, these augmentees train regularly with the JTF if it is organized on a standing basis.

(3) **Joint Planning Augmentation Cell (JPAC).** The JPAC is a tailored group of CBRN response joint planners. The cell is manned, equipped, and trained by JTF-CS to assist other JTF staffs or the DCE. JPAC members maintain currency in CBRN areas through professional education, participation in joint and multiagency exercises, and through planning for national special security event contingencies. The JPAC is able to focus an ad hoc JTF staff on how to employ joint forces in conducting CBRN response. The JPAC also assists the JTF with obtaining technical augmentation or dedicated reachback capability from DTRA, United States Army Medical Research Institute of Infectious Diseases (USAMRIID), United States Army Medical Research Institute of Chemical Defense (USAMRICD), United States Army Forces Command's (FORSCOM's) 20th Support Command, and the CDC. These experts maintain liaison and reachback capability for the JTF and JPAC to national-level expertise, while providing on-staff subject matter expertise. The JTF medical officer, in particular, should consult with these technical experts, as they are able to provide information critical to medical planning considerations.

(4) **Technical Augmentation and Liaison.** CBRN incidents entail operational and force health protection risks. The affected community and federal partners in the response may need technical advice and situational awareness in effects mitigation.

(a) **Defense Threat Reduction Agency.** DTRA provides planning support through deployable teams and real-time technical reachback. This includes expertise in CBRN incident modeling and potential consequences of CBRN incidents, as well as consequence management advisory teams (CMATs) to assist in all phases of CBRN incidents.

(b) **US Army Medical Research Institute of Infectious Diseases.** The USAMRIID representative provides expertise in epidemiology and biological warfare defense.

(c) **Centers for Disease Control and Prevention.** The CDC expert serves as the on-staff augmentation for national level EP and response, the Laboratory Response

Network, and Public Health emergency response, and has expertise on the Strategic National Stockpile.

(d) **20th Support Command (CBRNE).** The 20th Support Command is subordinate to US Army FORSCOM. Its representatives are CBRNE subject matter experts, can serve as liaison to the CJTF, and are knowledgeable of the command's capabilities and units.

(e) **US Army Medical Research Institute of Chemical Defense.** The USAMRICD representative provides an expert in the medical management of chemical casualties.

(f) **Air Force Technical Applications Center.** This center operates and maintains a global network of sensors called the United States Atomic Energy Detection System (USAEDS). Once the USAEDS senses a disturbance underground, underwater, in the atmosphere, or in space, the incident is analyzed for nuclear identification, and findings are reported to SecDef and the President through Headquarters US Air Force.

(g) **Armed Forces Radiobiology Research Institute (AFRRI).** The AFRRI representative provides an expertise in radiological and nuclear warfare defense, response, and treatment for radiological/nuclear casualties. For more discussion on the AFRRI, see Chapter III, "Foreign Consequence Management," paragraph 2c(4).

(5) **Boards, Centers, and Cells.** The CJTF may elect to organize boards, centers, and cells to facilitate a number of functions required of the JTF. To assist in this decision, the staff should determine what organizational structures have been formed within the JTF, and what organizational structures have been delegated to the CJTF by the supported CCDR. The CJTF then decides what boards, centers, and cells would be best suited to support the JTF mission and functions. The DCO is closely associated with the JTF and resides within the JFO as the DOD single point of contact under the NRF. JTFs typically will require planning, logistics, movement, medical fusion, current operations, future operations, communication, mortuary affairs, effects assessment, and intelligence coordination centers and boards. Larger incidents may also require joint mortuary affairs, movement control, contracting, PA, visitors, and a standing personnel reception center.

e. **CBRN Response Operations.** The JP 5-0, *Joint Operation Planning,* phasing model is adapted for domestic CBRN response operations as described below and depicted in Figure II-4.

(1) **Phase 0—Shape (Shape).** Phase 0 is continuous situational awareness and preparedness. Actions in this phase include interagency coordination, planning, identification of gaps, exercises, and PA outreach.

(a) This phase sets conditions for increased CBRN response interoperability and cooperation with interagency partners, through active engagement in planning, conferences, and exercises. These strategic- and theater-level objective activities continue through all phases. Preparedness of the designated units is the operational and tactical focus during this phase in order to ensure readiness conditions are sustained for execution of

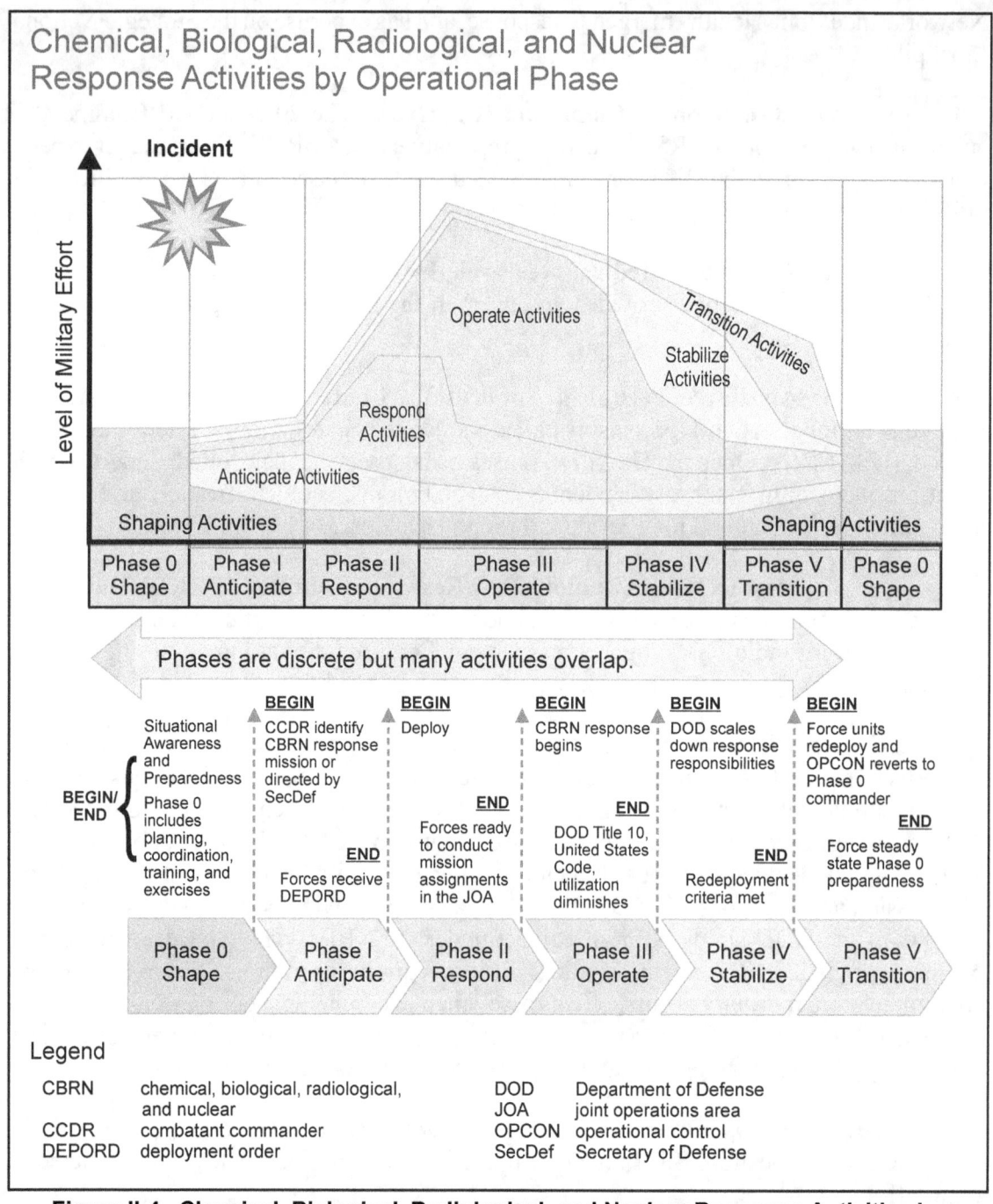

Figure II-4. Chemical, Biological, Radiological, and Nuclear Response Activities by Operational Phase

CBRN response operations and building command relationships. Units with designated C2 headquarters and the combatant command's Army Service component prepare to assume their mission. TF commanders focus on training and rehearsals for CBRN response, based on the joint mission-essential task list (JMETL) provided through the Army Service component command (ASCC) and the CCDR directed JMETL. Individuals and detachments receive training from experts on operations in a contaminated environment.

(b) Further, subordinate staffs, DCRF and C2CRE TF commanders, DCRF and C2CRE task forces, or others identify shortfalls and submit requests for additional capabilities through their parent headquarters. These staffs modify existing plans to fit their particular organization and capabilities and review the plans with the CJTF. This includes updating and submitting time-phased force and deployment data through the ASCC and their parent headquarters to USTRANSCOM. The TF commander pays particular attention to interoperability between elements from the other Services, and includes LNOs and other requirements.

(c) CBRN response units should be immunized to prevent unnecessary delays in response posture. Unit inoculation may occur at home base, an intermediate staging base, or the BSI based on availability of vaccine(s), time required for the vaccine to be effective, and time-distance criteria. Units must meet force health protection standards established in the operation or DEPORD prior to deployment into an operational area. For units stationed in an operational area, force health protection standards are met prior to employment. The CJTF should consider all these factors and recommend a viable force health protection course of action (COA) to the supported CCDR at the earliest available opportunity.

(d) Finally, the shaping phase includes a mission rehearsal exercise designed by USNORTHCOM/USPACOM and supported by USARNORTH/US Army Pacific, respectively. The phase ends with the identification of a potential CBRN response mission through indication and warning, SecDef direction, or the occurrence of a no-notice event.

(2) **Phase I—Deter (Anticipate).** Continued situational awareness is vital to understanding the CBRN response operation parameters. The situation may warrant, due to indications and warnings, the CAP process to begin before a CBRN incident occurs. Determination of joint force command structure, the DOD anticipated response, and early and thorough collaboration with federal departments and agencies, state governments (including respective NG TAGs, commanders), and localities is paramount. Alerting and preparing the joint force may be directed through a CJCS warning order, planning order, or alert order; however, CBRN incidents may also occur without warning, resulting in accelerated procedures and the first notification being an EXORD. This EXORD guidance may possibly even be verbal. In this case, the operations would move directly into phase II, with relevant phase I tasks still requiring to be performed. During this phase, the DCOs and United States Northern Command situational awareness teams (NSATs) are employed post incident to provide assessments to USNORTHCOM and situational awareness to the JFLCC.

(a) The assessment will determine the scope and magnitude of the incident; identify potential theater response forces; identify DCRF and C2CRE requirements to expedite response; and identify potential C2 node requirements. The senior individual of the assessment element serves as the CCDR's LNO to gain on-scene situational awareness and provide recommendations on the appropriate level of C2 and initial resources required for the CBRN response.

(b) The assessment element may include a staff judge advocate (SJA), CBRN, medical, PA, mortuary affairs, operations, plans, logistics, law enforcement, and communications officers and selected subject matter experts to assist in developing the assessment and recommending an appropriate response. USNORTHCOM's standing JTF in support of CBRN CM, JTF-CS, trains and prepares for this mission by maintaining a 24/7 on-call command assessment element capability. Other CCDRs have standing site assessment teams or survey and assessment teams prepared for this mission.

(c) Because the vast majority of Title 10, USC, capabilities for DSCA falls under USNORTHCOM, the JTF-CS NSAT procedures are included here as an example of assessment processes and actions. Following coordination with state civil and military officials (typically the state TAG or the NG JFHQ-State) and federal officials (to include the FCO, incident management assistance team, the DCO and other on-scene technical advisors), the NSAT makes an evaluation of potential shortfalls in federal and state capabilities, which may become requests for DOD assistance. The NSAT prepares its assessment shaped by its knowledge of CBRN effects, the harm or damage the effects may cause, and how to mitigate and manage the resulting consequences. The assessment identifies proposed methods of response, anticipated actions, and potentially required forces. Information gathered by the NSAT is developed, either independently or through the support of an appropriate joint planning group for CAP, into a commander's assessment using the Adaptive Planning and Execution format for a commander's estimate and forwarded to the CCDR. This document provides specific recommendations to the CCDR relative to the CBRN response effort, to include tailoring and supplementing the CBRN response force structure required to employ.

(d) The NSAT assessment helps the CCDR conduct the mission analysis and prepare the commander's estimate with a recommended DOD COA to be taken in support of the incident and recommended DOD resources and capabilities for anticipated mission assignments. The commander's estimate identifies force to task capabilities required to accomplish anticipated DOD mission assignments. With SecDef approval and through CJCS direction, these capabilities are identified by the Services, CCDRs, and the DOD agencies. The CJCS EXORD identifies the designated forces allocated to the CCDR and specifies the type of command authority (normally OPCON) in steady state for exercises and mission execution. Additionally, it provides approval of purpose, desired effect, and COA to be taken in support of federal agencies for the CBRN response.

(e) This phase ends when forces receive prepare-to-deploy orders and are staged and ready to deploy. Once a unit receives a DEPORD through its parent headquarters specifying OPCON by the receiving CCDR, the TF deploys LNOs to a location designated by the CJTF for establishing the JTF deployable headquarters. These LNOs provide C2 connectivity for dissimilar systems and pass situational assessments back to their TF as the situation develops. Simultaneously, each TF deploys an advance party to the BSI identified by the JFLCC or JFC for JRSOI and base support. JRSOI is the essential process that transitions deploying forces, consisting of personnel, equipment, and materiel arriving in theater, into forces capable of meeting the CCDR's operational requirements. The TF commanders should coordinate with the CJTF on rules for the use of force (RUF), arming status, law enforcement missions, intelligence support and restrictions, PA guidance, deployment priorities, and mission assignments (if known). Because of the nature of the most likely CBRN CM operations, forces will likely deploy into and remain in the JOA for the entire length of the CBRN response. Catastrophic incidents may require force rotation.

(3) **Phase II—Seize the Initiative (Respond).** The key to success during the respond phase is echeloning the required JTF resources at the appropriate time and place. Phase II executes deployment of forces to key theater nodes and to the JOA to save lives, minimize human suffering, and maintain public confidence. Speed and decisiveness are essential. The JFC establishes C2 of designated DOD Title 10, USC, forces, establishes a common operational picture, continues JRSOI, and validates and establishes a BSI. (See Appendix B, "Planning Considerations for Logistics and Other Services from Domestic Base Support Installations and Foreign Theater Assets.") Participation in the JRSOI is essential for mission accomplishment and protection of the joint force.

(a) Forces are prioritized to deploy for mission tasks that are directly involved in life saving and preventing further injury. These forces have the highest movement priority for CBRN response force deployment. Next in movement priority are forces that assess and establish operations or provide temporary critical life support. These forces subsequently become the forces necessary to establish and sustain operations. Biological incidents may or may not provide a clear point of origin. In this case, TF-Medical may be the primary effort and have priority in movement. Elements of TF-Operations normally have priority for movement in the force flow because they contain those capabilities needed to relieve and/or augment the efforts of first responders (i.e., monitoring, marking, decontamination, hot-zone extraction, security). TF-Operations is normally employed closest to the actual incident site.

(b) Forces for the JTF are transferred using a DEPORD to the CCDR, and command relationships are established as designated in the EXORD and/or OPORD. After coordinating with the BSI, the JTF commences JRSOI operations. Commanders should appoint a capable officer and staff to continue to manage unit arrival and JRSOI. As units complete JRSOI, they occupy their assigned operating bases and prepare for mission assignments. Leaders take every available opportunity to reinforce soldier skills they will need when operating in their operational areas, stressing protective measures, RUF, and situation awareness and reporting. TF commanders receive and integrate additional forces identified during phase II. They provide updates to the CJTF and keep the supporting installations informed.

(c) Phase II completion is generally marked by having forces deployed with enough C2 and unit-capability to safely and effectively begin operations. Depending on the situation, the CJTF may decide to move into phase III operations before all phase II objectives are complete and continue to work on phase II objectives while in phase III.

(4) **Phase III—Dominate (Operate).** In phase III, planning and execution efforts are synchronized and integrated with the efforts of the supported civil authorities, as well as other military operations that may be occurring simultaneously (e.g., technical nuclear forensics sample collection) within the same operational area. Phase III begins when DOD and/or NG forces begin executing mission assignments within the operational area. The coordinating agency typically assigns mission assignments to supporting or cooperating agencies for action. DOD accepts mission assignments as RFAs, which become mission assignments only after being received through the Office of the Executive Secretary of DOD, forwarded to the ASD(HD&ASA) and the JDOMS for validation and order processing, and then approved by SecDef. Once SecDef approves the request, an order is issued to

combatant commands, Services, and/or agencies to accomplish the mission. In the case of the DCRF and C2CRE, SecDef has authorized CDRUSNORTHCOM to approve the mission assignments as long as they are within the scope and capabilities of the DCRF and C2CRE. During this phase, the primary focus is on mission assignments that involve incident site lifesaving and injury prevention. Key tasks during this phase are hazard assessment, casualty search and extraction/rescue, ambulatory and non-ambulatory decontamination, emergency medical services, air and ground medical/casualty evacuation, and logistical support.

(a) The CJTF exercises OPCON over all designated DOD forces as directed by the CCDR's EXORD. The commander of a JTF-State exercises OPCON over all designated NG forces as directed by the approved EXORD or EMAC agreement. The JTF may task organize functionally, by Service components, or a combination of both, depending on the situation. The JTF is responsible for executing mission assignments using the allocated DOD forces within the designated operational area. The JTF-State is also responsible for executing mission assignments using NG forces within the designated operational area and requesting additional forces from the supported CCDR if those within the designated operational area are not adequate. The JTF receives mission assignments from the DCO/DCE after they have been validated. The JTF maintains force readiness and sustainment requirements for assigned forces in the designated operational area.

(b) The CJTF begins to assign missions to the JTF component commanders, who in turn task their units as they become available within the JOA. In some cases, mission assignments will be awaiting specialized units as they arrive. Each TF can expect to receive multiple missions together with a priority of effort. Commanders should conduct information engagement actions with residents and responders working near their forces.

(c) Certain units may work closely with highly specialized personnel from other agencies as part of their mission assignment. The TF commander may be required to support these agencies and should coordinate with them to assess the progress of operations.

(d) Normally Joint tactics, techniques, and procedures and mission essential task list conditions and standards derived from the Universal Joint Task List (UJTL) are adequate to meet the tactical expectation of civil authorities; however, in some circumstances, additional requirements may be established. Joint forces should expect some local authority coordination and periodic work oversight to confirm that projects are progressing on time and confirm that performance is to acceptable civil standards. Phase III ends when deployed Title 10, USC, Title 32, USC, and/or state active duty NG forces have completed the preponderance of incident site lifesaving mission assignments and the effort shifts to other state and/or federal mission assignments that have broader application to the JOA.

(5) **Phase IV—Stabilize (Stabilize).** Stabilization is marked by a scaling down of operations as DOD Title 10, USC, forces, Title 32, USC, NG, and/or state active duty utilization diminishes with the associated completion of a majority of incident site mission assignments.

(a) Great loss of property or life is no longer the state's major concern; rather, the priority shifts to support life sustaining operations. Key tasks during this phase are patient redistribution, logistical support, and ESF activities to minimize human suffering and enable community recovery. During this operational phase, all requests for forces have been identified and filled such that a smaller DOD C2 or a state-based NG C2 headquarters may be warranted. The JTF may engage in repositioning capabilities to locations throughout the operations area that support the primary agency requests. Determining whether DOD has met transition criteria requires close coordination and day-to-day interaction with the lead agency. TF commanders continue to exercise battle command while reviewing subordinate operations for ability to transition. Redeployment of selected uncontaminated DOD force capabilities no longer required for operations may begin; however, selected contaminated assets such as aircraft require GCC and International Civil Aviation Organization approval before transition begins. Success equals civil authorities ready to respond effectively to continuing requirements and assuming full response without degradation of operations.

(b) The phase ends when civil authorities are postured to transition to recovery operations and have the ability to accommodate surge requirements for treatment of casualties and critical life support. DCRF and C2CRE units redeploy and reconstitute.

(6) **Phase V—Enable Civil Authorities (Transition).** Transition functions begin when consequences of the CBRN incident have been mitigated and adequate support of civil authorities has been provided such that further support is no longer required.

(a) Civil authorities and the JTF, as well as the supported CCDR or supporting or supported JTF-State, agree to implement a seamless transition of operational responsibilities to a designated civil authority or a designated command. Civil authorities are postured for full responsibility for NRF recovery operations and have the ability to accommodate surge requirements. Well before this phase begins, TF and JTF planners develop transition criteria with specific measures of effectiveness for each mission assignment. As required, they modify reporting formats to indicate readiness for transition. Resource managers should pay particular attention to accountability for nonexpendable items that are to be turned over to a civilian agency as part of transition. Site clean-up is coordinated with federal, state, and local authorities, and HAZMAT is turned over for disposition. Lessons learned and after action reports are completed. Commanders review redeployment schedules and mode of transport details with their subordinates and ensure that leaders understand the schedule and requirements for a safe and efficient redeployment. Redeploying forces may require decontamination, and medical observation and evaluation based on the pathogen or hazard involved. Forces safely redeploy to home station to reset and reconstitute.

(b) The phase ends when all response forces are moved out of the JOA and when DOD Title 10, USC, Title 32, USC, or state active duty NG forces have transitioned all operations back to civil authorities and redeployed to home stations.

5. Unique Planning Considerations in the Domestic Operational Environment

a. **Base Support Installation.** A BSI is a military installation within the US or its territories controlled by any military Service or agency, in or near an actual or projected domestic emergency operational area, designated by DOD to provide military support for DOD and federal agency disaster response operation efforts.

(1) Resources provided by a designated BSI may include, but are not limited to marshalling and lay down areas, security forces, personnel and equipment reception and staging areas and facilities, personnel support, billeting, transportation, material handling equipment, maintenance, general supply and subsistence support, contracting support, communications support, and medical services.

(2) Logistic planners should consider appropriate Service and RC installations as potential BSIs that will facilitate JRSOI and sustainment of CBRN response units. Although the Services, when directed by SecDef, designate the appropriate BSI, locations for potential BSI should be based on previous site surveys, assessments, and mission analysis.

For more information on BSI planning considerations, see Appendix B, "Planning Considerations for Logistics and Other Services from Domestic Base Support Installations and Foreign Theater Assets."

b. **United States Army Corps of Engineers (USACE) Services.** USACE is the designated ESF #3 (Public Works and Engineering) coordinator and a primary agency as directed by the NRF. USACE can provide water, ice, construction materials, and engineer services when activated under ESF#3 and ESF#6 (Mass Care, Emergency Assistance, Housing, and Human Services). If ESF#3 or ESF#6 have not been activated, the JTF or DCO may request engineering capabilities through the CCDR to the components.

c. **Mortuary Affairs.** The joint force may aid federal and state agencies by providing mortuary affairs assistance. Any assistance provided will be IAW the NRF and existing civilian plans and local civilian direction.

(1) The primary responsibility for responding to mortuary affairs issues rests with state and local authorities. A local or state medical examiner and/or coroner (ME/C) will have the responsibility for leading the response effort. DOD mortuary affairs assets are usually employed in support of the ME/C. Other important state and local stakeholders who may have significant operational involvement include Office of Emergency Management, Department of Public Health, NG, state law enforcement, EPA, and fire department and HAZMAT units.

(2) Several conditions affect the ability of local and state officials to respond to mass fatality operations. Some of these factors include number of fatalities; quality and state of remains; the agent or agents (contaminated versus uncontaminated) present; location and size of the search and recovery area; conditions (weather, daylight, terrain); city and state resources available; and most important, public expectations. Within the construct of the civilian operation there are a number of different missions where joint forces may be asked to provide mortuary affairs assistance.

(3) Expected DOD mortuary operations include advisory support, search and recovery, reception, remains storage, contamination mitigation of remains, photography, fingerprinting, forensic dentistry, forensic pathology, family assistance, disposition of remains and personal effects, administration and logistic support. Decedent identification is an ME/C responsibility; DOD mortuary affairs assets support the identification process through forensic recovery and preservation of decedent identification material.

(4) For remains that cannot be decontaminated to a specified transportation level, protecting the health of Service members and the public takes precedence over rapid disposition. Temporary storage of remains in a refrigerated storage facility or interment of those contaminated remains that pose a threat to public health is recommended until remains can be safely handled.

(5) A phased mortuary affairs plan may be required to assist civil authorities in augmenting ME/C. Not all mortuary affairs assets are deployed for each mass fatality incident; the mortuary affairs response will be tailored to meet the needs of the local jurisdiction.

For additional information on mortuary affairs, see JP 4-06, Mortuary Affairs.

d. **Decontamination Planning.** The EPA is the ESF coordinator and primary agency responsible for hazardous waste. The USCG may also play a significant role as a primary agency for HAZMAT as defined by the NRF and the National Oil and Hazardous Substances Pollution Contingency Plan.

e. **Control Zones.** In CBRN response, control zones are established to ensure the safety of all responders and control access into and out of a contaminated area. The three zones established at a chemical, radiological, nuclear, and some biological incident sites (where there is a contaminated area such as may be the case with anthrax) are often referred to as the hot zone, the warm zone, and the cold zone. Figure II-5 depicts these control zones. In nearly all cases, the control zones will decrease in size with time as CBRN hazards naturally decrease. Once the characteristics of the hazard are understood, the control zones can be effectively altered to allow more mission flexibility.

(1) **Hot Zone.** The hot zone is an area immediately surrounding a hazardous material incident which extends far enough to prevent adverse effects from released contamination to personnel outside the zone. The level of risk and thus the included area is determined by the incident commander, accounting for characteristics of the hazards. The hot zone can also be referred to as the exclusion zone, red zone, or restricted zone and is the primary area of contamination. The hot zone is the area that the incident commander judges to be the most affected by the incident. This includes any area to which the contaminant has spread or is likely to spread. Primary contamination can occur when individuals enter this zone. Usually, no decontamination or patient care except evacuation is carried out in this zone. Access is only permitted to personnel who are properly trained and protected. The incident commander sets the perimeters of this zone after giving consideration to the type of agent, the volume released, the means of dissemination, the prevailing meteorological conditions, and the potential of local topographic characteristics to channel agent dispersal.

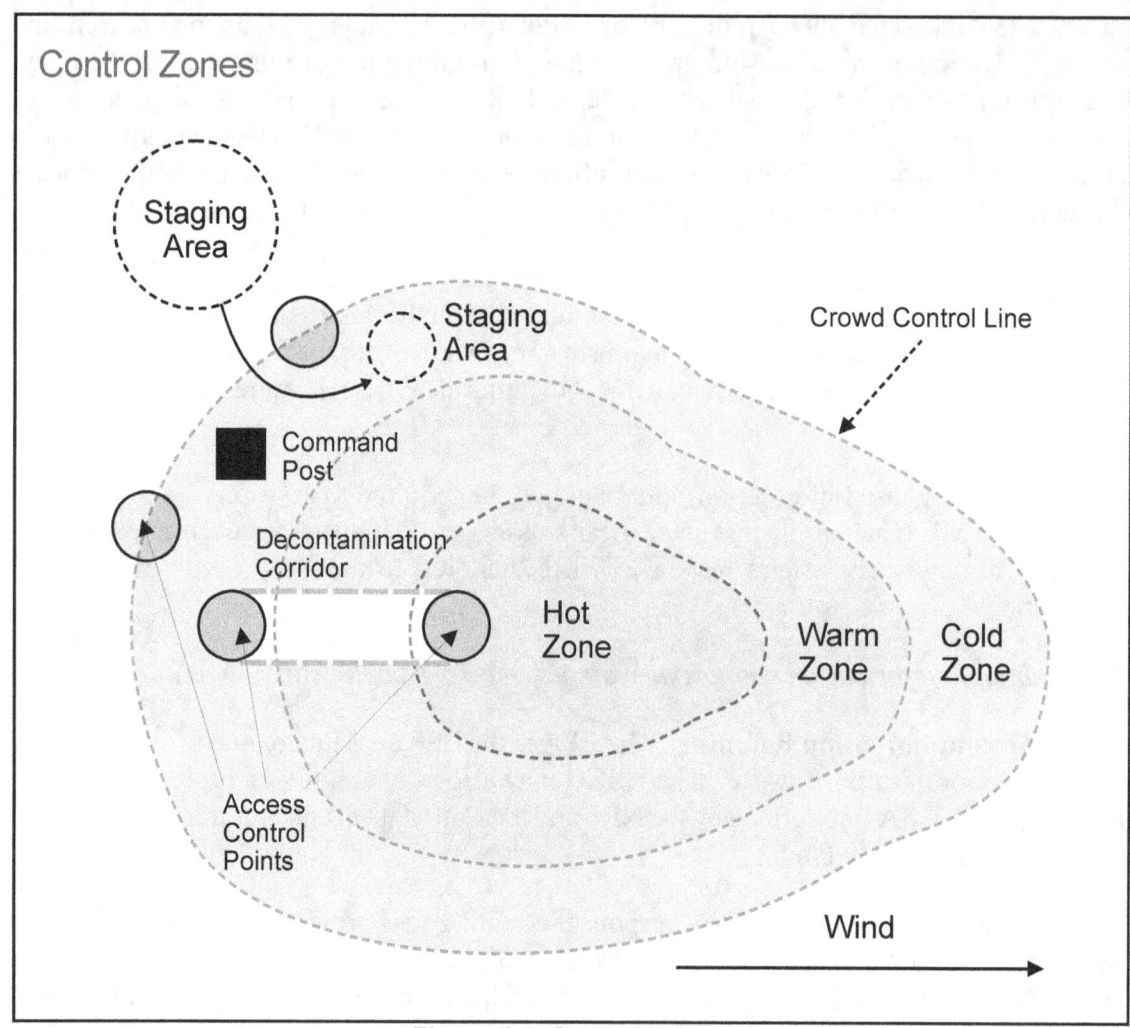

Figure II-5. Control Zones

Priorities within the hot zone may include conducting search and rescue, performing hazard mitigation, and identifying CBRN hazards or other physical obstacles to the entry point.

(2) **Warm Zone.** The warm zone includes control points for the access corridor and thus assists in reducing the spread of contamination. The warm zone can also be referred to as the decontamination zone, contamination-reduction zone, contamination-reduction corridor, yellow zone, or limited access zone. The warm zone is the area between the hot and cold zones where personnel and equipment decontamination and hot zone support take place. Management of the warm zone includes decontamination corridors where casualties, emergency responders, and equipment are decontaminated and where there is a risk of secondary contamination from objects or individuals brought from the hot zone. Maintaining access control points connecting the warm zone to the hot and cold zones and for the decontamination corridor assists in reducing the spread of contamination. Warm zone operation should be established in an area that is safe from downwind exposure and should include the bulk of the decontamination assets where survey teams are positioned and equipment decontamination is accomplished.

(3) **Cold Zone.** The cold zone is the area where the command post and support functions that are necessary to control the incident are located. It should be clean, meaning it is free of all contamination by HAZMAT, including discarded protective clothing and respiratory equipment. Contaminated casualties and emergency response personnel must be decontaminated before entering this zone. The cold zone is the area where the incident command post, staging areas for equipment, and other support functions that are necessary to control the incident are located upwind and uphill of the warm zone. The same basic considerations that are used for the hot and warm zones influence the extent of the cold zone. The cold zone must be readily accessible and provide the means for safety and rest. It must also be large enough to accommodate local, state, and federal CBRN response forces (if required) and to serve as the staging area for personnel and equipment. The operational priorities of the cold zone include providing C2 for operations being conducted in the warm and hot zones and ensuring that there is an area of security for emergency personnel and response forces conducting operations. Access to the different zones should be tightly controlled and limited to as few people as possible. Communication between work areas should be face-to-face whenever possible, particularly if the use of radios or other electronic devices (e.g., megaphones) is restricted because of the hazards involved.

(4) **Zone Control in Nuclear Detonations.** DHS has worked with partner agencies and emergency response partners to establish standard guidance for emergency planners with nuclear detonation specific response recommendations to maximize the preservation of life in the event of an urban nuclear detonation. The planning guidance summarizes recommendations based on the effects of a 10 KT nuclear detonation in an urban environment. The nuclear explosion's observable phenomena, in the area around ground zero, are linked to an accumulation of the hazards from pressure (blast), heat (thermal), and radiation as discussed in Chapter I, "Overview." These cumulative hazards make it more dangerous for rescue workers and less likely to find survivors the closer one moves toward the point of detonation. The observable phenomenon of damage to infrastructure and other objects provides a way to describe zones with rough approximation delineations that can assist planners and the initial emergency responders in managing risk before radiation levels have been measured and hazard areas marked. There are no clear boundaries between damage zones resulting from a nuclear detonation, but generally, the light damage zone is characterized by broken windows and easily managed injuries; the moderate damage zone by significant building damage, rubble, downed utility poles, overturned automobiles, fires, and serious injuries; and the severe damage zone by destroyed infrastructure.

For further guidance on the nuclear weapon effects, planning considerations, and zone control, refer to http://www.afrri.usuhs.mil/outreach/pdf/planning-guidance.pdf, for DHS Planning Guidance for Response to a Nuclear Detonation, *and JP 3-11,* Operations in Chemical, Biological, Radiological, and Nuclear (CBRN) Environments.

6. **Applicable Laws and Agreements in the Domestic Operational Environment**

a. **Key Executive and Legislative Guidance.** PPDs, Presidential study directives, Presidential decision directives, national security Presidential directives (NSPDs), homeland security Presidential directives (HSPDs), and executive orders (EOs) are the primary means by which the President issues national security policy guidance. These Presidential documents, national-level strategy documents, and laws provide the basis for the development of subordinate and implementing guidance by DOD agencies. A list of documents that provide guidance for CBRN response is contained in Appendix A, "Key Legal, Strategy, and Policy Documents and International Protocols." The following documents deserve special note due to their direct applicability to a domestic CBRN response:

(1) **HSPD-5, *Management of Domestic Incidents*.** HSPD-5 enhances the ability of the US to manage domestic incidents by establishing a single, comprehensive national incident management system. The NRF was developed as a result of HSPD-5 to integrate the family of federal domestic prevention, preparedness, response, and recovery plans into a single, all-discipline, all-hazards plan to unify the domestic incident management process. When the NRF is used, national interagency plans such as the National Oil and Hazardous Substances Pollution Contingency Plan, Mass Migration Emergency Plan, National Search and Rescue Plan, National Infrastructure Protection Plan, and National Maritime Transportation Security Plan are incorporated as supporting and/or operational plans. In addition to consolidating federal plans, the NRF establishes a National Operations Center, and the creation of a PFO, who may be appointed to represent the Secretary of Homeland Security at the incident site and the JFO. HSPD-5 also created NIMS to provide a consistent nationwide approach for federal, state, and local governments to work effectively and efficiently together to prepare for, respond to, and recover from domestic incidents.

(2) **PPD-8, *National Preparedness*.** This directive establishes policies to develop a national preparedness goal that identifies the core capabilities necessary for preparedness and a national preparedness system to guide activities that will enable the nation to achieve the goal. The national preparedness system will allow the nation to track progress of our ability to build and improve the capabilities necessary to prevent, protect against, mitigate the effects of, respond to, and recover from those threats that pose the greatest risk to the security of the nation.

(3) **The Robert T. Stafford Disaster Relief and Emergency Assistance Act.** The Stafford Act is the primary legal authority for federal participation in domestic DR. When incidents of national significance that are declared disasters or emergencies by the President occur, federal support to states is delivered IAW relevant provisions of the Stafford Act. A governor may request the President to declare a major disaster or emergency if the governor finds that effective response to the incident is beyond the combined response capabilities of the state and affected local governments. Based on the findings of a joint federal-state-local preliminary damage assessment indicating the damages are of sufficient severity and magnitude to warrant assistance under the act, the President may issue a major disaster or emergency declaration. The President may unilaterally provide federal emergency assistance under the Stafford Act when the President determines that an emergency exists for which the primary responsibility for response rests with the USG. Based upon the overwhelming nature of a no-notice catastrophic CBRN incident, the approval process will be expedited through federal levels. Federal assistance takes many forms—including the direct provision of goods and services, financial assistance (through insurance, grants, loans, and direct payments), and technical assistance—and can come from various sources. Under the NRF construct, DOD is designated a supporting agency for all ESFs and a cooperating agency for

a number of NRF support and incident annexes. DOD approved support under the Stafford Act is generally provided on a reimbursable basis. The ESF coordinators, located in the JFO, serve as the primary operational-level functional mechanisms to provide assistance to state, local, and tribal governments or to federal departments and agencies conducting missions of primary federal responsibility.

(4) **The Economy Act (Title 31, USC, Section 1535).** IAW the Economy Act or other applicable authorities, federal agencies participating in the NRF may provide federal-to-federal support by executing interagency or intra-agency reimbursable agreements. Federal agencies providing mutual aid support may request reimbursement from the requesting agency for eligible expenditures.

(5) **The National Strategy for Homeland Security, the National Strategy to Combat Weapons of Mass Destruction, and the National Strategy for Countering Biological Threats.** The National Strategy for Homeland Security complements the National Security Strategy (NSS) of the US by providing a road map for mobilizing and organizing the nation to secure the US homeland from terrorist attacks. This includes objectives around which society can mobilize, align, and focus on HS functions, align budgetary resources to the task of securing the homeland, and account for performance on HS efforts. The National Strategy to Combat Weapons of Mass Destruction also complements the NSS by expanding on the actions necessary to use strengthened nonproliferation to combat WMD proliferation, counterproliferation to counter WMD use, and WMD CM to respond to WMD use. The *National Strategy for Countering Biological Threats* provides a framework for future USG planning efforts that supports the overall *Biodefense for the 21st Century* (HSPD-10/NSPD-33), and complements existing White House strategies related to biological threat preparedness and response.

(6) **Posse Comitatus Act, Title 18, USC, Section 1385.** Under the PCA, federal military personnel in a Title 10, USC, duty status may not participate in law enforcement activities except as otherwise authorized by the Constitution or statute. For example, Congress specifically authorized military forces to engage in law enforcement activities as an exception to PCA when dealing with criminal investigations involving nuclear materials. See Title 18, USC, Section 831, and DODD 5525.5, *DOD Cooperation with Civilian Law Enforcement Officials.*

(7) **The Emergency Management Assistance Compact.** The EMAC is a congressionally approved interstate mutual aid compact that provides a legal structure by which states affected by an emergency may request assistance from other states. Signatories to the compact resolve potential legal and financial obstacles that states might otherwise encounter as they provide assistance to the stricken state or states. The compact sets out the responsibilities of the signatory states, provides authority to officials responding from other states (except that of arrest unless specifically authorized by the receiving state) equal to that held by residents of the affected state, ensures reciprocity in recognizing professional licenses or permits for professional skills, and provides liability protection (in certain areas) to responders from other states. The National Emergency Management Association, a professional association of state emergency managers, administers the compact. Since being ratified by Congress and signed into law in 1996 (Public Law 104-321), 50 states, the

District of Columbia, Puerto Rico, and the US Virgin Islands have enacted legislation to become members of EMAC. The compact establishes immunities, authorities, and liabilities for missions executed under its authority. It allows the states to rely upon each other in responding to, among other things, emergencies such as man-made or natural disasters, insurgencies, or enemy attack.

b. **Key DOD Guidance**

(1) **Implications.** DOD guidelines are promulgated in a variety of documents that include strategy documents, planning guidance, DODDs, and the CJCS policy documents. These documents are consistent with and complementary to the federal statutes and national security policy discussed earlier. DODDs specifically address missions for HD and CS operations to include CBRN response. The following documents, further discussed in Appendix A, "Key Legal, Strategy, and Policy Documents and International Protocols," are of special note:

(a) The Strategy for Homeland Defense and Civil Support that builds on the concept of an active, layered defense outlined in the National Defense Strategy (NDS).

(b) The DODD 3025 series of directives that provide policy on and responsibilities for CS activities.

(c) Chairman of the Joint Chiefs of Staff Instruction (CJCSI) 3125.01, *Defense Support of Civil Authorities (DSCA) for Domestic Consequence Management Operations in Response to a Chemical, Biological, Radiological, Nuclear, or High-Yield Explosive (CBRNE) Incident,* provides operational and policy guidance for US military forces supporting domestic CBRN response operations to prepare for and respond to the effects of a threatened or actual CBRN situation.

(2) **Special Considerations.** The following discussion provides general guidelines for functional areas that are associated with CBRN response. Commanders should be aware of the specific legal implications of special considerations.

(a) **Intelligence Oversight Information Collection, Sharing, and Handling**

<u>1</u>. In light of today's changing environment, commanders and their staffs should carefully consider the different rules when planning domestic operations.

<u>2</u>. The SJA role is especially important during domestic operations as the parameters under which DOD operates are different in the US than they are overseas. The military commander's need for information and intelligence within the homeland is on the rise—force protection information and counterintelligence integrated into domestic operations are expected due to a heightened awareness of potential terrorist threats. These needs and expectations pose unique issues in the information and intelligence gathering arena. DOD intelligence components are restricted by a set of rules referred to as intelligence oversight, governed and regulated by DODD 5240.01, *DOD Intelligence Activities,* and DOD 5240.1-R, *Procedures Governing the Activities of DOD Intelligence Components that Affect United States Persons.* Everyone else in DOD, is subject to a

different set of rules governed by DODD 5200.27, *Acquisition of Information Concerning Persons and Organizations not Affiliated with the Department of Defense*. Therefore, the commander must direct his need for information or intelligence to the right component—the component with the capability and authority to achieve the commander's intent. Determining the nature of the data and the right unit to gather it are areas that often require SJA input.

(b) **Military Information Support Operations.** US law and DOD policy prohibit DOD from using military information support units to conduct operations against US persons. However, assets can be used to help disseminate critical information to the civilian population. DOD PA units may use military information support personnel and equipment to support activities such as information dissemination, printing, reproduction, distribution, and broadcasting.

(c) **Use of Weapons and RUF**

<u>1</u>. CJCSI 3125.01, *Defense Support of Civil Authorities (DSCA) for Domestic Consequence Management Operations in Response to a Chemical, Biological, Radiological, Nuclear, and High-Yield Explosive (CBRNE) Incident*, Enclosure F, establishes a presumption that units deployed to CBRN incident sites will not carry arms. Units may deploy to CBRN incident sites with their weapons in storage in the event that the unit is subsequently authorized to carry arms by SecDef or is deployed from the CBRN site to an assignment where weapons are authorized. Military commanders are responsible to ensure that weapons and ammunition are properly stored and physically secured. Military members providing security for stored weapons and ammunition at military facilities during CBRN response operations may carry their weapons while performing their normal security duties.

<u>2</u>. JFCs should be thoroughly knowledgeable regarding the standing rules for the use of force (SRUF) IAW CJCSI 3121.01B, *Standing Rules of Engagement/Standing Rules for the Use of Force for US Forces (U)*. National and local decisions about force protection conditions (FPCONs) may affect decisions regarding the arming policy. The decision to implement a particular FPCON is a CJTF command decision. The CJTF may request a higher FPCON from the CCDR if warranted by threat level assessments for the JOA. FPCON is based on an assessment of the vulnerability of JTF personnel or facilities, criticality of personnel or facilities, availability of security resources, impact on operations and morale, damage control considerations, and other international or US actions. Deterrent measures may include requesting SecDef authorization to arm the response forces along with taking other additional security measures based on local FPCON.

(d) **Immediate Response.** The DOD policy on immediate response addresses the authority delegated to DOD component or military commanders to provide immediate assistance to civil authorities to save lives, prevent human suffering, or mitigate great property damage in the event of imminently serious conditions resulting from any civil emergency or attack.

<u>1.</u> Immediate response is situation-specific and may or may not be associated with a declared or undeclared disaster. The potentially catastrophic nature of CBRN incidents would most likely lead to DOD forces conducting some CBRN response activities under immediate response authority, but there are no policy exceptions or special authorities for CBRN response. A JFC, responding to a SecDef approved DSCA mission and/or EXORD, is like any other DOD military commander and may find the need to exercise his/her immediate response authority with available forces. This is particularly relevant in the event of a second terrorist attack or TIM release within the JOA, since trained medical and specialized CBRN assessment/response teams are on the scene and able to rapidly respond to time-sensitive requests from the civil sector.

<u>2.</u> It is important for commanders to understand that **the policy is limited, restrictive, and conditional.** The situation must be a bona fide emergency that overwhelms the ability of civilians to respond and meets the restrictions criteria within DOD and Service directives. As soon as practical, the military commander, or responsible official of a DOD component or agency rendering such assistance, reports the request, the nature of the response, and any other pertinent information through the chain of command to the National Military Command Center (NMCC). The GCC should also be notified when the NMCC is notified. IAW state law and NGB policy, state officials may also direct immediate response assistance by Title 32, USC, NG personnel. Immediate response requests in the event of a CBRN incident may include, but are not limited to:

<u>a.</u> Rescue, evacuation, and emergency medical treatment of casualties, maintenance or restoration of emergency medical capabilities, and safeguarding the public health.

<u>b.</u> Emergency clearance of debris, rubble, and explosive ordnance from public facilities and other areas to permit rescue or movement of people and restoration of essential services.

<u>c.</u> Detection, assessment, and containment (initial steps taken to facilitate emergency evacuation and public awareness warnings).

<u>d.</u> Roadway movement control and planning.

<u>e.</u> **Emergency Response.** An action that commanders or individuals may take in extraordinary emergency circumstances where prior authorization is impossible, and where the delay or absence of a quick response to save lives, prevent human suffering, protect property and the environment, or meet basic human needs may contribute to greater danger, tragedy, or misfortune.

<u>f.</u> Emergency restoration of essential public services (including fire-fighting, water, communications, transportation, power, and fuel).

For more information on immediate response authority, see JP 3-27, Homeland Defense, *JP 3-28,* Defense Support of Civil Authorities, *and DODD 3025.18,* Defense Support of Civil Authorities.

(e) **Memoranda of understanding (MOUs)** for mutual assistance are often established between military installations and local communities. If an installation commander receives a request for assistance directly from local civil authorities prior to the President declaring a major disaster or emergency, the requesting agency should be referred to the local/state emergency management channels, unless an immediate response condition exists or a mutual assistance agreement is in effect. Installations may have entered into earlier mutual assistance agreements with the local community in the areas of fire-fighting, HAZMAT, medical evacuation and/or other areas, as appropriate. Dependent upon circumstances, this type of support may not be considered immediate response. Accordingly, RFAs under mutual assistance MOUs must be considered IAW applicable DOD and Service directives.

c. **National Response Framework Guidance.** The NRF is a guide to how the nation conducts all-hazards response. It is built upon **scalable, flexible, and adaptable coordinating structures** to align key roles and responsibilities across the nation. It describes specific authorities and best practices for managing incidents that range from the serious but purely local, to large-scale terrorist attacks or catastrophic natural disasters.

(1) The NRF explains the common discipline and structures that have been exercised and matured at the local, tribal, state, and national levels over time. It describes key lessons learned from Hurricanes Katrina and Rita, focusing particularly on how the USG is organized to support communities and states in catastrophic incidents. Most important, it builds upon NIMS, which provides a consistent template for managing incidents.

(2) The term "response" as used in the NRF includes immediate actions to save lives, protect property and the environment, and meet basic human needs. Response also includes the execution of emergency plans and actions to support short-term recovery. The NRF is always in effect, and elements can be implemented as needed on a flexible, scalable basis to improve response.

(3) The NRF is comprised of the core document, the ESF, Support, and Incident Annexes, and the partner guides.

(a) **Core Document.** The core document describes the doctrine that guides the national response, roles and responsibilities, response actions, response organizations, and planning requirements to achieve an effective national response to any incident that occurs.

(b) **Emergency Support Function Annexes.** Appendix B, Department of Defense Roles and Responsibilities for Emergency Support Functions, of the NRF, groups federal resources and capabilities into 15 functional areas that are most frequently needed in a national response.

(c) **Support Annexes.** The support annexes describe essential supporting aspects that are common to all incidents (e.g., financial management, volunteer and donations management).

(d) **Incident Annexes.** The incident annexes address the unique aspects of how agencies respond to seven broad incident categories (e.g., biological, nuclear, radiological).

(e) **Partner guides** provide ready references describing key roles and actions for local, tribal, state, federal, and private-sector response partners.

d. **Security and Prosperity Partnership of North America (SPP).** The SPP is a US Presidential initiative with DOD equities. The SPP agreement, designed to reduce barriers on trade and facilitate economic growth while improving the security of the continent, was signed on 23 March 2005 by the President of the United States, the Prime Minister of Canada, and the President of Mexico. DHS and the Homeland Security Council are the lead agencies for the agreement's security components, with DOD as a supporting agency. The SPP Action Plan addresses goals and objectives associated with HS to include "protection, prevention, and response." One of the goals of the agreement is to "develop and implement a common approach to critical infrastructure protection, response to cross-border terrorist incidents, and as applicable, natural disasters." This includes a dual-binational (US/Canada and US/Mexico) objective on emergency management cooperation to develop and implement joint plans for cooperation in incident response, as well as conduct joint training and exercises in hazard response. This drives the development of plans to build and strengthen mechanisms, protocols, and agreements for communicating and coordinating hazard response for mutual assistance and cooperation in the event of natural and technological/industrial disasters or malicious acts involving CBRN devices and hazards.

CHAPTER III
FOREIGN CONSEQUENCE MANAGEMENT

> *"Abroad, when requested by a host nation, the President may authorize and the Secretary of Defense may direct DOD support to US Government (USG) foreign consequence management (FCM) operations. For all consequence management activities, the military must be prepared either to support or lead consequence management operations, as directed."*
>
> **National Military Strategy to Combat Weapons of Mass Destruction**
> **13 February 2006**

1. General

a. FCM is assistance provided by the USG to an impacted nation to mitigate the effects of a deliberate or inadvertent CBRN incident. From the national level, FCM encompasses USG efforts to assist partner nations to respond to incidents involving CBRN contaminants and the coordination of the US interagency response to a request from a partner nation following an incident involving CBRN contaminants. DOD's CBRN response includes efforts to protect its citizens and its Armed Forces abroad, as well as those of its friends and allies, in order to mitigate human casualties and to provide temporary associated essential services. Primary responsibility for responding to a foreign CBRN incident resides with the impacted nation, unless otherwise stipulated under relevant international agreements. Unless otherwise directed by the President, DOS leads FCM operations and is responsible for coordinating the overall FCM response. When requested by DOS and directed by SecDef, DOD supports FCM operations by performing CBRN response activities to the extent allowed by law and subject to the availability of forces.

b. Any FCM response typically includes a number of USG departments and agencies in addition to DOD. In the case of a CBRN incident, the ability of the USG to assist an impacted nation government and its affected population is determined by the nature of the CBRN incident, the resources available to provide assistance, and the time required to deploy to the vicinity of the incident. FCM operations may be conducted concurrently with foreign DR and humanitarian assistance (HA) operations. FCM operations generally occur in a permissive environment, but the relevant GCC is responsible for force protection requirements for US military personnel. Figure III-1 depicts the basic FCM relationships.

c. A foreign nation that endures a significant CBRN incident requiring external assistance may first request assistance from neighboring states, regional allies, and regional or international organizations that have the capacity to deliver that assistance in a timely manner. The USG may be asked to provide assistance, or the USG may offer assistance, as part of a bilateral or international response to the CBRN incident. It is unlikely that the USG would be the only foreign entity providing assistance.

For further guidance on foreign assistance, refer to JP 3-29, Foreign Humanitarian Assistance*.*

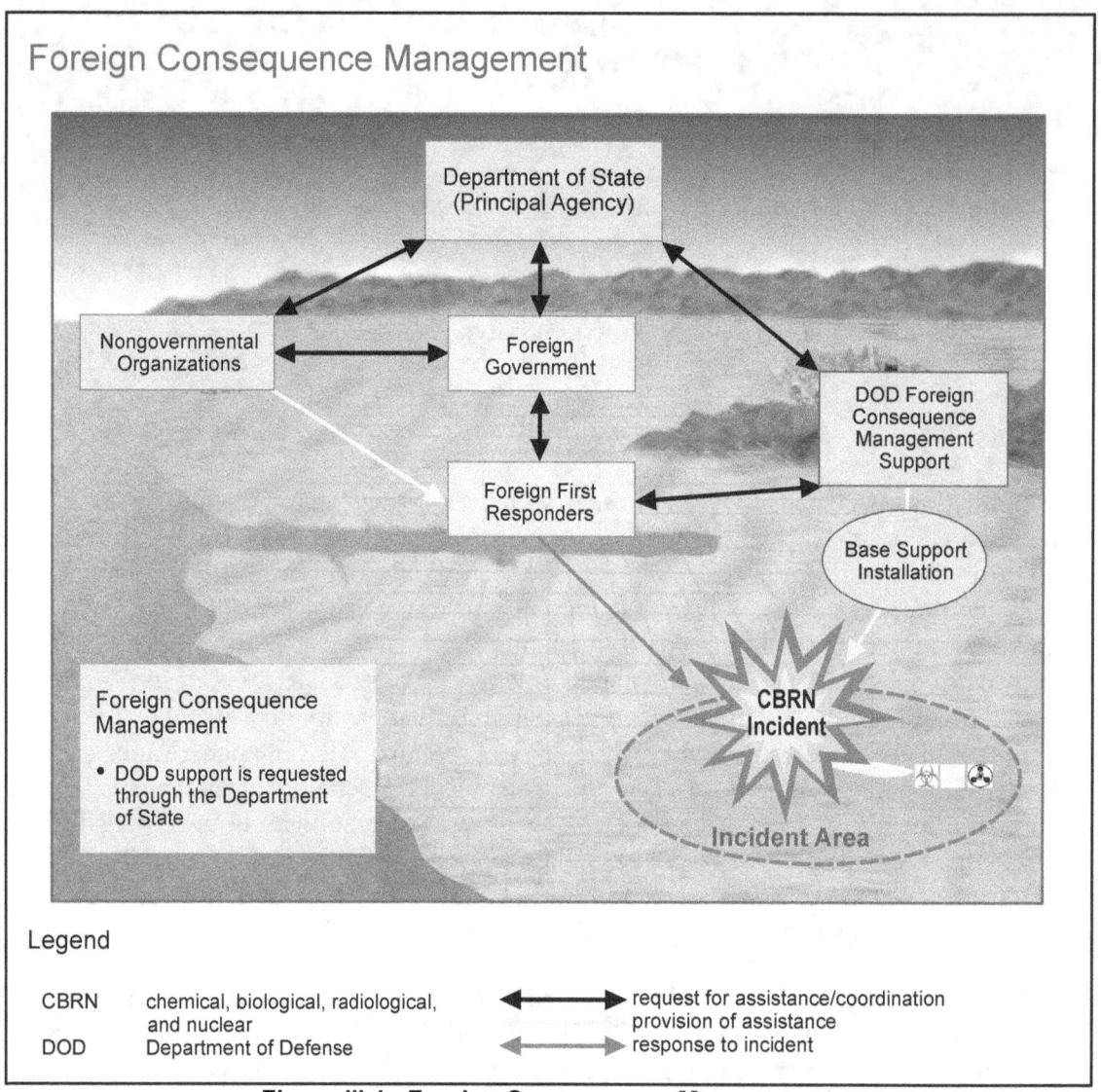

Figure III-1. Foreign Consequence Management

d. **Limits on the Scope of Operations of FCM.** FCM applies to foreign incidents involving the deliberate or inadvertent release of CBRN materials, including TICs and TIMs. It does not apply to the following activities:

(1) Acts of nature or acts of man that do not involve CBRN materials. Response to such incidents is conducted as foreign DR or HA operations IAW DODD 5100.46, *Foreign Disaster Relief.*

(2) CBRN incidents that are the direct result of US military operations in a foreign country where DOS does not have an established presence. See Chapter IV, "Department of Defense-Led Chemical, Biological, Radiological, and Nuclear Consequence Management," for additional information.

(3) CBRN incidents that occur and are contained on DOD installations and facilities overseas for which DOD retains primary responsibility under relevant international

agreements or arrangements IAW DODI 2000.18, *Department of Defense Installation Chemical, Biological, Radiological, Nuclear, and High-Yield Explosive Emergency Response Guidelines*, and DODI 6055.17, *Department of Defense Installation Emergency Management (IEM) Program*.

e. **United States Government Offer of Assistance Process.** The impacted nation's response may or may not be sufficient to mitigate the hazards from a CBRN incident. Support requests for foreign assistance may begin immediately after an incident. During this period, the US embassy in the country, the applicable GCC, and other USG entities need to begin to obtain situational awareness related to the nature and magnitude of effects from the CBRN incident. The USG may also begin considering whether to proactively offer assistance to the impacted nation.

f. **Request for Assistance Process**. Figure III-2 depicts both the FCM request for assistance and FCM processes. Once the impacted nation determines additional capabilities are required, the impacted nation notifies the US embassy with a request for assistance and provides known information about the incident.

(1) The COM, frequently the ambassador, notifies DOS in Washington, DC. DOS makes internal DOS and National Security Staff notifications and dispatches a foreign emergency support team (FEST) and/or a consequence management support team (CMST) to the US embassy. Additionally, DOS begins logistics, transportation, and other support coordination with the country team. It is expected that the country team will inform the relevant GCC, who will dispatch a liaison element to work with the country team to assess the situation, identify potential support requirements, and begin the flow of information through the combatant command to the NMCC.

(2) The National Security Staff coordinates interagency deliberations to assess the request and determine whether the US will honor it; identify what specific support will be provided and which agencies will provide that support; and develop initial guidance for responding organizations. During this period it is expected that response elements from other nations and international organizations will also start deployment to the country stricken by the CBRN incident.

(3) Following interagency coordination, the National Security Staff provides guidance to executive departments and other organizations to initiate the formal USG response under FCM. The country team out of the US embassy increases coordination with the impacted nation regarding the specific support the US will provide and finalizes logistics, transportation, and legal negotiations.

(4) Specific requests for DOD support are submitted to the OSD Executive Secretary or verbally through the NMCC with a follow-on formal request to the OSD Executive Secretary. Upon receipt of a request, DOD assesses it against specific request criteria, issues appropriate orders, and coordinates for the movement of tasked resources. DOD identifies command relationships, and the supporting commands coordinate the provision of identified resources. The supported combatant command identifies a TF

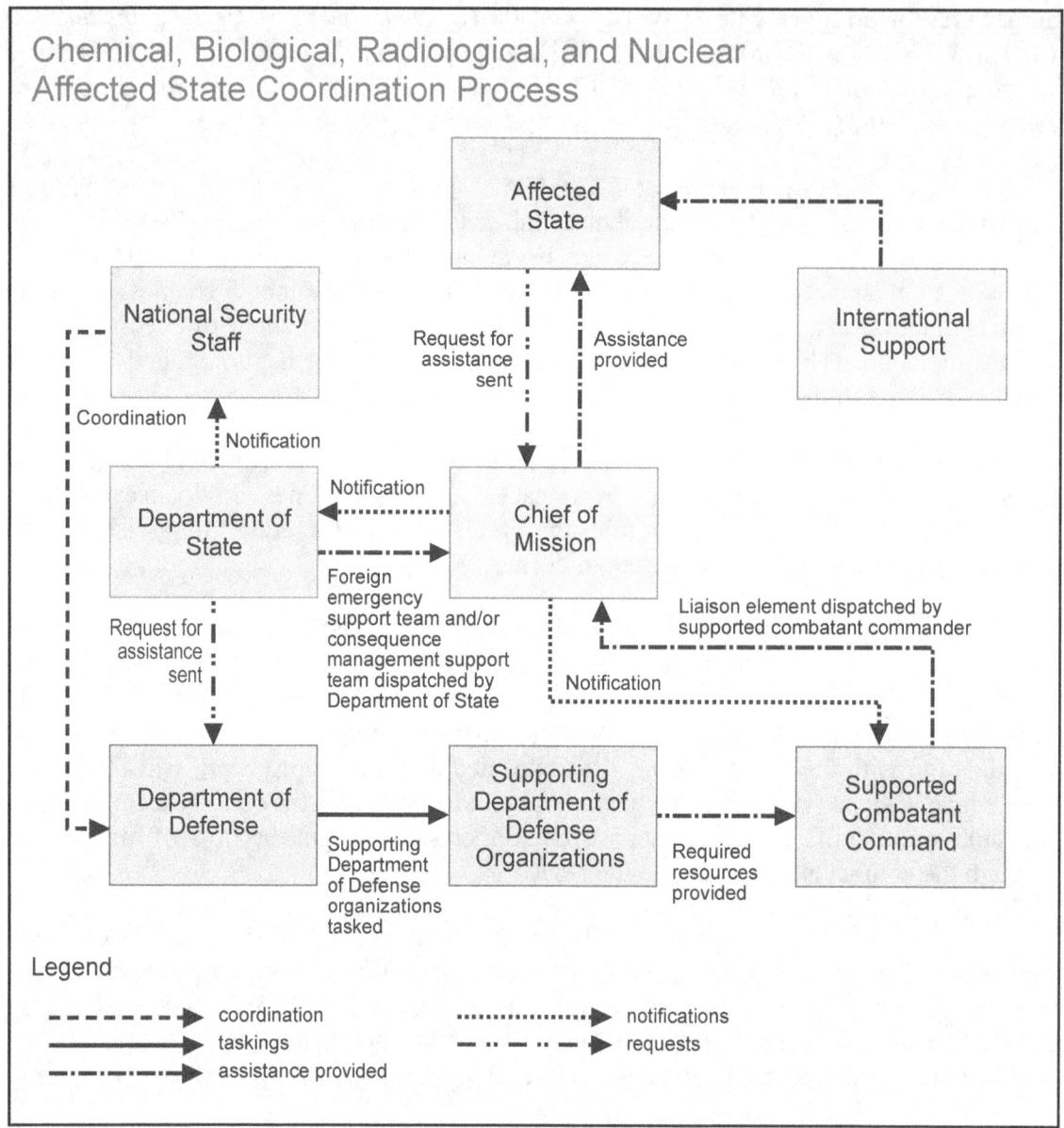

Figure III-2. Chemical, Biological, Radiological, and Nuclear Affected State Coordination Process

organization, develops C2 guidance, and coordinates resource deployment with the country team.

g. **Request for Assistance/Offer of Assistance Assessment Criteria.** OSD and Joint Staff offices, in coordination with the supported GCC, will use the criteria outlined below to assess potential offers of, and requests for, assistance and provide a coordinated recommendation to SecDef.

FOREIGN CONSEQUENCE MANAGEMENT DURING OPERATION TOMODACHI

The disaster from a 9.0 magnitude earthquake, 46-foot tsunami, and catastrophic damage to the Fukushima Dai'ichi Nuclear Power Plant on Honshu Island, Japan, in March 2011 required the first foreign consequence management (FCM) support response by US forces. This incident ultimately resulted in the voluntary departure of American citizens from Japan, significant loss of life, and displacement of Japanese citizens, and a Level 7 Major Accident—the highest level—on the International Nuclear Event Scale.

United States Pacific Command (USPACOM) established Joint Support Force – Japan (JSF-J) to plan and execute several different missions concurrently including; humanitarian assistance and disaster relief (HA/DR), FCM, departure of Department of Defense (DOD) dependents and force protection of US military bases. Adding to the complexity, HA/DR and FCM operations were conducted bilaterally with the government of Japan and the Japanese Ministry of Defense.

In order to support FCM operations, JSF-J employed a combination of USPACOM forces and chemical, biological, radiological, and nuclear assets resourced from outside the joint operations area including staff augmentation from the Defense Threat Reduction Agency and Joint Task Force-Civil Support, the Air Force Radiological Assessment Team, the Army Area Medical Laboratory, and one Initial Response Force from the Marine Corps Chemical, Biological Incident Response Force. In addition, unilateral response operations were required of JSF-J forces in addition to FCM response.

The radiological contamination from the nuclear power plant required unique and complex analysis of the potential radiation hazard areas and short- and long-term radiation hazard to US forces and citizens. Differing national and international standards of radiation exposure, hazard modeling, exclusion zones, response procedures, and units of radiation measurement were issues faced by the response community. Those issues coupled with the lack of reliable information of the state of the damaged reactors demonstrate that there can be uncertainty in situational awareness in FCM response operations.

The concurrent execution of various mission areas (FCM, HA/DR, departure of DOD dependents, and force protection) demonstrates that joint force commanders should be prepared to adapt to any dynamic situations that arise during response.

Various Sources

     (1) Legality—compliance with US and international laws and bilateral and multilateral agreements.

     (2) Lethality—potential use of force by or against DOD assets.

(3) Risk—to national security (if the USG does or does not provide the requested assistance), the potential to effect US interests across national instruments of power, and to the health and safety of forces supporting FCM operations.

(4) Cost and Reimbursement—availability of funds, potential for reimbursement, and impact on DOD budget.

(5) Readiness—impact on DOD's ability to perform its primary mission and availability of appropriate forces.

(6) Appropriateness—whether or not DOD can and should perform the mission. Factors to be considered include the contributions provided by other USG departments or agencies, other nations, and international and private organizations.

(7) CCDR input—GCC issues regarding mission execution and impact of the mission on country-specific and regional policies, plans, and initiatives.

(8) Timeliness—ability to get requested capabilities where they are needed in a timeframe that can make a positive difference.

2. Roles, Responsibilities, Authorities, and Assets

a. Roles and Responsibilities

(1) **Impacted Nation.** Primary responsibility for responding to, managing, and mitigating the consequences of a foreign CBRN incident resides with the affected nation's government. When overwhelmed, the impacted nation is responsible for requesting foreign assistance and sharing all relevant information about the CBRN incident with international partners.

(2) **The Department of State.** Unless directed otherwise by the President, DOS coordinates all USG support to an affected nation. DOS typically serves as the LFA for FCM; however, DOS frequently coordinates support through the US Agency for International Development. After such an FCM support request by DOS is approved by SecDef, DOD commences its support to the affected nation as part of the overall USG response. This support may include negotiation of landing and/or overflight diplomatic clearances for contaminated or formerly contaminated aircraft.

(3) **The US Embassy/Chief of Mission.** The US COM (normally the ambassador) is the President's top representative in the affected nation. Normally, all USG support to the affected nation will be coordinated by the responsible COM and country team. All matters requiring DOS review or approval should be submitted to the COM.

(4) **The National Security Council/Staff.** The National Security Council through the National Security Staff coordinates interagency deliberations during any FCM response to determine whether the US will honor a potential affected nation request, identifies what specific support will be provided and which agencies will provide that support, and develops initial guidance for responding organizations.

(5) **The Assistant Secretary of Defense for Global Security Affairs.** The ASD(GSA) serves as the principal advisor to SecDef and the USD(P) on matters concerning any portion of the DOD response within a FCM operation. As such, the ASD(GSA) is responsible for developing, coordinating, and overseeing all aspects of associated policy. The ASD(GSA) also serves as the OSD office of primary responsibility for the review of all CJCS plans, instructions, and manuals related to CBRN response activities and exercises for the foreign operational environment. The ASD(GSA) represents SecDef on all FCM policy matters outside of DOD; provides policy oversight for the planning and pre-positioning of DOD FCM assets for foreign incidents, including but not limited to, international athletic events, summits, and conferences; and finally serves as the principal coordinator of DOD FCM exercises with the interagency.

(6) **Chairman of the Joint Chiefs of Staff.** The CJCS serves as the principal military advisor to SecDef and the President in preparing for and responding to a foreign CBRN incident. The CJCS assesses whether US force capabilities are able to support FCM operations and develops US military strategy, policy, and positions to support operational planning for a CBRN response. The CJCS reviews all requests and provides recommendations for DOD support to USG FCM operations, and ensures military planning is accomplished to support DOS in preparing for and responding to a foreign CBRN incident.

(7) **Geographic Combatant Commanders.** Each GCC has the inherent responsibility to provide support to DOS, the lead for FCM, unless otherwise directed by the President. Each GCC develops plans for FCM within their assigned AOR and is prepared to deploy a liaison element to the vicinity of the incident site to liaise with the US embassy and to provide situational awareness to the supported CCDR. Each GCC identifies a headquarters element to provide the initial incident response and serve as the initial C2 element of DOD for FCM operations within their respective AOR. When in a supporting role, CCDRs provide requested forces and assets to the supported GCCs. The GCCs develop interface procedures for exchanging CBRN response-related operational support requests between the COM, Joint Staff, their subordinate commanders, and higher headquarters. The interface procedures should include affected nation to DOS, DOS to DOD, DOD to supported CCDRs, and supported to supporting CCDRs' protocols, and reside in theater plans or standard operating procedures.

For more information, see CJCSI 3214.01, Defense Support for Chemical, Biological, Radiological, and Nuclear Incidents on Foreign Territory.

(8) **Commander, US Strategic Command.** Consistent with USSTRATCOM's role to integrate and synchronize DOD's efforts in combating WMD, advises the CCDRs and Joint Staff on the capabilities available to assist in FCM operations.

(9) **Commander, US Transportation Command.** When directed by SecDef, USTRANSCOM is prepared to move selected DOD forces and identified elements, equipment, supplies, and other commodities and those of other USG departments and agencies, the impacted nation, and international partners in support of a President-directed FCM and/or other military CBRN CM assistance operations.

(10) **Commander, US Special Operations Command.** Is prepared to deploy selected forces to support the GCC during Presidential-directed FCM and/or other military CBRN CM assistance operations. Provides special operations assets to the supported combatant command as requested and approved by SecDef.

(11) **Service Chiefs.** When directed by SecDef, provide forces (to include forces from the RC) as part of the supported GCC's response during a CBRN incident. These forces may consist of, but are not limited to, specialized personnel, teams, or units that have been trained and equipped to provide support in the warm and hot zone and conventional forces that will operate in the cold zone; and force protection elements, transportation units, logistics activities, air assets, and research and medical capabilities.

(12) **Defense Threat Reduction Agency.** DTRA provides operational and technical advice and support to DOD components and other USG departments and agencies, as requested and approved regarding FCM operations. This is accomplished through training and exercises, the deployment of CBRN CMATs, and operational planning assistance. DTRA also provides modeling, predictions, assessments, publications, training, lessons learned, analysis, and other support as required. DTRA provides technical reachback through the DTRA Operations Center, a 24/7 WMD and CBRN national reachback and situational awareness facility, for all technical support. During FCM, DTRA liaises with other technical support providers and the intelligence community to meet support requests.

(13) **Installation Commanders.** As in the US, if a CBRN incident occurs, US commanders on foreign territory may, when requested by the impacted nation, exercise their immediate response authority; however, it is more restrictive (limited to saving lives) than within the homeland (see CJCSI 3214.01, *Military Support to Foreign Consequence Management Operations for Chemical, Biological Radiological, and Nuclear Incidents*). DOD has independent statutory authority (Title 10, USC, Section 404) to respond to overseas man-made or natural disasters when necessary to prevent loss of life. Under EO 12966, SecDef provides such assistance at the direction of the President, or in consultation with the Secretary of State; however, in emergency situations to save human lives, when there is not sufficient time to seek prior concurrence from the Secretary of State, DOD may provide assistance, and advise and seek the concurrence of the Secretary of State as soon as practicable thereafter (see also DODD 5100.46, *Foreign Disaster Relief*).

(14) **NGOs and the Private Sector.** NGOs are private, self-governing, not-for-profit organizations dedicated to alleviating human suffering; and/or promoting education, health care, economic development, environmental protection, human rights, and conflict resolution; and/or encouraging the establishment of democratic institutions and civil society. Private sector is an umbrella term that may be applied in the US and in foreign countries to any or all of the nonpublic or commercial individuals and businesses, specified nonprofit organizations, most of academia and other scholastic institutions, and selected NGOs. While many of these organizations are very capable of performing HA tasks, there is a great diversity of capabilities between the various NGOs and private sector entities. For planning purposes, it should be assumed that these various agencies and entities will desire to participate in HA aspects of FCM operations. It should also be expected that various organizations will interact with the responsible combatant command military elements in

differing degrees and manners, from cooperative to indifferent. These organizations often need to work separate from the USG to maintain the ability to be neutral in the conflict.

b. **Authorities.** In the event of a CBRN incident affecting foreign territory, various authorities exist to govern the response. The two major laws which govern US responses to foreign CBRN incidents are the International Disaster Assistance section of the Foreign Assistance Act (FAA) (Title 22, USC), and the military humanitarian response authorities set forth in Title 10, USC. In addition to a review of these authorizing laws, various restrictions on US foreign aid should be considered before any response or assistance is provided.

(1) **The Foreign Assistance Act of 1961** provides authorization for USG foreign aid programs. Section 2292 of the FAA authorizes the President "to furnish assistance to any foreign country, international organization, or private voluntary organization, on such terms as he may determine, for international disaster relief and rehabilitation, including assistance relating to disaster preparedness, and to the prediction of, and contingency planning for, natural disasters abroad." Additionally it states, "In carrying out the provisions of this section the President shall insure that the assistance provided by the United States shall, to the greatest extent possible, reach those most in need of relief and rehabilitation as a result of natural and man-made disasters." The types of assistance that may be provided under this section are not enumerated; however, assistance relating to disaster preparedness is expressly approved.

(2) **EO 12966** authorizes the military to respond to a CBRN incident in a foreign operational environment either at the direction of the President, with the concurrence of the Secretary of State, or on its own initiative to save human lives in emergency situations where there is insufficient time to consult with the Secretary of State. EO 12966 is analogous to the military's immediate response authority for domestic disasters. When conditions resulting from any emergency or attack in a foreign country require immediate action, local military commanders may take such actions as necessary to save lives. When such compelling conditions exist and time does not permit prior approval from higher headquarters, commanders or officials acting under **"immediate response authority"** may take necessary action to respond to requests from local affected nation authorities or the US COM. Following their immediate response actions, commanders report to their higher headquarters of assistance being provided by the most expeditious means available, and seek approval or additional authorizations as needed. The GCC notifies the affected US COM at the time of higher headquarters notification.

c. **Assets.** The following paragraphs identify organizations that could respond to an FCM incident:

(1) **Foreign Emergency Support Team.** The FEST is a DOS-led interagency support team that can be deployed immediately in support of the US embassy in response to actual or suspected terrorist incidents. The Office of the Coordinator for Counterterrorism exercises responsibility for the management of the FEST. The FEST is task-organized depending on the incident and may include DOD elements that provide support to the US embassy, consulate, or mission for foreign emergency operations. The appropriate GCC provides liaison, and as required technical support to the FEST. A small FCM advisory

component should be on the FEST whenever CBRN materials are involved. DOD provides additional support as required through the supported combatant command.

(2) **Consequence Management Support Team.** The CMST is a DOS-led interagency support team that can be deployed pre- or post-incident. The CMST provides CBRN CM advice, assistance, and support to a US embassy, consulate, or mission in country. It can be deployed in lieu of or as a subordinate element to the FEST. It is comprised of subject matter experts from DOS and other USG departments and agencies as required. The CMST provides FCM situation assessments to the USG and affected nation, as appropriate, and with the COM, coordinates the USG response for DOS. Upon approval by SecDef, DOD provides support to the CMST through the appropriate GCC as requested by DOS.

(3) **DTRA Consequence Management Advisory Team.** The CMAT deploys to provide joint technical support to the supported commander with expertise in CBRN response procedures, requirements, resources, C2, health physics, PA, legal affairs, and specialized technical information. The CMAT is able to task-organize and deploy to support commanders in the technical aspects of CBRN accidents or incidents. The incident tailored force has secure communications, trained technical experts, hazard prediction modeling capability, and rapid reachback capability.

(4) The **US Armed Forces Radiobiology Research Institute** can provide DOD technical support capability for nuclear and radiological incidents or accidents. An AFRRI medical radiobiology advisory team (MRAT) responds as part of the DTRA CMAT and is available at all times. The MRAT can provide on-site training to health professionals on the management of nuclear or radiological casualties. The team provides state-of-the-art expertise and advice to commanders and primary care providers following a nuclear or radiological accident (nuclear weapons, reactor, or radiological material). The MRAT provides access to biodosimetry and bioassay support to incident responders and local health authorities.

(5) The **United States Air Force Radiation Assessment Team (AFRAT)** is a globally responsive, specialty asset team that provides health physics and radiological support in response to radiation incidents and accidents. AFRAT provides subject matter experts to support planning, surveillance, analysis, and assessment to mitigate radiation and operational risks resulting from radiation/nuclear incidents. The team provides field radioanalytical support. It measures, analyzes, and interprets environmental and occupational samples for its radioactivity content, providing expert guidance on the type and degree of radiological hazards that face deployed forces. The AFRAT performs radioanalytical analysis on environmental samples (such as swipes, soil, water, air, and foodstuffs) and occupational samples (such as urine and feces). Analysis results are interpreted for the effect on deployed forces and noncombatants. The information is compiled for use by command and medical authorities on dose avoidance, dose reduction, and dose assessment; risk of communication; and additional requirements for effective CBRN CM.

(6) **US Marine Corps Chemical-Biological Incident Response Force.** CBIRF is a unit that was created to deploy on short notice in response to CBRN incidents. CBIRF consists of specially trained personnel and specialized equipment suited for operations in a wide range of contingencies. CBIRF is designed to minimize the effects of a CBRN incident through detection, identification, search and extraction, technical rescue, mass casualty decontamination, medical triage, and emergency medical support.

(7) The **United States Army 20th Support Command (CBRNE)** is the operational headquarters for Army CBRN specialized units. The 20th Support Command is the primary Army force provider of specialized CBRNE capabilities. It conducts CBRNE operations in support of the CCDR, JFC, Army, and provides support to federal agencies as required; provides C2 of assigned CBRN forces; provides CBRNE technical advice and assistance; and maintains a technical reachback assistance capability.

A more comprehensive listing of military capabilities, assets, and units for support to CBRN CM operations can be found in FM 3-11.21/MCRP 3-37.2C/NTTP 3-11.24/AFTTP (I) 3-2.37, Multi-Service Tactics, Techniques and Procedures for Chemical, Biological, Radiological, and Nuclear Consequence Management Operations.

Additionally, the Interagency Combating Weapons of Mass Destruction Database of Responsibilities, Authorities, and Capabilities (INDRAC) *(http://indrac.dtra.mil) identifies responsibilities, authorities, and capabilities across the full spectrum mission for combating WMD, serving as a single focal point of information and references on combating WMD and CBRN CM assets.*

3. Command Relationships

a. SecDef designates the supported and supporting combatant command relationships, and the supported CCDR establishes the command relationships of assigned forces for each specific CBRN response. The DOD supports the LFA during USG FCM operations unless otherwise directed by the President. DOD forces remain under the C2 of the supported CCDR. DOS retains responsibility for coordination among USG entities.

b. **Command and Control Element Considerations.** Important considerations for commanders of C2 elements include:

(1) **Assessment and Response.** JTF-CM assessment and response requirements may include:

(a) Incident site surveillance and initial assessments.

(b) Incident site control, to include entry and exit management.

(c) Assistance with decontamination of personnel, equipment, facilities and/or terrain. The JTF-CM assessment and response element may provide initial assistance to the affected nation in decontamination services. The JTF-CM assessment and response element should scope planning for potential decontamination services providing protection for public health and safety, keeping in mind that protracted clean-up efforts will be performed by the affected nation.

(d) Analysis and recommendations to the COM, USG departments and agencies, and affected nation for near-term management of the incident.

(e) Temporary provision of essential service support. This support may include providing assistance in critical infrastructure restoration or assistance in initial site clean-up and debris removal. Note, however, that long-term recovery efforts are the responsibility of the affected country.

(f) In the event of a radiological incident, a radiological control team may be needed to provide health physicists and/or other technical assistance (radiation control and safety).

(g) Risk communications coordination to include developing strategy, addressing operational issues, and ensuring consistent messaging across the JTF. Assistance with this task can be sought through the US Army Public Health Command or Service equivalents.

(h) Coordination of information sharing protocols among data producers and data users in order to maintain a common operational picture among participating agencies. Provision of a share point or similar unique information clearinghouse that is access controlled and available to all participating agencies is recommended.

(2) **Transportation and Logistics.** Transportation and logistics may include the following:

(a) Pre-positioning materials and supplies for use by the JTF.

(b) Providing transport support, to include aviation, ground, and, if necessary, waterborne assets. Assisting the affected nation in the coordination of transportation.

<u>1</u>. Depending upon the condition of the remaining transportation infrastructure including roads and railroads, rotary-wing aviation and ground units may be able to assist in the movement of personnel, supplies, debris, and equipment in and around the incident area. The CCDR and CJTF should anticipate such assistance requests.

<u>2</u>. The use of a maritime support detachment is dependent upon waterway and helicopter/aerial access of incident site and JTF transportation requirements.

(c) Providing contract support to the JTF.

(d) Coordinating logistic support for the other components of the JTF.

(e) Providing medical evacuation transportation support.

1. USTRANSCOM will not transport contagious and contaminated casualties within the aeromedical patient movement system. In extreme circumstances, there may be a requirement to move contagious index cases (approximately two) for evaluation or critical medical care. If patient movement is required, prior approval must be given by the involved GCCs, Commander USTRANSCOM, and SecDef in consultation with medical authorities.

2. Rotary-wing assets may be able to provide the most efficient means to move non-contaminated casualties within the vicinity of the incident site.

3. Both fixed-wing and high speed waterborne assets can be used to quickly move casualties intertheater and intratheater depending upon the locations of the affected areas and the condition of surviving transportation infrastructure (e.g., airfields, ports, railroads).

(f) Establish policy for the disposition of contaminated or formerly contaminated US materiel and equipment including aircraft, vehicles, and other major end items. Note that this may apply in the HN, a third party nation, or CONUS.

(g) Establish policy for the maintenance of contaminated or formerly contaminated US materiel and equipment including aircraft, vehicles, and other major end items. Supporting elements should be notified that although the item may have been decontaminated to standard, there may be remaining contamination in internal areas and components not normally accessible during routine operations. Note that this may apply in the HN, a third party nation, or CONUS.

(3) **Health Service Support.** Assess health risk of CBRN hazards and provide recommendations to mitigate risk. HSS tasks may include the following:

(a) Triage of casualties.

(b) Treatment for casualties and responders.

(c) Augmentation to existing medical treatment facilities IAW status-of-forces agreements (SOFAs).

(d) Assistance in medical administration and management during an incident.

(e) Collection of medical specimens as required for laboratory analysis and identification.

(f) Patient tracking/patient movement/evacuation teams for coordination purposes.

(g) Distribution of medical supplies.

(h) Administration of medical countermeasures, to include immunizations and prophylaxes, as required. Medical countermeasure administration may require the establishment of a point of dispensing for mass prophylaxis operations.

(i) Stress management.

(j) Patient decontamination.

(k) Detection.

(l) For radiological incidents, a radiological advisory medical team specifically trained in radiological health matters may be needed to provide on-site assistance and guidance to the CJTF and local medical authorities.

(m) For biological incidents, consider the following specific augmentation:

1. The US Army chemical and biological advisory team provides on-site advice for chemical-biological casualty care.

2. The aeromedical isolation team consists of physicians, nurses, medical assistants, and laboratory technicians specially trained to provide care to and transport for patients with diseases caused by infectious agents.

3. The US Army Special Medical Augmentation Response Teams have transformed to US Army Specialized Medical Response Capabilities (SMRC) in order to meet DOD requirements for anticipated HD and DSCA missions. The US Army SMRC-aeromedical isolation team composition has transformed to just a consultant role. The primary responsibility for contingency casualty movement has transitioned to the US Air Force.

(n) Develop policy and guidance on health monitoring of exposed and/or contaminated Service members or other impacted US citizens. This may encompass short, intermediate, and/or long-term monitoring and follow-up.

(o) Ensure coordination of force health protection measures with DOS and other USG and HN departments and agencies. Careful consideration should be given to higher order effects associated with force health protection measures.

(4) **Civil-Military Operations.** Civil-military operations tasks may include the following:

(a) Assistance in supporting the interface between the affected nation government and outside assets.

(b) Assistance in dealing with displaced civilians.

(c) Interorganizational coordination.

(5) **Security.** Security tasks may include the following:

    (a) Providing force protection and security for JTF, as required.

    (b) Protecting US citizens and casualties.

    (c) Implementing appropriate AT measures.

    (d) Establishing early warning systems within the JTF operational area.

    (e) Providing convoy and patient transport security.

Guidelines for establishing a JTF and standing JTF headquarters can be found in JP 3-33, Joint Task Force Headquarters.

4. Affected Nation Considerations

a. An affected nation is one that has requested support to mitigate the effects of a CBRN incident. The affected nation has primary responsibility for responding to, managing, coordinating other nations' augmenting support, and mitigating the consequences of a CBRN incident within its borders. A major part of any FCM operation is augmenting affected nation operations, not replacing them. In order to avoid duplication of effort, affected nation capabilities need to be determined. In the aftermath of a CBRN incident, it may be difficult to determine which government ministry is performing certain functions. The US embassy within the country should be able to assist in identifying such details. To assist in the clarification of duties, a list of typical government ministries is provided below, although exact names will vary in each country.

(1) Ministry of interior; in many countries this ministry performs the national crisis response mission.

(2) Ministry of agriculture typically has the responsibility for rural development and water conservation, as well as land resources.

(3) Ministry of defense is typically responsible for ensuring the defense of the country by coordinating defense-related matters with the Services, as well as the applicable branches of government.

(4) Ministry of finance is typically responsible for the administration of the finances of the affected nation government, regulation of expenditures of the government, and concerned with all economic and financial matters affecting the country as a whole.

(5) Ministry of foreign affairs typically prepares the affected nation foreign affairs policy and represents the interests of the affected nation government outside of its borders.

(6) Ministry of health is typically the health authority in the affected nation responsible for the coordination of the affected nation health care policy (if applicable) and sanitation.

(7) Ministry of trade and industry is typically responsible for providing safe working conditions, administrating laws and regulations related to trade and industry, and dialogues with enterprises, organizations, and other authorities.

(8) Ministry of justice is typically concerned with the creation and implementation of the affected nation laws, as well as advising the other ministries regarding these laws.

(9) Ministry of labor is typically responsible for the affected nation employment policy, administration and personnel policy, competition and income policy, and matters concerning living standards.

(10) Ministry of the environment typically handles issues such as pollution control, nature conservation, and waste management and minimization.

(11) Ministry of public works and housing is typically responsible for affected nation programs that address housing needs; improves and develops communities; and enforcement of applicable housing and other public welfare laws.

(12) Ministry of social development is typically entrusted with the welfare, social justice, and empowerment of the disadvantaged and marginalized section of the society.

(13) Ministry of transportation typically ensures a fast, safe, efficient, accessible, and convenient transportation system that meets affected nation interests.

(14) Ministry of education typically oversees the quality of education in the affected nation and prepares students for employment in the affected nation environment.

b. **Negotiations Regarding Use of Specialized Equipment and Facilities.** In the case of a foreign CBRN incident, highly specialized equipment such as decontamination systems, mobile laboratories, field hospitals, medical equipment, and facilities for temporary accommodation of persons may be necessary. However, the affected nation may have safety, interoperability, or other issues with the importation and use of such equipment in a CBRN response. For instance, US responders may have difficulty importing specialized chemical, biological, and radiological detection equipment into foreign countries. Unless prior agreements are in place, it may be necessary for the US to negotiate with the affected nation at the time of the incident based on the specific equipment required for that incident. Without adequate procedures in place in advance to manage such concerns, responders may have to rely on such ad hoc negotiations to import and/or use equipment necessary for an effective response. Ideally, relevant multinational CBRN CM training exercises can be used to identify any such special requirements and establish the necessary agreements prior to an actual incident occurring.

c. The affected nation will likely have its own guidelines for decontamination. For instance, within the US, the EPA provides guidance on cleanup levels for radioactive sites and trains other US departments and agencies to prepare for such emergencies. However, international standards may also apply to a foreign CBRN incident.

5. Joint and Multinational Force Considerations

a. **Rules on the Use of Force/Rules of Engagement (RUF/ROE).** CJCSI 3121.01, *Standing Rules of Engagement/Standing Rules for the Use of Force for US Forces (U),* outlines the DOD standing rules of engagement (SROE) and SRUF for US forces. In general, when conducting FCM, SROE should be applied. However, CCDRs may augment SROE with supplemental measures or by submitting supplemental measures to SecDef for approval. Commanders also notify SecDef of restrictions placed on approved ROE/RUF.

b. During FCM, commanders at all levels have the inherent right and obligation to defend their units and other US forces at all times against a "hostile act or demonstrated hostile intent."

c. US forces under the OPCON or TACON of a multinational force will follow the ROE of the multinational force for mission accomplishment if authorized by SecDef. Any inconsistencies between the multinational ROE and US ROE will be submitted through the chain of command for resolution. Prior to resolution, US forces will follow US ROE. Additionally, US forces will remain bound by international agreements to which the US is a party regardless of whether the other members of the multinational force are party to the agreements. However, international agreements, e.g., SOFAs, "may never be interpreted to limit US forces right of self-defense." Self-defense, specifically unit self-defense, can be extended to, and includes persons, vessels, or aircraft receiving emergency assistance from US aircraft or vessels.

Enclosure A of CJCSI 3121.01, Standing Rules of Engagement/Standing Rules for the Use of Force for US Forces (U), *details SROE policy and provides implementation guidance for the application of force for mission accomplishment and the exercise of self-defense. It also addresses SROE for US forces operating with multinational forces.*

d. **Multinational Operations.** The US has standing agreements with some foreign governments that allow for the sharing of high-level intelligence (e.g., special category), but in all cases, the release of classified information to multinational partners is made IAW the national disclosure policy (NDP). Detailed guidance is provided to the senior US commander by the chain of command IAW National Security Decision Memorandum 119, *Disclosure of Classified United States Military Information to Foreign Governments and International Organizations,* and NDP-1, *National Policy and Procedures for the Disclosure of Classified Military Information to Foreign Governments and International Organizations.* During the integration of multinational partners into operations, commanders and planners should identify operational restrictions on those forces due to relevant US laws, policies, treaties, and agreements.

JP 2-01, Joint and National Intelligence Support to Military Operations, *and JP 3-16,* Multinational Operations, *contain detailed discussions of sanitization and foreign disclosure procedures.*

e. **Civil-Military Operations Center (CMOC).** The ability of the JTF to work with all organizations and groups is essential to mission accomplishment. A good working relationship between military forces, USG departments and agencies, civilian authorities, involved international and regional organizations, and the population is therefore important. Conceptually, the CMOC is the meeting place of these elements, represented by US Service liaisons, military liaisons from participating countries, Office of Foreign Disaster Assistance representatives, DOS personnel, affected nation representatives, and representatives from the United Nations (UN), NGOs, and IGOs. More than one CMOC may be established in a JOA, and each is task organized based on the mission. The organization of the CMOC is theater and mission dependent—flexible in size and composition. During large-scale hazards assessment operations, if a headquarters operations center is formed by the affected nation or UN, the CMOC becomes the focal point for coordination between participating military and civilian agencies.

For further guidance on the interagency process, refer to JP 3-57, Civil-Military Operations, *and JP 3-08,* Interorganizational Coordination During Joint Operations. *Additional guidance on multinational operations is found in JP 3-16,* Multinational Operations.

6. **Unique Planning Considerations in a Foreign Operational Environment**

The phases of FCM are derived from CJCSI 3214.01, *Military Support to Foreign Consequence Management Operations for Chemical, Biological, Radiological, and Nuclear Incidents.* As in the domestic operational environment, CBRN response is based on a six-phase construct; however, phase names and associated activities differ from the JP 5-0, *Joint Operation Planning,* model. It is unlikely that all forces will shift from each of these phases to the next phase simultaneously. It is more likely that some forces will be still working the last issues associated with one phase as other components are commencing activities within the next phase. The six phases are listed below:

a. **Phase 0 (Shape).** This is a continuous phase. The intent of this phase is to ensure DOD is organized, trained, equipped, and prepared to support USG efforts to minimize the effects of CBRN incidents on foreign soil. Key tasks of this phase include partner engagement, interagency coordination, plans development, training, exercise, and constant monitoring for a developing crisis. DOD will assist DOS in shaping the environment through theater security cooperation, information operations, partner capacity building and other engagement activities on both a country and regional basis in an effort to prevent or avert a CBRN incident and to enhance partner capabilities to effectively manage the effects of a CBRN incident if such an incident cannot be prevented. Additionally, combatant commands should coordinate response, support, and situational awareness processes, procedures, and requirements with US embassies within their AOR.

b. **Phase I Deter (Situation Assessment and Preparation).** Transition to phase I occurs on reliable indications and warning of a CBRN incident or upon notification that an incident has occurred. Phase I includes those actions required to conduct situation assessment and preparation, including the timely and accurate assessment of the CBRN situation, preparation for deployment, and deployment of selected advance elements. This may include but is not limited to the GCC LNO or team. Phase I ends when the nature and scope of the CBRN situation and initial response force requirements are defined. Additionally, any limited initial response to a CBRN incident conducted by DOD commanders operating under immediate response authority would likely occur during phase I.

c. **Phase II Seize the Initiative (Deployment).** Phase II begins with SecDef-approved CJCS deployment and/or EXORD designating the intermediate and/or forward staging bases and establishing formal command relationships (i.e., supported and supporting commanders). The order serves as the formal authority for the deployment of forces. Phase II completion is generally marked by having forces deployed with enough C2 and unit capability to safely and effectively begin operations. Depending on the situation, the CJTF may decide to move into phase III operations before all phase II objectives are complete and continue to work on phase II objectives while in phase III.

d. **Phase III Dominate (Assistance to Affected Nation Authorities).** Phase III begins with the arrival of required military assistance at the incident location and supporting locations and ends with the determination that DOD support is no longer required or appropriate. Commanders begin planning immediately for transition to affected nation and civilian agencies, including USG, other international governments, donors, and NGOs, and should identify the necessary or minimum conditions to initiate transition to other agencies.

e. **Phase IV Stabilize (Transition to Affected Nation and/or Other Agencies).** Although planning for transition of CBRN CM activities begins as soon as practical following the initial response, phase IV begins with the formal implementation of the transition plan for those tasks and responsibilities being accomplished by DOD and ends when directed by SecDef or the affected nation has assumed full responsibility for response activities.

f. **Phase V Enable Civilian Authorities (Redeployment).** Phase V begins with the redeployment of US military forces involved in CBRN CM operations or the formal transition of those forces to a purely DR or HA mission. Phase V is complete when all forces have returned to their previous military posture or completed transition to other missions.

7. Applicable International Laws and Agreements

a. **Legal Guidance.** The complexity of FCM policies, treaties, and agreements requires continuous involvement of the SJA or appropriate legal advisor with the planning, control, and assessment of operations. Because of the international nature of FCM efforts, this will also include continuous interorganizational coordination to establish the legal authorities, capabilities, and limitations associated with engaged organizations.

(1) The SJA should be involved throughout the planning process, including mission analysis and COA development, to ensure that the relevant GCC is aware of potential FCM related legal issues. For instance, multinational partners, allies, and affected nations will have their own treaty obligations and laws that may significantly differ from our own and restrict or prohibit their participation in FCM operations. The SJA can advise of potential associated issues, such as consequences of execution and harmful environmental impacts,

collateral damage, or other FCM-related legal issues that should be considered during the response effort.

(2) The SJA should address FCM-related legal issues associated with joint operations during both the mission analysis and the planning processes. FCM-related legal issues should be outlined in appendix 4 (Legal) to annex E (Personnel) and should reflect the description of legal support required to sustain the mission as developed during the planning process. Protecting enemy prisoners of war and third country nationals from CBRN hazards are examples of two such issues.

b. **International Law and Agreements.** International law, policies, treaties, and agreements to which the US is a signatory identify certain rights and obligations that may affect joint operations. These legal requirements may pose constraints and restraints. They shape the design of operations and campaigns that deal with support to an FCM mission.

For further guidance on legal support, refer to JP 1-04, Legal Support to Military Operations. *For additional background on legal issues unique to FCM operations, refer to the DTRA* Foreign Consequence Management Legal Deskbook.

CHAPTER IV
DEPARTMENT OF DEFENSE-LED CHEMICAL, BIOLOGICAL, RADIOLOGICAL, AND NUCLEAR CONSEQUENCE MANAGEMENT

> **DOD [Department of Defense] Led CM [Consequence Management] Operations.** *In both domestic and foreign environments, CM actions are initiated at the national level with DOD providing support as directed by the President or SecDef [Secretary of Defense]. DOD forces may, however, be directed to lead [these] operations as a direct result of US military operations in a foreign country where DOS [Department of State] does not have an established presence.*
>
> **Joint Publication 3-40, *Combating Weapons of Mass Destruction***
> **10 June 2009**

1. General

a. DOD conducts CBRN CM to mitigate hazards in support of operations or to support others in response/recovery (when required/as directed). All DOD CBRN CM capabilities are designed to be used in support of military operations. Like any other DOD capability, these military assets may be used in support of civilian operations or joint or multinational forces, as directed. Mitigating the hazard reduces the threat to personnel, facilitates freedom of action, and supports mission completion. In the majority of cases, DOD supports DOS in the conduct of FCM and DHS for domestic CBRN CM. However, during combat operations or in specific instances where DOS or DHS is unable or incapable of leading the USG effort, DOD could be given primary mission responsibility. DOD-led CBRN CM can occur in either domestic CBRN CM or FCM. DOD may be delegated or tasked with leading a USG CBRN CM effort.

b. For DOD, the CBRN environment is hazard-focused and may involve deliberate, prolonged actions in and around the hazard area to support response and recovery efforts. While some hazard mitigation can be conducted by conventional forces, CBRN CM operations to address the source of the hazard often require specialized training and equipment.

c. DOD-led CBRN CM operations are generally conducted in one of two situations. DOD may be directed to coordinate the USG CBRN CM response in a permissive or uncertain environment where the DOS has no established diplomatic presence in the JOA to facilitate LFA activities, or there is no functioning HN government, to meet FCM requirements. The US military will lead CBRN CM operations conducted concurrently with military operations in hostile environments consistent with strategic planning guidance.

d. These unique conditions require the JFC to assume primary responsibility for planning, managing, and mitigating the incident until conditions permit transfer of responsibility as the lead USG agency for FCM to DOS or another authority. In these cases, the JFC becomes the de facto USG lead for the initial FCM response using available assets. The JFC requests additional support from the USG and other nations through DOS for follow-on operations. The conditions within the operational environment may range from active combat operations to crisis response in limited contingency in responding to or in mitigating the effects of, such an incident. DOD transitions DOD-led CBRN CM activities as soon as feasible to an appropriate civilian governmental authority.

e. Strategic and operational objectives drive the priority of DOD-led CBRN CM operations in relation to other ongoing military operations. JFC's should plan DOD-led CBRN CM operations as a complex contingency or branch operation executed in any environment to:

(1) Facilitate accomplishment of overall military objectives.

(2) Reduce the effect of a CBRN incident on combat operations.

(3) Provide assistance to civilian populace affected by a CBRN incident.

(4) Facilitate transfer to stability operations.

f. In general, DOD-led CBRN CM operations occur in one of the following two operational contexts:

(1) In response to CBRN incidents on foreign territory where DOS does not have an established diplomatic presence or there is no functioning HN government DOD may be required to act as the LFA for FCM requests to coordinate the USG response including in-country activities and actions to minimize the effects of WMD use/CBRN hazards. Requested activities and actions will be assessed based on the following criteria: legality, lethality, risk, cost and reimbursement, readiness, appropriateness, GCC input, and timeliness to provide recommendations to SecDef and facilitate coordination of the USG response through DOS and interagency partners.

(2) CBRN CM operations conducted concurrently with military operations include:

(a) CBRN CM assistance to the local populace within the operational area.

(b) CBRN CM operations at APODs/SPODs to maintain force projection capacity.

(c) Activities to minimize potential collateral effects from targeting adversary WMD capabilities.

(d) CBRN CM activities as a result of US, allied, or adversary military operations that result in the release of CBRN or TIMs.

2. Roles and Responsibilities

Roles, responsibilities, and relationships for DOD-led CBRN CM differ from those listed in Chapter II, "Domestic Chemical, Biological, Radiological, and Nuclear Consequence Management." The following information applies only to DOD-led CBRN CM:

a. **Office of the Secretary of Defense.** OSD coordinates JFC requests for support and forces with other USG departments and agencies and coordinates through DOS for support from partner nations and NGOs. OSD coordinates with the interagency for the transition or transfer of responsibility of CBRN CM operations to other USG departments and agencies, international agencies, or other countries, as appropriate. OSD coordinates with both DOS and the Joint Staff to obtain international legal authorities, protocols, standards, and agreements and multinational support for operations. Additionally, OSD coordinates with DOS to notify the Organization for the Prohibition of Chemical Weapons of discoveries or destruction of chemical weapons materials and former production facilities.

b. **Chairman of the Joint Chiefs of Staff.** CJCS through the Joint Staff coordinates with combatant commands and Services to make sure that DOD-led CBRN CM operations are executed in compliance with domestic, international, and foreign laws, policies, treaties, and agreements. They assist with interagency support for operations and assist in planning and exercising activities within the interagency process. They also coordinate and provide intelligence support to the CCDRs for threat identification and prioritization. When required after SecDef approval, CJCS publishes appropriate EXORDs for DOD-led CBRN CM operations.

c. **Geographic Combatant Commanders.** GCCs plan and execute DOD-led CBRN CM operations within their AORs. They incorporate DOD-led CBRN CM operations into their operational plans. GCCs also provide for intratheater movement of specialized personnel and equipment and coordinate transportation of suspect or confirmed CBRN-related material, to include weapons, agents, delivery systems, and infrastructure for short- to long-term storage, protection, dismantlement, destruction, or disposal. This includes tracking, documenting, accounting, and reporting WMD material, facilities, and personnel discovered, stored, or destroyed in the AOR. CCDRs coordinate with OSD and the Joint Staff to plan for transition or transfer of responsibility of DOD-led CBRN CM operations to other multinational forces or nation-states. Finally, they coordinate with OSD and the Joint Staff to ensure operations are in compliance with US obligations under international laws, policies, treaties, and agreements.

d. **Defense Threat Reduction Agency.** DTRA provides operational and technical advice and support to DOD components and other USG departments and agencies, as requested and approved regarding CBRN CM operations. This is accomplished through training and exercises, the deployment of CBRN CM advisory teams, and operational planning assistance. DTRA also provides modeling, predictions, assessments, publications, training, lessons learned, analysis, and other support as required. DTRA provides technical reachback through the DTRA Operations Center, a 24/7 WMD and CBRN national reachback and situational awareness facility for all technical support. During CBRN CM, DTRA liaises with other technical support providers and the intelligence community to meet support requests.

3. **Command Relationships**

The JFC coordinates the response to a CBRN incident in the assigned JOA. The JFC requests additional support through the appropriate GCC. For large incidents, a JTF-CM as described in Chapter III, "Foreign Consequence Management," should be considered for the response. The GCC coordinates with DOS for support from other USG departments and agencies or foreign countries. For DOD-led CBRN CM, the JFC is the supported commander. JFCs should take into consideration that other USG departments and agencies may not be accustomed to working in a supporting capacity to DOD.

4. Joint Force Considerations

a. In the context of DOD-led CBRN CM operations, the appropriate JFC assumes responsibility for the execution of operations within the JOA when a CBRN incident requiring a response occurs. The GCC approves end states for these operations by phase within the JOA. One major objective is to conduct DOD-led CBRN CM operations without jeopardizing critical military operations and objectives; however, commanders should plan for the diversion of combat forces and possible changes to overall end states and objectives due to the significance of a CBRN incident.

b. Providing assistance to civilian populace affected by a CBRN incident is an important aspect of these operations. Assistance may include, but is not limited to:

(1) Saving lives and preventing human suffering.

(2) Providing support to displaced personnel.

(3) Preventing/reducing additional damage.

(4) Providing mortuary affairs support.

(5) Providing emergency mitigation of CBRN hazards.

(6) Providing minimum emergency restoration of life supporting services.

(7) Conducting a noncombatant evacuation operation.

5. Planning Considerations During Military Operations

a. GCC theater security cooperation activities (phase 0) support DOD-led CBRN CM operations by facilitating interaction with partner nation military forces to identify partner capabilities, build partner capacity, and increase interoperability. Planning for DOD-led CBRN CM should build on these activities and incorporate the experience gained in working with partner nations in operations.

b. DOD-led CBRN CM operations may be required to facilitate combat operations, and depending on the nature and purpose of the activities, may require coordination with response operations of multiple countries, partners, and a wide variety of international organizations and other NGOs. JFCs should be aware of the following planning considerations:

(1) Integration of specialized US military forces, USG departments and agencies, and contractors.

(2) Integration of partner nation support and forces.

(3) Support and integration of NGOs.

(4) Development of a strategic communication plan.

c. Coordination between DOD and other USG departments and agencies, NGOs, and IGOs will also be important aspects of any DOD-led CBRN CM operation. Regardless of the status of an impacted nation government or partner nations, IGOs and NGOs will have significant equities in the operation; therefore, JFCs should anticipate considerable interagency and intergovernmental coordination requirements.

(1) Operations will likely be subject to monitoring by various government agencies or IGOs; therefore, planners should anticipate receiving specific US national level guidance. As DOD-led CBRN CM operations may involve significant interactions with foreign civilian authorities and IGOs that do not normally operate in a supporting role to DOD, the JFC should strongly consider forming a CMOC or supplementing an existing CMOC with appropriate FCM expertise. In addition to IGO participation, the CMOC often involves multinational partners that possess unique FCM capabilities.

For further guidance on CMOCs, refer to JP 3-57, Civil-Military Operations. *Additional guidance on multinational operations is found in JP 3-16,* Multinational Operations.

(2) As with USG departments and agencies, NGOs and IGOs may have significant equities and capabilities; planning for their participation in a hostile or uncertain environment is challenging. Some of these agencies may demand to participate regardless of the risk, and others may not be willing to participate until a permissive environment exists.

d. DOD-led CBRN CM operations can occur at any point in a campaign; therefore, these operations should be considered as a branch to contingency operations. DOD-led CBRN CM-related activities are conducted in the following phases, which differ from traditional operational phases as found in JP 5-0, *Joint Operation Planning*:

(1) **Phase 0 (Shape).** This is a continuous phase. The intent of this phase is to ensure DOD is organized, trained, equipped, and prepared to minimize the effects of CBRN incidents on foreign soil. Key tasks of this phase include planning response capabilities within the joint force, identifying possible partner nation FCM capabilities, incorporating DOD-led CBRN CM scenarios into training and exercises, and developing intelligence on friendly, neutral, and enemy CBRN threats in the operational area.

(2) **Phase I Deter (Situation Assessment and Preparation).** Transition to phase I occurs on reliable indications and warnings of a CBRN incident or upon notification that an incident has occurred. Phase I includes those actions required to conduct a timely and accurate assessment of the CBRN situation, preparation for deployment, and deployment of selected advance elements. Phase I ends when the nature and scope of the CBRN situation

and initial response requirements are defined. The response spectrum may include technical expertise, specialized teams, or entire units. Conventional forces will also be needed to carry out non-CBRN tasks (medical, transportation, security, etc.). Any limited initial response to a CBRN incident conducted by DOD commanders operating under immediate response authority would likely occur during phase I. Plans should also include HA/DR considerations for those affected by the CBRN incident or its cause.

(3) **Phase II Seize the Initiative (Deployment).** Phase II begins with the deployment of designated forces and the establishment of formal command relationships between supported and supporting commanders. Depending on the nature and scope of the hazard, forces may continue to flow for some time (days, weeks, or even months). Commanders begin planning immediately for redeployment and transition to civilian agencies, including USG, other international governments, donors, and NGOs, and should identify the necessary or minimum conditions needed to effect the transition. Phase II ends when the first capability arrives and is operational.

(4) **Phase III Dominate (Mitigate Hazard Effects).** Phase III begins with the initialization of efforts to mitigate hazard effects. These efforts may include lifesaving operations, personnel and equipment decontamination, actions to stop or reduce the source of contamination, and actions to support associated HA/DR efforts as a result of the CBRN incident. Remediation (return to a pre-contaminated state) is usually not possible by DOD forces. Rather, the control of the hazard site and reduction to the threat to forces and any nearby civilians is the goal. When (due to operations) transition is not possible, the area will be marked to protect forces and any civilians in the area. Phase III ends when the on-scene commander determines that the incident site is under positive control.

(5) **Phase IV Stabilize (Transition to Close the Incident Site).** Phase IV begins initiation of the redeployment plan. The situation contained, the effort is now made to reduce the personnel needed to continue mitigation efforts. When possible, HN, NGO, or USG personnel may replace functions performed by DOD personnel. Otherwise, efforts will be made to mark the area to reduce any residual threat to personnel or civilians in the area. Phase IV ends when the mitigation of the incident is at such a point where it is determined that no or minimal personnel are needed to maintain security of the site.

(6) **Phase V Enable Civilian Authorities (Redeployment).** Phase V begins with the redeployment of the bulk US military forces involved in CBRN CM operations or the formal transition of those forces to a purely DR or HA mission. Phase V is complete when all forces have returned to their previous military posture or completed transition to other missions.

6. General Planning Considerations

a. **Overall Planning Considerations**

(1) Many important DOD-led CBRN CM activities take place as shaping (phase 0) activities and are included in theater campaign plans, regional combating WMD plans, and contingency plans. Many are executed as part of the theater security cooperation strategy,

but provide direct support to DOD-led CBRN CM. These activities include joint, interagency, bilateral and multinational CBRN CM or FCM exercises and training; efforts to build partner CBRN CM capacity; and consultation with partner nations and local authorities.

(2) International law, policies, treaties, and agreements to which the US is a signatory identify certain rights and obligations that may affect DOD-led CBRN CM operations. These legal requirements may pose constraints and restraints and shape the planning and execution of operations.

(a) The complexity of international laws, US policies, treaties, and agreements requires the involvement of the SJA or appropriate legal advisor with planning and execution.

(b) This will also include consultation with other USG departments and agencies, multinational partners, impacted nation governments (if applicable), and IGOs to establish the legal authorities, capabilities, and limitations associated with their organizations.

(c) Policies for the disposition of contaminated human remains to meet health-based clearance requirements for contamination mitigation, safety requirements for transportation, and environmental/diplomatic requirements for temporary interment in theater.

(3) To protect both DOD forces and civilian populations, DOD-led CBRN CM mission planning should address both immediate and long-term effects of dispersed CBRN hazards. Planning should include the capability for CBRN hazard identification and assessment, protection, avoidance, and decontamination. Considerations include but are not limited to the following:

(a) Procedures for the temporary or permanent disposition of human remains and equipment and materiel that cannot be decontaminated or that does not meet agreed upon cleanliness standards.

(b) Medical obligations under international law. DOD should be prepared to lead activities necessary to accomplish medical obligations under international law when indigenous capacity does not exist or is incapable of assuming responsibility. Once legitimate civilian authority is prepared to conduct and sustain this medical support, US military forces transition to provide support, as required or necessary. Medical planning considerations include the following:

1. Planning for medical assistance to be provided to indigenous populations, multinational forces, USG employees, contractors, and as appropriate, IGOs and NGOs.

2. Policies for contaminated mass casualty decontamination. Policies and procedures should include provisions for casualty decontamination and evacuation both in

and out of the area of operations. Procedures and provisions for processing family pets are also an important consideration in catastrophic incidents.

(c) Planning should include specific meteorological and oceanographic products and information support. These products are important components of modeling and simulation analysis used to predict hazard areas and estimate casualties during operations.

(d) An effective communications strategy aids the commander in the conduct of DOD-led CBRN CM operations and responses. This plan should inform affected civilian and military populace, reduce panic and restore order, and provide information consistent with overall mission objectives. Communications planning should include common themes and messages to reassure local populations and promote effective communications between the JFC commander and partner nations, IGOs, and NGOs.

b. **Additional Planning Guidance**

(1) **Flexibility.** Geographic combatant commands and JTFs should be given maximum flexibility to both render assistance and continue conduct of their primary mission. Assistance that allows mission flexibility during conduct of DOD-led CBRN CM includes:

(a) Assessment of the incident site (e.g., agent preliminary identification, initial damage assessment, perimeter of incident identified).

(b) Timely cordoning off of the contamination site.

(c) Emergency medical treatment on civilians (triage).

(d) Providing incident information for subsequent public information broadcasts or warnings.

(e) Decontamination of casualties.

(f) Providing biological agent outbreak information to surveillance and disease reporting offices.

(g) Facilitating transition to responding international health organizations or indigenous health care elements.

(h) Conducting shipment and administration of vaccines to civilian populations in the event of a biological agent breakout (e.g., smallpox) while DOS or non-US health organizations have limited access due to a nonpermissive environment.

(2) **Use of Partner Nation Forces.** Use of partner nation CBRN CM assets, with emphasis on those elements not fully engaged with combat operations, should be planned and coordinated, if possible, prior to the start of combat operations. Many partner nation forces have significant capabilities and trained forces to assist in reducing or mitigating the impact of CBRN hazards on affected indigenous civilian populations. These forces can be

used to reinforce indigenous nation first response capabilities, conduct initial assessments of the incident, conduct incident scene C2, conduct limited medical treatment, and conduct limited decontamination.

(3) **Nonpermissive Environment Factors.** Due to the nature of the environment in which DOD-led CBRN CM operations occur, the following specific details need to be covered during JFC planning:

(a) Additional force protection is provided for elements in direct support of the CBRN CM operation.

(b) Medevac resources, both air and land, are available for both the CBRN CM force and for possible civilian CBRN casualties.

(c) Communications are adequate for CBRN CM operations during simultaneous combat operations and have as little priority competition as possible.

(d) Intelligence and counterintelligence capabilities are focused on the CBRN incident to reduce its impact or eliminate future incidents.

(e) PA and information operations that reduce the civilian population panic, support the early return of civilian authority to the management of the CBRN-related incident, and facilitate the release of US and partner nation forces to the conduct of the primary combat operation.

c. **Assessments.** There are several assessments available to a commander to assist with overall planning. These include:

(1) **Operational Environment Assessment.** An operational environment assessment provides the commander information on the threat, the physical environment, and the political environment. Decision support tools may be used in conjunction with this information to assist predictive modeling.

(a) The threat assessment identifies what enemy or adversary the force may face during a DOD-led CBRN CM operation, if in a hostile environment. The threat assessment also addresses the types of agents and hazards and includes occupational and environmental health assessments.

(b) The physical environment includes terrain, weather, and characteristics of the geographical area. Characteristics include critical infrastructure, hazard sites, and zone analysis considerations. Analysis of urban areas within the JOA can facilitate the complex transition from combat operations to CBRN CM when required.

See JP 3-06, Joint Urban Operations, *for detailed discussions in urban areas.*

(c) The political environment includes applicable impacted nation agreements, SOFAs, and other sovereignty issues that may apply.

(2) **Capabilities Assessment.** Capabilities assessment provides an assessment of the JFC's ability to conduct DOD-led CBRN CM and includes plans, organization, manpower, equipment, logistics, medical, training, leadership, and readiness.

(3) **Vulnerability Assessment.** A vulnerability assessment is an evaluation of the organization's strengths and weaknesses compared with the operational environment and CBRN threat. Vulnerability analyses of key APOD, SPOD, and JRSOI sites, to include proximity of TIM storage facilities or sites, are used to develop measures to reduce the organization's vulnerability to identified CBRN threats. The ultimate purpose of a vulnerability assessment is to help ensure that adequate defensive and CBRN CM assets are available.

(4) **Risk Assessment.** These assessments attempt to quantify the level of risk that exists in the conduct of DOD-led CBRN CM operations. In certain incidents, such as high radiation hazards, the risk may preclude mission accomplishment.

(5) **Criticality Assessment.** The criticality assessment evaluates a command's missions and functions/capabilities and determines mission impact or consequence of loss of assets that support execution of the command's missions.

(6) **Threat Assessment.** The threat assessment provides an assessment on the adversary's CBRN capability. This threat can come from nation states and non-state actors alike, sometimes simultaneously, and may occur in a variety of forms. These include deliberate attacks or accidental releases.

See JP 3-40, Combating Weapons of Mass Destruction, *CJCSI 3214.01,* Military Support to Foreign Consequence Management Operations, *and the DTRA* Foreign Consequence Management Planning Guide *for additional planning considerations for DOD-led CBRN CM missions.*

Response to US nuclear weapon incidents and other nuclear or radiological incidents involving materials in DOD custody is a special case and may or may not be led by DOD. These responses are conducted IAW NSPD 28, United States Nuclear Weapons Command and Control, Safety, and Security; *the NRF, where applicable; NIMS, where applicable; and appropriate DOD instructions and plans.*

See DODD 3150.08, Response to Nuclear and Radiological Incidents, *and DOD 3150.8-M,* Nuclear Weapon Accident Response Procedures (NARP), *for further information.*

APPENDIX A
KEY LEGAL, STRATEGY, AND POLICY DOCUMENTS AND INTERNATIONAL PROTOCOLS

1. Legal, National Strategy, and National Policy Guidance

a. **Key Executive and Legislative Guidance.** The following documents are key references when addressing the CS mission area, to include CBRN CM:

(1) **The White House Notice,** *Continuation of Emergency with Respect to Weapons of Mass Destruction.* Reissued every year since 1994, the notice concerns EO 12938, and as amended, that a national emergency exists because of the worldwide threat posed by the proliferation and potential use of WMD.

(2) **PPD-1,** *Organization of the National Security Council System,* establishes the process and structure for the national security council system.

(3) **HSPD-1,** *Organization and Operation of the Homeland Security Council,* established the Homeland Security Council to ensure coordination of all HS-related activities among the executive departments and agencies and promote the effective development and implementation of all HS policies.

(4) **HSPD-3,** *The Homeland Security Advisory System,* provides the guidelines for a comprehensive and effective means to disseminate information regarding the risk of terrorist acts to federal, state, and local authorities and the American people. This document establishes the five threat conditions and their respective protective measures.

(5) *National Strategy to Combat Weapons of Mass Destruction* states, "As part of our defense, the United States must be fully prepared to respond to the consequences of WMD use on our soil, whether by hostile states or by terrorists. We must also be prepared to respond to the effects of WMD use against our forces deployed abroad and to assist friends and allies." Refer to the classified version of this strategy and its applicable annex for details concerning WMD CM.

(6) **HSPD-5,** *Management of Domestic Incidents,* assigns the Secretary of the DHS as the PFO for domestic incident management to coordinate the USG's resources utilized in response to, or recovery from terrorist attacks, major disasters, or other emergencies. Additionally, HSPD-5 established the NIMS to provide a consistent nationwide approach for federal, state, and local governments to work effectively and efficiently together to prepare for, respond to, and recover from domestic incidents.

(7) **PPD-8,** *National Preparedness,* is aimed at strengthening the security and resilience of the US through systematic preparation for the threats that pose the greatest risk to the security of the Nation, including acts of terrorism, cyberspace attacks, pandemics, and catastrophic natural disasters.

(8) **Federal Strategic Guidance Statement for Chemical Attacks in the United States.** The strategic guidance statement, issued pursuant to HSPD-8, Annex 1 (National

Preparedness), guides USG efforts in addressing chemical attacks based on the applicable National Planning Scenarios along with threats of attacks using other possible chemical weapons.

(9) **HSPD-9,** *Defense of United States Agriculture and Food,* establishes a national policy to defend the agriculture and food system against terrorist attacks, major disasters, and other emergencies.

(10) **HSPD-10,** *Biodefense for the 21st Century*, outlines the essential pillars of our biodefense program and provides specific directives to further strengthen the significant gains put in place during the past three years. These pillars include threat awareness, prevention and protection, surveillance and detection, and response and recovery, which include response planning, mass casualty care, risk communication, medical countermeasures, and decontamination.

(11) **HSPD-14,** *Domestic Nuclear Detection*, seeks to protect against the unauthorized importation, possession, storage, transportation, development, or use of a nuclear explosive device, fissile material, or radiological material in the US, and to protect against attack using such devices or materials against the people, territory, or interests of the US.

(12) **HSPD-15,** *US Strategy and Policy on the War on Terror[ism]* (U), discusses the coordination of all instruments of national power to meet six US goals for the war on terrorism: deny terrorists resources, enable partner nations to counter terrorism, combat WMD, defeat terrorists and their organizations, counter support for terrorism in coordination with partner nations, and establish conditions that counter ideological support for terrorism.

(13) **HSPD-18,** *Medical Countermeasures Against Weapons of Mass Destruction*, describes the principles from which national guidance is derived for addressing the challenges presented by the diverse CBRN threat spectrum, optimizing the investments necessary for medical countermeasures development, and ensuring that USG activities significantly enhance domestic and international response and recovery capabilities. Mitigating illness and preventing death from CBRN threats are the principal goals of the USG medical countermeasure efforts.

(14) **HSPD-19,** *Combating Terrorist Use of Explosives in the United States,* establishes a national policy, and calls for the development of a national strategy and implementation plan, on the prevention and detection of, protection against, and response to terrorist use of explosives in the US.

(15) **HSPD-20,** *National Continuity Policy*, establishes a comprehensive national policy on the continuity of USG structures and operations and a single national continuity coordinator responsible for coordinating the development and implementation of federal continuity policies. The policy establishes "national essential functions," prescribes continuity requirements for all executive departments and agencies, and provides guidance for state, local, territorial, and tribal governments and private sector organizations in order to ensure a comprehensive and integrated national continuity program that will enhance the

credibility of the USG national security posture and enable a more rapid and effective response to and recovery from a national emergency.

(16) **HSPD-21,** *Public Health and Medical Preparedness*, establishes a national strategy for public health and a medical preparedness strategy which builds upon principles set forth in HSPD-10, *Biodefense for the 21st Century.* The directive sets forth policy enabling the provision of public health and medical needs of the American people in the case of a catastrophic health incident through continual and timely flow of information and rapid public health and medical response that marshals all available nation capabilities and capacities in a rapid and coordinated manner.

(17) **HSPD-22,** *Domestic Chemical Defense (U),* establishes a national policy and directs actions to strengthen the ability of the US to prevent, protect from, and respond to, and recover from terrorist attacks employing toxic chemicals and other chemical incidents.

(18) **The NSS and the National Military Strategy (NMS).** The NSS establishes broad strategic guidance for advancing US interests in the global environment through the instruments of national power. The NSS and the NMS continue to reflect the first and fundamental commitment to defend the Nation against its adversaries.

(19) **The National Strategy for Homeland Security.** Prepared for the President by the Office of Homeland Security, this document lays out the strategic objectives, organization, and critical areas for HS. The strategy identifies critical areas that focus on preventing terrorist attacks, reducing the nation's vulnerabilities, minimizing the damage and recovering from attacks that do occur.

(20) **National Strategy for Countering Biological Threats.** Issued by the National Security Council, this strategy guides efforts to prevent acts of bioterrorism or other significant outbreaks of infectious disease by reducing the risk of misuse of the life sciences or derivative materials, techniques, or expertise that will result in the use or intent to use biological agents to cause harm. It also complements existing policies, plans, and preparations to advance the USG's ability to respond to public health crises of natural, accidental, or deliberate origin.

(21) **National Strategy for Combating Terrorism.** Expands on the National Strategy for Homeland Security and the NSS by expounding on the need to destroy terrorist organizations, win the war of ideas, and strengthen America's security at home and abroad. While the national strategy focuses on preventing terrorist attacks within the US, this strategy is more proactive and focuses on identifying and defusing threats before they reach our borders. The direct and continuous action against terrorist groups can disrupt, degrade, and destroy their capability to attack the US.

(22) **National Strategy for Pandemic Influenza.** Issued by the Homeland Security Council, this strategy presents the USG approach to address the threat of PI. It outlines how the nation prepares, detects, and responds to a pandemic by documenting the responsibilities of federal, state, and local governments; private industry; international partners; and American citizens.

(23) **Strategy for Homeland Defense and Civil Support.** Establishes strategic guidance for securing the US from direct attack with an active, layered defense. Expands on the NDS by establishing a lead, support, and enable construct in organizing DOD objectives. Provides specific objectives to support managing the consequences of CBRN and bulk HE use resulting in mass casualties.

(24) *Foreign Assistance Act of 1961.* Establishes DOS as LFA for USG assistance to a foreign country during a disaster and describes the procedures for conducting that relief as well as the congressionally authorized funding.

(25) **Uniting and Strengthening America by Providing Appropriate Tools Required to Intercept and Obstruct Terrorism Act** (US Patriot Act of 2001 [as amended]). This act enhances domestic security against terrorism. It eases some of the restrictions on foreign intelligence gathering within the US and affords the US intelligence community greater access to information discovered during a criminal investigation.

(26) **The Robert T. Stafford Disaster Relief and Emergency Assistance Act, (Title 42, USC, Sections 5121–5207).** The Stafford Act provides for assistance by the USG to the states in the event of natural and other disasters and emergencies. It is the primary legal authority for federal participation in domestic DR. Under the Stafford Act, the President may direct federal agencies, including DOD, to support DR. DOD may be directed to provide assistance in one of three different scenarios: a Presidential declaration of a major disaster, a Presidential order to perform emergency work for the preservation of life and property, or a Presidential declaration of emergency.

(27) **The Economy Act (Title 31, USC, Section 1535).** The Economy Act authorizes federal agencies to provide goods or services on a reimbursable basis to other federal agencies when more specific statutory authority to do so does not exist.

(28) **Posse Comitatus Act (Title 18, USC, Section 1385).** This statute limits the use of federal military personnel to perform civilian law enforcement activities. The PCA generally prohibits the use of US Army and US Air Force active duty (Title 10, USC), personnel for civilian law enforcement activities, except as authorized by the US Constitution or by statute. DOD policy extends the prohibitions of the PCA to US Navy and Marine Corps active duty (Title 10, USC) personnel. Specifically prohibited activities include interdiction of a vehicle, vessel, aircraft, or similar activity; search and/or seizure; arrest, apprehension, "stop-and-frisk" detentions, and similar activities; and use of military personnel for surveillance or pursuit of individuals, or as undercover agents, informants, investigators, or interrogators. DODD 5525.5, *DOD Cooperation with Civilian Law Enforcement Officials*, sets forth several forms of military assistance to civilian authorities, which are allowed under the PCA. Further, DODD 5525.5, *DOD Cooperation with Civilian Law Enforcement Officials,* details express statutory exceptions to the PCA, such as the Insurrections Act and emergency assistance involving WMD, which, upon appropriate notifications and approval, allow for the otherwise prohibited use of federal forces to support civilian law enforcement activities during CBRN CM operations.

(29) **Title 10, USC (Armed Forces).** Title 10, USC, provides guidance on the Armed Forces. Guidance is divided into five subtitles. One covers general military law and one each for the US Army, US Navy and US Marine Corps, the US Air Force, and the RC. Chapter 18 (Sections 371–382) of Title 10, USC, is entitled and governs Military Support for Civilian Law Enforcement Agencies. Title 10, USC, Section 375, directs SecDef to promulgate regulations that prohibit "direct participation by a member of the Army, Navy, Air Force, or Marine Corps in a search, seizure, arrest, or other similar activity unless participation in such activity by such member is otherwise authorized by law."

(30) **Title 14, USC (Coast Guard).** Sections 2, 19, 89, 141, and 143, define the statutory authority of the USCG during HS missions.

(31) **Title 32, USC (National Guard).** Specifically, statutes in Title 32, USC, authorize the use of federal funds to train NG members while they remain under the C2 of their respective state governors. In certain limited instances, specific statutory or Presidential authority allows for those forces to perform operational missions funded by the USG, while they remain under the control of the governor. Examples of those exceptions include the employment of WMD-CSTs, civil defense missions, and the President of the United States-directed airport security mission.

(32) ***Memorandum of Understanding Between the Intelligence Community, Federal Law Enforcement Agencies, and the Department of Homeland Security Concerning Information Sharing, 4 March 2003.*** This agreement provides a framework and guidance to govern information sharing, use, and handling among the following individuals and their agencies: Secretary of Homeland Security, Director of National Intelligence, the Attorney General, and any other organization having federal law enforcement responsibilities (other than those that are part of the DHS). The agreement mandates minimum requirements for information sharing, use, and handling and for coordination and deconfliction of analytic judgments.

(33) **Memorandum of Agreement Between DOD and DHS on Use of the USCG Capabilities and Resources in Support of the NMS, 23 May 2008.** This agreement provides for the identification of certain national defense capabilities of the USCG and improves the process by which the USCG serves as a force provider for DOD missions.

(34) **National Response Framework.** The NRF focuses on response and short-term recovery, and articulates doctrine, principles, and architectures by which the US prepares for and responds to all-hazard disasters across all levels of government. The NRF and supporting annexes are available at www.fema.gov/nrf.

(35) **Inter-Departmental Memorandum of Understanding for Foreign Consequence Management Preparedness and Response.** The purpose of this MOU is to synchronize and integrate USG FCM efforts. The MOU details the USG's goals and objectives relating to FCM and provides policy relating to roles and responsibilities of departments and agencies to prepare for and respond to a CBRN incident on foreign soil.

b. **Key DOD Guidance.** The following discussion identifies a number of key documents to make commanders and planners more aware of material that may assist in the planning and execution of the CBRN mission areas.

(1) **Unified Command Plan.** The UCP provides basic guidance to all unified CCDRs; establishes their missions and responsibilities; delineates the general geographical AORs for GCCs; and specifies functional responsibilities for functional CCDRs.

(2) **National Defense Strategy.** NDS establishes and directs how to accomplish broad strategic objectives. Provides HD implementation guidelines.

(3) **The National Military Strategy (NMS) to Combat WMD** describes WMD consequence management as one of the eight military mission areas to combat WMD; it illustrates and explains how WMD consequence management contributes to the success of the military strategic objective.

(4) **National Military Strategic Plan for the War on Terrorism.** This National Military Strategic Plan for the War on Terrorism constitutes the comprehensive military plan to prosecute the global war on terrorism for the Armed Forces of the United States. It is the plan that guides the contributions of the combatant commands, the Military Departments, combat support agencies and field support activities of the United States to protect and defend the homeland, attack terrorists and their capacity to operate effectively at home and abroad, and support mainstream efforts to reject violent extremism.

(5) **DODD 2000.12,** *DOD Antiterrorism Program.* This directive updates policies and assigns responsibilities for implementing the procedures for the DOD AT program. It establishes CJCS as the principal advisor and focal point responsible to SecDef for DOD AT issues. It also defines the AT responsibilities of the Military Departments, commanders of combatant commands, DOD agencies, and DOD field activities. Its guidelines are applicable for the physical security of all DOD activities both overseas and in the homeland.

(6) **DODD 2000.15,** *Support to Special Events.* DODD 2000.15, *Support to Special Events,* provides definitions for a special event and support and outlines policy guidelines and responsibilities for DOD support of special events. It allows for the DOD component to designate a special events coordinator who is charged with providing timely information and technical support to the ASD (HD&ASA).

(7) **DODD 2060.2,** *Department of Defense (DOD) Combating WMD Policy.* This directive recognizes the need for Services to be prepared to support CWMD operations and directs Services to organize, train, and equip their forces to support them.

(8) **The DODD 3025 series of directives, instructions, and manuals** provides policy on and responsibilities for CS activities. As a result of the terrorist attack on September 11, 2001, the USG changed how it supports state, local, and tribal authorities in responding to incidents and events. In conjunction with the changes to the federal response DOD modified how it supports the federal response.

(9) **DODD 3025.18,** *Defense Support of Civil Authorities.* DODD 3025.18, *Defense Support of Civil Authorities,* provides guidance for the execution and oversight of DSCA when requested by civil authorities approved by the appropriate DOD official or as directed by the President. It authorizes immediate response authority for providing DSCA when requested and authorizes emergency authority for the use of military force under dire situations.

(10) **DODD 3025.12,** *Military Assistance for Civil Disturbances.* DODD 3025.12 *Military Assistance for Civil Disturbances,* provides guidance on CS activities for civil disturbances and civil disturbance operations, including response to terrorist incidents, and covers the policy and procedures whereby the President is authorized by the Constitution and laws of the US to employ the Armed Forces to suppress insurrections, rebellions, and domestic violence under various conditions and circumstances. Planning and preparedness by the USG and the DOD for civil disturbances are important due to the potential severity of the consequences of such incidents for the nation and the population.

(11) **DODD 3150.08,** *DOD Response to Nuclear and Radiological Incidents.* This directive promulgates policy and assigns responsibilities for DOD CBRM CM response to US nuclear weapon incidents and other nuclear or radiological incidents involving materials in DOD custody IAW the guidance in NSPD-28, *US Nuclear Weapons Command and Control, Safety, and Security,* the NRF, and the NIMS.

(12) **DODD 5100.46,** *Foreign Disaster Relief,* details DOD policy for conducting DR operations which covers the scenarios of FCM and DOD-led CBRN CM on foreign soil.

(13) **DODD 5200.27,** *Acquisition of Information Concerning Persons and Organizations not Affiliated with the Department of Defense.* This directive establishes the Defense Investigative Program general policy, limitations, procedures, and operational guidance pertaining to the collecting, processing, storing, and disseminating of information concerning persons and organizations not affiliated with DOD.

(14) **DODD 5240.01,** *DOD Intelligence Activities.* This directive is the primary authority used as guidance by DOD intelligence personnel and those performing an intelligence or counterintelligence function to collect, process, retain, or disseminate information concerning US persons.

(15) **DOD 5240.1-R,** *Activities of DOD Intelligence Components That Affect United States Persons.* This regulation sets forth procedures governing the activities of DOD intelligence components that affect US persons, to include the collection, retention, processing, and dissemination of US persons' information.

(16) **DODD 5525.5,** *DOD Cooperation with Civilian Law Enforcement Officials.* This directive assigns responsibilities and provides policy and procedures to be followed with respect to support provided to federal, state, and local law enforcement efforts.

(17) **DOD Manual 3150.8-M,** *Nuclear Weapon Accident Response Procedures (NARP).* This manual is issued under the authority of DODD 3150.8, *DOD Response to Nuclear and Radiological Incidents.* It provides a concept of operations as well as functional

information necessary to execute a comprehensive and unified response to a nuclear weapon accident. It provides information for planners and response elements to understand the overall response concept and roles of DOD and the Department of Energy/National Nuclear Security Administration.

(18) **DODI 2000.18,** *Department of Defense Installation Chemical, Biological, Radiological, Nuclear, and High-Yield Explosive Emergency Response Guidelines.* This instruction implements policy, assigns responsibilities, and prescribes procedures to establish and implement a program for a worldwide DOD installation hazard response to manage the consequences of a CBRN and bulk HE incident. It provides guidance for the establishment of a CBRN and bulk HE preparedness program for emergency responders at all DOD installations. It also prescribes that DOD installation emergency responders must be prepared to respond to the effects of a CBRN or bulk HE incident to preserve life, prevent human suffering, mitigate the incident, and protect critical assets and infrastructure.

(19) **DODI 2000.21,** *Foreign Consequence Management.* This document establishes policy and assigns responsibility for DOD support to USG FCM operations in response to a foreign CBRN and bulk HE incident.

(20) **DODI 3001.02,** *Personnel Accountability in Conjunction With Natural or Manmade Disasters.* This instruction establishes policy and assigns responsibilities for accounting and reporting of specified DOD-affiliated personnel, within CONUS and outside the continental United States, following a natural or man-made disaster.

(21) **DODI 6055.17,** *DOD Installation Emergency Management (IEM) Program.* This instruction is a reference for response of a DOD installation to a CBRN incident.

(a) Establishes policy, assigns responsibilities, and prescribes procedures for developing, implementing, and sustaining installation emergency management (IEM) programs at DOD installations worldwide for "all hazards" as defined in the glossary. Establishes the goals of the DOD IEM Program as follows:

1. Prepare DOD installations for emergencies.

2. Respond appropriately to protect personnel and save lives.

3. Recover and restore operations after an emergency.

(b) Aligns DOD emergency management activities with NIMS, the National Preparedness Guidelines, and the NRF.

(c) Establishes the DOD Emergency Management Steering Group.

(22) **DODI 6200.03,** *Public Health Emergency Management within the Department of Defense.* Establishes DOD guidance IAW applicable law and ensures mission assurance and readiness by protecting installations, facilities, personnel, and other assets in managing the impact of public health emergencies caused by all-hazards incidents.

(23) **CJCSI 3121.01,** *Standing Rules of Engagement/Rules for the Use of Force for US Forces (Classified).* This instruction provides the SRUF to be employed by US forces in a Title 10, USC, status performing DSCA missions.

(24) **CJCSI 3125.01,** *Defense Support of Civil Authorities for Domestic Consequence Management Operations in Response to a Chemical, Biological, Radiological, Nuclear, and High-Yield Explosives Incident.* This instruction provides operational and policy guidance and instructions for US military forces responding to domestic CBRN and bulk HE incidents. This instruction applies only to domestic operations. This instruction is of specific importance to the geographic combatant commands with domestic CBRN and bulk HE responsibilities. It identifies that domestic support encompasses both deliberate and inadvertent CBRN and bulk HE situations including terrorism, acts of aggression, industrial accidents, and acts of nature. It recognizes that these operations may be conducted by US military forces under immediate response authority and in support of the designated LFA.

(25) **CJCSI 3214.01,** *Defense Support for Chemical, Biological, Radiological, and Nuclear Incidents on Foreign Territory.* This instruction provides guidance for US military forces supporting USG-led FCM operations and DOD-led CBRN CM operations in response to a CBRN incident.

(26) **Guidance for Employment of the Force (GEF).** The GEF and the Joint Strategic Capabilities Plan (JSCP) inform DOD how to employ, and in part manage, the force in the near term. The GEF provides strategic planning guidance and identifies security cooperation focus areas for campaign planning—both foreign language for US forces and English skills for allies.

(27) **Joint Strategic Capabilities Plan.** The JSCP provides guidance to the CCDRs and the Joint Chiefs of Staff to accomplish tasks and missions based on current military capabilities. It apportions limited forces and resources to CCDRs, based on military capabilities resulting from completed program and budget actions and intelligence assessments. The JSCP provides a coherent framework for capabilities-based military advice provided to the President and SecDef.

2. Key International Legal Documents

  a. **Canada-United States (CANUS) Agreements**

(1) **Canada-United States Integrated Lines of Communications (ILOCs) Agreements.** The CANUS ILOCs agreements facilitate cooperation in training and operations and provides for reciprocal logistical support, supplies, and/or services in nonroutine situations.

(2) **Canada-US Agreement for Enhanced Military Cooperation.** Under this agreement, both countries work together on contingency plans for defending against and responding to possible threats in Canada and the US including natural disasters and potential terrorist attacks.

(3) **Temporary Cross-Border Movement of Land Forces Between the United States and Canada Agreement.** This agreement provides principles and procedures for temporary cross-border movement of land forces between the two nations.

(4) **Canadian–United States Regional Emergency Management Agreements.** Emergency management officials in Canada and the US have regional mutual assistance agreements to manage emergencies or disasters when the affected jurisdiction(s) requests assistance in response to natural disasters, technological hazards, man-made disasters, and civil emergencies. These agreements are compliant with the *Agreement between the Government of the United States and the Government of Canada on Cooperation in Comprehensive Emergency Planning and Management.* These agreements promote unity of effort with civil authorities in planning and executing military support to civilian authorities. Three regional agreements implement regional emergency management mutual assistance covering specific states and provinces:

(a) Pacific Northwest Emergency Management Agreement.

(b) Prairie Region Emergency Management Assistance Compact.

(c) International Emergency Management Assistance Memorandum of Understanding.

(5) **Joint Radiological Emergency Response Plan (JRERP).** The CANUS JRERP establishes the basis for cooperative measures to deal effectively with a potential or actual peacetime radiological incident involving Canada, the US, or both countries. The JRERP will apply whenever a potential or actual radiological incident occurs that can affect both countries or, although affecting one country, is of a magnitude that the affected country may need to request assistance from the other. The JRERP is designed to:

(a) Alert the appropriate federal authorities within each country of the existence of a threat from a potential or actual radiological incident.

(b) Establish a framework of cooperative measures to reduce, to the extent possible, the threat posed to public health and safety, property, and the environment.

(c) Facilitate coordination between organizations of the federal government of each country in providing support to states and provinces affected by a potential or actual radiological incident.

(6) **Inland Pollution Contingency Plan,** June 1998. The US EPA and Environment Canada recognize that there is a high probability that there will be a spill or other release of oil or HAZMAT along the common border between Canada and the US. The CANUS Joint Inland Pollution Contingency Plan provides for cooperative measures for dealing with accidental and unauthorized releases of pollutants that cause or may cause damage to the environment along the shared inland boundary and that may constitute a threat to the public health, property, or welfare. The Inland Plan is made up of five regional annexes or regional plans.

b. **Military Agreements**

(1) **Canada–US Civil Assistance Plan.** The CANUS Civil Assistance Plan provides a framework for the military of one nation to provide support to the military of the other nation in the performance of CS operations.

(2) **Quadripartite Standardization Agreements (QSTAGs).** The military forces of the US, United Kingdom, Canada, Australia, and New Zealand have agreed to adopt certain standard operational concepts in various QSTAGs. The military forces further agreed to consult and wherever possible, reach mutual agreement, before introducing changes to these agreements.

(3) **North Atlantic Treaty Organization (NATO) Standardization Agreements (STANAGs).** STANAGs are promulgated by the Director, NATO Standardization Agency. No departure may be made from these agreements without informing the tasking authority in the form of a reservation at the time of ratification. Ratifying nations have agreed that national orders, manuals, and instructions implementing these STANAGs will be developed. The aim of these agreements is to provide guidelines to commanders about operational issues. Participating nations agree that NATO armed forces will adopt the standards outlined in each agreement.

c. **Security and Prosperity Partnership of North America.** The SPP agreement, designed to reduce barriers to trade and facilitate economic growth while improving the security of the continent, was signed on 23 March 2005 by the President of the United States, the Prime Minister of Canada, and the President of Mexico. DHS and the Homeland Security Council are the lead agencies for the agreement's security components, with DOD as a supporting agency. The SPP Action Plan addresses goals and objectives associated with HS to include "protection, prevention, and response." This includes a dual-binational (US/Canada and US/Mexico) objective on emergency management cooperation to develop and implement joint plans for cooperation in incident response, as well as conduct joint training and exercises in hazard response. This includes the development of a plan to build and strengthen mechanisms, protocols, and agreements for communicating and coordinating hazard response for mutual assistance and cooperation in the event of natural and technological/industrial disasters or malicious acts involving CBRN and bulk HE devices and hazards.

d. **Multi-Service Tactics, Techniques, and Procedures**

(1) **FM 3-11.21/MCRP 3-37.2C/NTTP 3-11.24/AFTTP(I) 3-2.27,** *Multi-Service Tactics, Techniques, and Procedures for CBRN Consequence Management Operations.* DOD personnel responding to a CBRN incident may be responsible for CBRN CM and/or crisis planning and may be required to execute plans across the conflict spectrum. This publication provides a reference for planning, resourcing, and executing CBRN CM in support of domestic or foreign agencies responding to a CBRN incident.

(2) **FM 3-11.34/MCWP 3-37.5/NTTP 3-11.23/AFTTP(I) 302.33,** *Multi-Service Tactics, Techniques, and Procedures for Installation CBRN Defense.* This publication

provides doctrine and tactics, techniques, and procedures for planning, resourcing, and executing CBRN defense for various military installations as part of an overarching installation protection program. This manual incorporates the joint doctrine elements for CWMD, to include counterproliferation passive defense functions of CBRN sense, shape, shield, and sustain. It also ties installation CBRN defense to CBRN CM doctrine.

e. **International Agreements that Affect US CBRN Activities with Mexico**

(1) **Basel Convention on the Control of Transboundary Movements of Hazardous Wastes and their Disposal.** The Basel Convention on the Control of Transboundary Movements of Hazardous Wastes and their Disposal is the most comprehensive global environmental agreement on hazardous and other wastes. While the US is not a party to the agreement, it is a signatory and conducts activities with many of the convention's 178 parties to help protect human health and the environment against the adverse effects resulting from the generation, management, transboundary movements, and disposal of hazardous and other wastes.

(2) **Convention on the Transboundary Effect of Industrial Accidents.** This convention applies to the prevention of, preparedness for, and response to industrial accidents capable of causing transboundary effects, including the effects of such accidents caused by natural disasters, and to international cooperation concerning mutual assistance, research and development, exchange of information, and exchange of technology in the area of prevention of, preparedness for, and response to industrial accidents.

(3) **International Convention on Oil Pollution Preparedness** provides emergency response planning for oil pollution incidents.

(4) **The Organisation for Economic Co-Operation and Development Guiding Principles for Chemical Accident Prevention, Preparedness, and Response.** A comprehensive document to help public authorities, industry, and communities worldwide prevent and prepare for accidents involving hazardous substances resulting from technological and natural disasters, as well as sabotage.

APPENDIX B
PLANNING CONSIDERATIONS FOR LOGISTICS AND OTHER SERVICES FROM DOMESTIC BASE SUPPORT INSTALLATIONS AND FOREIGN THEATER ASSETS

1. Purpose

a. The planning considerations contained in this appendix will assist commanders and their staffs in conducting mission analysis, preparing to meet logistics and other service support requirements, and coordinating the potential use of a military installation for support of DOD forces during CBRN response operations. These are considerations and not requirements. They are not unique to CBRN response, but the difficult nature of responding to the catastrophic no-notice incidents described in this publication make it appropriate that they be contained here. Managing the consequences of a CBRN incident often means that lifesaving forces deploy and are employed before the JFCs logistics structure is established.

b. Depending on the physical location of the APOD and/or SPOD, the questions concerning airfield or port suitability may be analyzed separately or in conjunction with base support planning. Some requirements may be adequately met or even better suited to the operation when obtained from impacted nation or local community capabilities rather than from a US controlled installation.

c. Serving as a BSI is a uniquely domestic function of DOD Service and defense agency installations because the GCC has limited or no control over resources on installations within the US and territories. This is particularly true for CDRUSNORTHCOM who, by special SecDef restriction, does not have the authority to assume OPCON of forces within the US during an emergency. SecDef establishes the supported/supporting relationship through an EXORD at the time of incident (or anticipation thereof) to task the specific installation to serve as a base for military forces engaged in either HD or CS operations. These planning considerations are helpful in selecting a BSI and arranging for necessary support.

d. CBRN response operations in the foreign- or DOD-led military operational environments will find these planning considerations of value even when the affected country has unique relationships with the US in terms of access and support.

e. **Planning.** All GCCs have the responsibility to plan coordinated responses to the possible use of WMD in their AORs. GCC plans for WMD CM are developed IAW DOD policies and law. These guidance documents are listed in Appendix A, "Key Legal, Strategy, and Policy Documents and International Protocols."

(1) **Plan.** The JFC plans CBRN CM actions to isolate and contain the physical effects, assure security, promote freedom of action, save lives, and provide essential services to continue operations. One of the most important aspects of planning is anticipating the need to coordinate and integrate joint, multinational, interagency, and HN actions. Planning should include the transition efforts to civil authority as soon as possible when supporting another agency or department other than DOD.

(2) **Prepare.** Preparing and posturing actions set the conditions for successful execution of response operations. Preparation activities happen both before and after the incident.

(a) **Phase 0 mission analysis is critical to support the JFC's response operation.** Pre-incident activities are designed to collect and analyze militarily significant information on the operational environment such as industrial hazards (friendly, neutral, and enemy) in the operational area and any WMD actors' intent. **Mission analysis includes** indicators and warnings focused on attack preparation and detection to provide early warning for response asset preparation and facilitating a rapid response to any intentional use of WMD or accidental release of any CBRN material. **Advance situational assessment teams should be developed to facilitate JTF entry through communication with the COMs.** Additional preparation tasks may include directing intelligence activities to include provision of indicators and warning of WMD attack for non-domestic operational areas; collaboratively assessing and monitoring the operational situation; developing and exercising C2 structures to integrate components (medical, logistics, engineering, security, communications), as well as any other partners and interagency support; integrating partner capabilities (first responder equipment, training, personal decontamination supplies, health care facilities, etc.) to maximize effectiveness; conducting exercises; providing passive defense capabilities that will allow all the interactive forces to maintain the necessary operational tempo; and identifying specialized individuals, teams, and forces needed to provide CBRN CM support.

(b) Plan for post-incident activities to allow sensor and intelligence assets to begin surveillance of the affected area for the detection, identification, characterization, support to attribution forensics activities, and analysis of the CBRN hazards. Once the hazard and contaminated "hot zones" are established, the joint force concentrates upon hazard prediction and attribution analysis. The JFC also focuses upon the prevention of further injury, death, or illness. Post-incident operations include those designed to establish the extent and composition of a CBRN incident. This effort increases the commander's awareness and feeds his understanding of the incident and its effect on the force.

(3) **Execute.** The JFC may provide politico-military support to establish a secure environment that allows for the delivery of assistance and the introduction of civilian relief resources. A secure environment could include protection from the effects of contaminants as well as protection from external threats that may destabilize the affected area. **Execution also includes supporting efforts to concurrent operations brought about by the CBRN incident.**

(4) **Assess.** The JFC assesses progress along each response line of operation that may be part of the plan. The assessment facilitates the transition of response, remediation, and restoration efforts to civil authorities as desired conditions are met. Collected forensic information assists in establishing attribution for the incident to support appropriate follow-on action.

2. Checklists

Planning considerations should take into account, at a minimum, the following areas related to the key functions of logistics, service support, and other enabling requirements of the JFC in a CBRN response. Those items that are solely domestic or foreign are annotated appropriately.

a. General

(1) Is there a concise concept of the purpose of the supporting installation? Is there a description of the functions that the installation is to support?

(2) What forces have been identified to support the operation? Has the deployment flow been analyzed to determine time phasing for induction of logistic elements?

(3) What are the key assumptions the supporting installation operates under?

(4) Is the installation a RC base? If so, what will be required to activate personnel to provide required support (e.g., mobilization and man-days)? Is funding available for activation?

(5) Where is the incident response coordination center? For domestic response, where is the established JFO in the affected area? For foreign- or DOD-led military operations, where is the impacted nation emergency operation center, or where will the JTF-CM be located?

(6) Where are non-DOD equipment, personnel, and materials arrival and staging areas? For domestic CBRN incidents, where is the location(s) of the nearest FEMA incident support base(s)? For FCM, where are the nearest APOD, SPOD, and JRSOI points?

(7) How long will the supporting installation be expected to provide support to the JFC?

(8) Where will the BSI headquarters be established? *(Domestic only)*

(9) Where is the support installation location relative to incident or venue?

(10) Is the installation identified to support other agencies or organizations simultaneously? What is the current or projected utilization?

(11) What are the proper coordination procedures to arrange for support?

(12) What CBRN response capabilities are resident in the state and local jurisdictions? *(Domestic only)*

(13) Where are FEMA, state, and local staging areas? What is their capacity?

(14) What CBRN response capabilities are resident in the impacted nation? Will the impacted nation offer use of military/civilian facilities? *(Foreign only)*

(15) What mutual support agreements are in place for state/local support? (*Domestic only*)

(16) What mutual support agreements are in place for impacted nation support? (*Foreign only*)

(17) Develop the annex T, "Consequence Management," for operation plans consistent with the Joint Operation Planning and Execution System format.

b. **Airfield Suitability**

(1) Is the APOD contaminated or is the APOD in danger of becoming contaminated (weather, high threat)? If contaminated, can airlift operations be accomplished without contaminating the aircraft?

(2) Is the APOD capable of handling the flow of forces and material moving in/out and around the operational area?

(3) Are the personnel and cargo reception and staging capabilities of the airfield capable of handling the deployment flow for onward movement? (Refer to JP 3-35, *Joint Deployment and Redeployment Operations.*)

(4) Is a contingency response element needed to manage air mobility activities?

(5) What is the current condition of the airfield? What are the runway lengths? What is the current usage/throughput of the airfield? What is the working and parking maximum (aircraft) on ground?

(6) Can the airfield support medical evacuation and utility helicopter operations?

(7) Is the weight bearing capacity of the airfield sufficient to handle the type of aircraft that will be used for movement?

(8) What impact does weather have on airfield operations? Night operations?

(9) Are adequate personnel and equipment assets available to assist in arrival/departure airfield control group operations? What materials handling equipment (MHE) is available? Where can additional MHE be acquired (via contract and/or closest military installations)?

(10) Is support available for mobile aeromedical staging facilities?

(11) Is sufficient refueling capability/bulk fuel available? What is the resupply turn-around time? Has a stand-by bulk fuel vendor been requested?

(12) Is direct support aircraft maintenance available?

(13) What are the characteristics and capabilities of the main supply routes (MSRs) that access the airfield? Can the MSRs support over/out-sized vehicles? Have over/out-

sized vehicles been identified? Who handles DD Form 1266 (request for Special Hauling Permit)?

(14) What other nearby military or civilian airfields are available?

(15) What is the threat level?

(16) What type of physical security is available at the airport?

(17) Are security personnel available?

(18) After review of threat, vulnerability, and criticality assessments, what force protection measures are needed?

(19) Coordinate with the appropriate military legal advisor to ensure that the operative RUF *(domestic only)* or ROE *(foreign only)* are properly tailored for the situation.

(20) Are air traffic control and fire/crash/rescue available?

(21) What type of aircraft does the airfield support?

(22) What types of navigational aids are available?

(23) Can the airfield support aircraft decontamination operations if required?

c. **Supply**

(1) Does the site have adequate supply support capabilities in place to sustain the forces in the operational area?

(2) What supply capabilities are available? Will military augmentation be required?

(3) What is the process to establish requisition flow? What type of automated or non-automated requisition system is used? How will the forces tie into that system?

(4) What supply support is available for common-user items in relation to the standard categories of supply? What type of storage, handling, shipping, security, and safety measures and procedures are in place? Is cold storage available?

(5) What distribution capability is available? What MHE is available? Can it be moved to support multiple locations to include potential forward operating bases (FOBs)?

(6) Is fuel storage and distribution available to support the rolling stock and potential FOBs?

(7) What type of local support is available for FOBs or intermediate staging bases?

(8) Are other DOD assets available (for instance DLA) that can assist the supporting installation?

d. **Maintenance Support**

(1) Does the site have adequate maintenance capabilities in place to sustain the units in the operational area?

(2) What maintenance capability is available to support primarily automotive, communications, and medical equipment? Will military augmentation be required?

(3) What are the procedures for disposal of contaminated fuel, oils, antifreezes, and other HAZMAT? Is there an environmental office available?

(4) Is local support available for repair parts?

e. **Transportation**

(1) Can the site accommodate deployment, sustainment, and redeployment flow and facilitate movement of units in/out and around the operational area?

(2) What transportation capability is available?

(3) What other transportation capabilities (rail lines or marine ports) are available to support military operations?

(4) What transportation tracking systems are in place? What automation is available for in-transit visibility/total asset visibility?

(5) Are loading ramps available? If so, what are their capabilities (i.e., weight, width restrictions)? Are the ramps fixed or portable?

(6) What are the characteristics and capabilities of the MSRs that access the base? What are the primary and secondary routes? What are the dimensions and classifications of bridges/tunnels along the routes? Are there any restrictions or chokepoints? What routes are identified for evacuation? What are the grades of the primary and secondary routes?

(7) What is the availability of installation transportation motor pool assets (truck, bus, passenger vehicles)? Are drivers available for these assets? Are rental vehicles available?

(8) Does the installation transportation officer (ITO) have contract capability with local vendors (truck, bus, passenger vehicles) to support a surge?

(9) Are the personnel and cargo reception and staging capabilities of the installation capable of handling the deployment flow for onward movement? (Refer to JP 3-35, *Joint Deployment and Redeployment Operations.*)

(10) Will the ITO be able to support redeployment operations of DOD forces?

(11) What are the procedures for and availability of ground refueling?

(12) Who will provide transportation management services to coordinate personnel and material movements into, within, and out of the JOA?

(13) Who will provide daily operations briefings?

(14) Who will provide technical guidance to subordinate units and civilian agencies?

(15) Who will coordinate and deconflict transportation movement mission assignments?

(16) Who will monitor freight and passenger movement by all modes in the JOA?

(17) Who will coordinate transit clearances for highway movement?

(18) Will there be a joint movement center (JMC) in the JOA?

(19) What tracking systems will the JMC have access to?

(20) Who will monitor flow and velocity in the supply distribution system?

(21) Will an individual responsible for special assignment airlift mission validation be located in the JMC?

(22) Will unit movement officers back brief the ITO on the deployment plan?

(23) Has the unit created load plans for air movement/rail movement/sea movement?

(24) Has the unit completed appropriate HAZMAT declarations?

(25) Has the unit completed appropriate country clearances? (*Foreign only*)

f. **Engineering, Environmental, and Public Works**

(1) What engineering assets are in place and available to support forces in the operational area?

(2) What are the water planning factors in use on the installation? Will sufficient water support be available to support the DOD forces? What procedures are used to ensure the water is potable?

(3) What are the procedures for trash collection and disposal?

(4) What are the procedures for hazardous waste collection and disposal?

(5) What environmental rules and procedures are in place?

(6) Will the installation be able to handle the additional energy usage requirements or will supplemental generators be required?

(7) What force protection considerations will require engineer support to implement?

(8) What electrical power sources are available that may require voltage converters for DOD use? (*Foreign only*)

g. **Health Services**

(1) Does the site have adequate health service (medical, preventive medicine, dental, medical logistics, ground and aeromedical evacuation) support capabilities in place to sustain the forces in the operational area?

(2) What medical assets are available and what capabilities do they have?

(3) Is there a primary and secondary hospital available? What number of medical field units, operating rooms, and hospital beds are available? What type and how many medical specialists are available?

(4) Are there ground and air ambulances available? Has an air ambulance helipad been identified? What are the grid coordinates and physical location?

(5) Is medical supply available?

(6) Is there a pharmacy available? What types of medicine are in short supply/not generally available?

(7) What are the availability and power requirements of mobile drug/blood registration storage units?

(8) What medical capabilities exist in the local community?

(9) Are patient decontamination capabilities available?

(10) What are the diseases endemic in the local population and vectors present in the area?

(11) Is there adequate electrical, water, drainage, and space to accommodate up to an expeditionary medical support +25 (25-bed rapid response medical package)?

(12) Do medical practitioners require licensing and credentialing to practice on the supporting installation? (*Foreign only*)

h. **Communications**

(1) Does the support installation have look angles (latitude, azimuth, elevation, and longitude) to access required satellites?

(2) What are the building specifics that may affect the communications at the command post? Considerations:

(a) Detailed description of proposed site (include drawings and photos).

(b) Building composition.

(c) Roof composition.

(d) Roof shape.

(e) Roof access.

(f) Window description.

(g) Power.

(h) Phone and data lines.

(i) Location of trees surrounding buildings.

(j) Location of antennas surrounding buildings.

(k) Telephone lines and numbers.

(l) Can a communication room be secured?

(3) What are the antenna placement factors that may affect the communications at the command post? Considerations:

(a) Selected location of tactical radios from antenna location (distance will depend on type and capabilities of available radios).

(b) Location of radio antennas of other units within area without interfering with each other.

(c) Recommended radio room set up and location.

(d) Recommended coax cable runs.

(e) Recommended antenna grounds.

(f) Placement (use roof as last resort).

(g) Location of power lines which may affect signal strength.

(4) Power planning considerations:

(a) Communications room/closet number/location.

(b) Type of power available (110 volts/60 hertz or 220 volts/50 hertz).

(c) Type of outlets available (two-prong or three-prong).

(d) Location of circuit breaker boxes.

(e) Access available to breakers.

(f) Circuit breaker numbers.

(g) Backup power.

(h) Type of power (generator, auto switching) and how long will it last?

(i) Power test plan.

(5) JFC communication requirement considerations:

(a) Defense Switch Network or commercial voice (prefix, number, extension). Commercial will be required if DOD communications are required to support commercial or government civilian agencies.

(b) Commercial Internet, NIPRNET, or SIPRNET requirements. (Commercial will be required if DOD communications are required to support commercial or government civilian agencies).

(c) Tactical single channel radios (primarily used for DOD-to-DOD communications).

(d) Radio bridging capability (used to bridge disparate communication capabilities such as single channel tactical radios into commercial cell phones, etc).

(e) Satellite phone requirements.

(f) Communications on-the-move (enables communications while en route to the incident area or other locations).

i. **Public Affairs**

(1) What type of PA assistance is available in the incident area or, if using a military facility, what military support is available? What PA personnel are already there?

(2) Is there an appropriate non-classified facility for use by PA as well as members of the media? Is it separate from the main JOC area?

(3) Is there a facility large enough to host a news conference that could include hundreds of media representatives?

(4) Does this facility offer Internet and cable/satellite television access? Does it have the capacity for multiple Internet connections so that all PA staff and supporting personnel have access? Is there enough capacity to allow media to use workstations if necessary?

(5) Does the facility have adequate electrical plugs and wiring to support PA equipment?

(6) What kinds of major media outlets (television, radio, print) are in the area?

j. **Other Services**

(1) Is there a contracting office on the installation? What local contracting procedures are in place? What existing contracts are in place to support the major items previously listed?

(2) Is financial management support available? Who is tracking costs associated with contracting and installation support?

(3) Is there adequate infrastructure to support billeting and food service? If not, what contract lodging and food service options are available? How many can be handled per day at the current capacity?

(4) Is there an adequate location to locate a JOC?

(5) Are hardstand facilities available to support several large command operations centers?

(6) What is the availability of laundry, shower, and latrine facilities? Will the installation provide portable facilities as required?

(7) Are exchange facilities available?

(8) Is there adequate infrastructure in place to support C2 communications requirements?

(9) Are there adequate force protection and security procedures in place? Will this require military augmentation?

(10) What are the procedures for receiving mail?

(11) What type of RS is available?

(12) Are adequate security forces and trained security augmentation forces available to:

(a) Secure the site (mark areas around the site clearly)?

(b) Provide convoy security on to the installation or from one area of the installation to another for containment of the crisis? If convoys are required to travel outside of the installation, are there additional security requirements to protect from looting, vandalism, etc?

(c) Implement force protection tasks as assigned.

(d) Provide weapons and ammunition storage facilities.

(13) Is there a CBRN response capability resident on the installation?

(14) Is there a fire-fighting capability resident on the installation?

(15) What intelligence support/infrastructure is available?

(16) Is there an emergency 911 system in place? (*Domestic only*)

(17) Can the support installation coordinate off-installation law enforcement support/escort?

APPENDIX C
DEPARTMENT OF DEFENSE DOMESTIC CHEMICAL, BIOLOGICAL, RADIOLOGICAL, AND NUCLEAR RESPONSE ENTERPRISE ASSETS

1. General

a. The DOD CBRN Response Enterprise focuses on life-saving activities and includes AC and RC forces. The following forces constitute the DOD CBRN Response Enterprise. All elements described below consist of assigned and allocated units, standardized to ensure they contain the required capabilities for that type element, and are trained and ready to deploy as a coherent element within prescribed timelines. WMD-CSTs, CERFPs, and HRFs are NG units in their respective states. The DCRF, C2CRE A, and C2CRE B are allocated to USNORTHCOM in the Global Force Management Allocation Plan. Figure C-1 identifies these units.

b. NG forces in the WMD-CSTs, CERFPs, or HRFs responding to an incident under state active duty or Title 32, USC, authorities, such as governor deployment, interstate compact agreement, or EMACs request. Forces allocated to the DCRF and C2CRE A and B will conduct operations in Title 10, USC, status under federal control. The command and control structures in response to an incident are dependent on the nature and size of the incident.

c. DOD CBRN Enterprise Mission. When directed (by SecDef for federal military forces and by the governor[s] concerned for NG forces under state C2), the DOD CBRN Response Enterprise conducts CBRN response operations within the US and its territories to support civil authorities in response to CBRN incidents in order to save lives and minimize human suffering.

2. Response Forces

a. **National Guard WMD-CSTs.** WMD-CSTs respond to a CBRN incident by providing a rapid response capability in the event of an intentional or unintentional release of CBRN threats and hazards. There are WMD-CSTs assigned to the NG. These are a high priority, rapid response unit made up of 22 full-time Title 32, USC, Active Guard and Reserve Army and ANG personnel assigned. These units were established by Congress, certified by SecDef to Congress after they meet DOD certification guidelines. By statute, each WMD-CST operates under the control of the governor, in Title 32, USC, status, and can be employed as a state asset without DOD authorization. TAG will direct employment of the WMD-CST to support either a state response or to provide support to another state's response, if requested. Further, under Presidential mobilization, WMD-CST could be employed as part of the Title 10, USC, force package. Per direction of OSD, the NGB has established a national level response plan which provides a designated number of WMD-CSTs for a rapid response to WMD incidents and national disasters. On site, a WMD CST is prepared to conduct continuous operations for 72 hours, using organic assets.

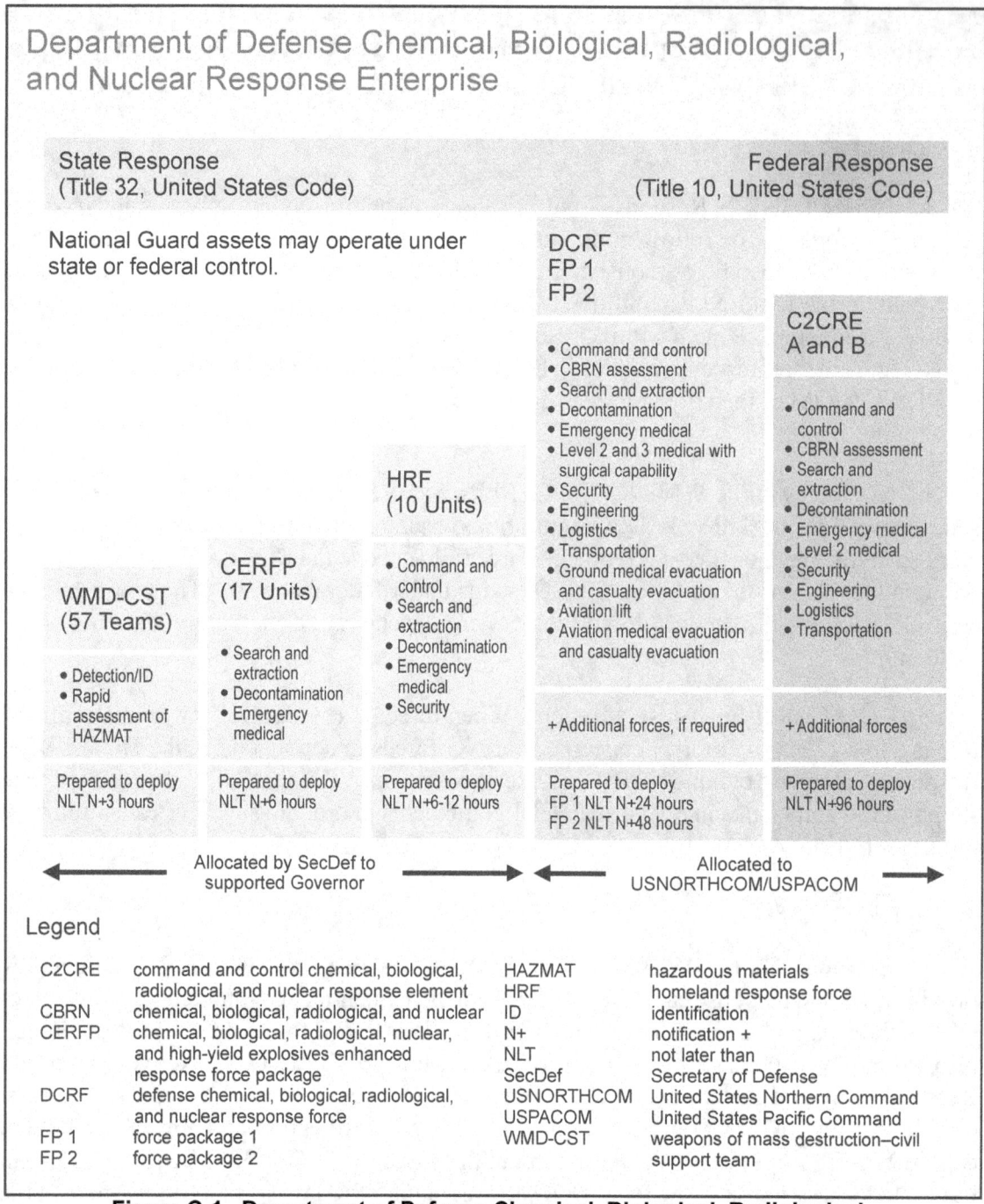

Figure C-1. Department of Defense Chemical, Biological, Radiological, and Nuclear Response Enterprise

(1) The WMD-CST mission is to support civil authorities at a domestic incident site by identifying CBRN hazards/substances, assessing current or projected consequences, advising on response measures, and assisting with appropriate requests for state support to facilitate additional resources. This includes the intentional or unintentional release of CBRN and natural or man-made disasters in the US that result, or could result, in the catastrophic loss of life or property.

(2) WMD-CSTs are assigned to USNORTHCOM for training and readiness oversight (TRO) which is provided by USARNORTH. For WMD-CSTs in Hawaii, Guam, and Alaska, USPACOM has TRO, which is executed by US Army Pacific.

b. **National Guard CERFPs.** The CERFP mission is, on order, to respond to a CBRNE incident or other catastrophic event and assist local, state, and federal departments and agencies in conducting CBRN CM by providing capabilities to conduct personnel decontamination, emergency medical services, and casualty search and extraction. There are 17 CERFPs, consisting of 186 total personnel each, for a total of 3,162 personnel, to include 5 Active Guard and reserves and 5 full-time equivalents, per CERFP. (This number does not include the 11 ANG fatalities search and recovery team personnel.) They are a state and federal NG capability. Personnel who augment the CERFPs are not in a Title 32, USC, "operational status," which means they cannot assemble and deploy until the governor orders the unit members into state active duty. Units assigned to each of the 17 CERFPs remain under the control of the governor of the state in which they reside. Governors exercise their executive authority through TAGs. Out-of-state CERFP support is requested from the state EOC IAW interstate agreements or EMACs. The NG JFHQ-State JOC may enter the governor's request into the Joint Information Exchange Environment (JIEE) for coordination with the several states and NGB. Requests are coordinated with other states and NGB based on a supporting/supported relationship and operational or TACON provided by the gaining supported state IAW established MOAs or other agreements. In some circumstances, the President may federalize NG assets, to include HRFs, CERFPs, and WMD-CSTs. CERFP capabilities are casualty search and extraction, emergency medical triage, treatment, and patient stabilization, and mass casualty decontamination, in a contaminated environment to support the incident commander's IAP objectives.

c. **National Guard HRFs.** The HRF mission is, on order, alert, assemble, and deploy within 6–12 hours of notification in response to a CBRN incident to save lives, mitigate human suffering, and prepare for follow-on forces in support of civil authorities. Capabilities include search and extraction, casualty decontamination, emergency medical triage and treatment, security element, and C2. There are 10 HRFs, one existing within each FEMA region, consisting of 566 personnel in each HRF with 25percent full time manning in each, for a total of 5,660 personnel. The HRFs will be sourced from the existing Army and Air NG force. NG units that are selected as part of the HRF remain under the direction and control of the governor of the state in which they reside. Governors exercise their command, operational authority, or TACON of military forces through TAGs. Requests for out-of-state HRF support is requested from the state EOC IAW interstate agreements or EMAC (via a Requisition A) of which all states are signatories. The NG JFHQ-State JOC may enter the governor's request into the JIEE for coordination with other states and NGB. Requests are coordinated with other states and NGB based on a supporting/supported relationship and OPCON or TACON provided by the gaining/supported state IAW established MOAs or other agreements. The authority to notify, deploy, and employ an HRF, in almost all cases, is vested in the independent, sovereign state governors who control the NG capabilities with the understanding that HRFs are designed to be regional and national assets that support CBRN CM nationwide. In some circumstances, the President may federalize NG assets, to include HRFs, CERFPs, and WMD-CSTs. Capabilities include search and extraction, mass casualty decontamination, emergency medical triage and patient stabilization treatment, security, and C2 in a contaminated environment to support the incident commander's IAP objectives. Each HRF has a medical treatment area with no holding capacity. In addition, HRFs provide C2 and planning for all organic and attached units (WMD-CSTs and CERFPs) and provide security for CBRN site locations. They also coordinate and synchronize CBRN operations for designated areas and decontamination sites. The HRFs are the center of gravity for the DOD CBRN Response Enterprise integration in their respective FEMA region's states' planning.

d. **JTF-Civil Support.** JTF-CS serves as the CBRN response headquarters for the DCRF. JTF-CS provides planning, training, and coordination for CBRN response operations. It serves as lead planning authority for development of operational JTF and tactical TF level CBRN response operation plans and develops projected CBRN response and DSCA force requirements and structures to support mission requirements for all CBRN national planning scenarios. JTF-CS is the C2 element responsible for executing domestic CBRN response by responding to federal request for assistance IAW the NRF and DOD policy to provide immediate actions to save lives, protect property and the environment, and meet basic human needs. The domestic CBRN response focuses on the operational to tactical levels in order to rapidly integrate and synchronize DOD capabilities in support of civil authorities.

e. **Defense Chemical, Biological, Radiological, and Nuclear Response Force.** The DCRF includes approximately 5,200 personnel sourced primarily from the AC (multi-Service). DCRF capabilities include CBRN incident assessment, search and rescue, decontamination of DOD personnel and equipment, evacuee and casualty decontamination, emergency medical, Role 2 medical care (patient triage, along with trauma and emergency medical care), patient holding, ground and rotary-wing air patient movement, Role 3 medical care (surgical and intensive care), force health protection measures, military personnel and equipment operational security, site accessibility horizontal engineering, logistics, general support to enhance lifesaving and reduce human suffering, C2 aviation lift, mortuary affairs, and transportation. The DCRF is designed to employ these capabilities in multi-function packages in order to provide critical lifesaving capabilities in a synchronized manner. There are two force packages, Force Package 1 (2,100 personnel) and Force Package 2 (3,100 personnel). Commander, JTF-CS, has the flexibility to task organize the DCRF based on the situation and mission in order to provide the most effective support to a CBRN response.

f. **C2CRE A and B.** The two C2CREs will include approximately 780 personnel each and be sourced from the AC and RC. C2CRE A and C2CRE B will contain much smaller elements of many of the capabilities contained in the DCRF. When directed, the C2CREs will begin initial operations, but must be quickly augmented with additional capabilities to sustain operations. These additional capabilities may include federalized NG assets (including WMD-CSTs, CERFPs, and HRFs) or forces from the AC and RC. Dedicated C2CRE capabilities include CBRN assessment, search and rescue, decontamination, emergency medical, Role 2 medical, engineering, C2, logistics, and transportation.

3. Unity of Effort in the Department of Defense Chemical, Biological, Radiological, and Nuclear Response Enterprise

The DOD CBRN Response Enterprise is only a small part of the national response. An effective, unified national response requires layered, mutually supporting capabilities. The NRF systematically coordinates private sector and NGO capabilities with those of local, tribal, state, and federal for commitment in response to a CBRN incident. If requested, SecDef is responsible for assisting DHS and the NRF primary and coordinating agencies in CBRN response operations for a domestic CBRN incident. The synergistic construct of the DOD CBRN Response Enterprise supports unity of effort by facilitating a rapid and echeloned response providing redundancy of critical lifesaving capabilities and a layered integration of NG resources reinforced by federal capabilities.

Intentionally Blank

APPENDIX D
REFERENCES

The development of JP 3-41 is based upon the following references:

1. General

    a. The Constitution of the United States.

    b. Title 10, USC (Armed Forces).

    c. Title 10, USC, Sections 331–336.

    d. Title 10 USC, Section 382 (Emergency Situations Involving Chemical or Biological WMD).

    e. Title 10 USC, Section 404 (Foreign Disaster Assistance).

    f. Title 14 USC (USCG).

    g. Title 18, USC, Section 831 (Prohibited Transactions Involving Nuclear Material).

    h. Title 18, USC, Section 1385 (Posse Comitatus Act).

    i. Title 22, USC (Foreign Assistance Act).

    j. Title 31, USC, Section 1535 (Economy Act).

    k. Title 32, USC, (National Guard).

    l. Title 42, USC, Section 5170 (The Public Health and Welfare).

    m. Public Law 84-99 (Flood Control and Coastal Emergency Act).

    n. Public Law 100-707 (Stafford Disaster Relief and Emergency Assistance Act).

    o. Public Law 107-56 (USA Patriot Act).

    p. Public Law 107-296, 116 Stat. 2135 (Homeland Security Act of 2002).

    q. EO-12966, *Foreign Disaster Assistance*.

    r. HSPD-1, *Organization and Operation of the Homeland Security Council*.

    s. HSPD-3, *The Homeland Security Advisory System*.

    t. HSPD-4/NSPD-17, *National Strategy to Combat Weapons of Mass Destruction*.

    u. HSPD-5, *Management of Domestic Incidents*.

v. PPD-8, *National Preparedness.*

w. HSPD-9, *Defense of United States Agriculture and Food.*

x. HSPD-10, *Biodefense for the 21st Century.*

y. HSPD-14, *Domestic Nuclear Detection.*

z. HSPD-15, *US Strategy and Policy on the War on Terrorism (U).*

aa. HSPD-18, *Medical Countermeasures Against Weapons of Mass Destruction.*

bb. HSPD-19, *Combating Terrorist Use of Explosives in the United States.*

cc. HSPD-20, *National Continuity Policy.*

dd. HSPD-21, *Public Health and Medical Preparedness.*

ee. HSPD-22, *Domestic Chemical Defense (U).*

ff. NDP-1, *National Policy and Procedures for the Disclosure of Classified Military Information to Foreign Governments and International Organizations.*

gg. NSPD-28, *United States Nuclear Weapons Command and Control, Safety, and Security.*

hh. National Security Decision Memorandum 119, *Disclosure of Classified United States Military Information to Foreign Governments and International Organizations.*

ii. NSS.

jj. *The Effects of Nuclear Weapons*, Glasstone and Dolan, DOD.

kk. National Strategy for Homeland Security.

ll. National Strategy for Combating Terrorism.

mm. National Strategy to Combat Weapons of Mass Destruction.

nn. National Strategy for Countering Biological Threats.

oo. National Strategy for Pandemic Influenza.

pp. NSPI Implementation Plan.

qq. NRF Resource Center: http://www.fema.gov/NRF.

rr. NRF: http://www.fema.gov/pdf/emergency/nrf/nrf-core.pdf.

ss. NRF, Catastrophic Incident Annex.

tt. 4 March 2003, Memorandum of Understanding Between the Intelligence Community, Federal Law Enforcement Agencies, and the Department of Homeland Security Concerning Information Sharing.

uu. Planning Guidance for Response to a Nuclear Detonation.

vv. JFO Standard Operating Procedures and JFO Field Operations Guide: http://www.fema.gov/emergency/nrf/jobaids.htm.

ww. NIMS Resource Center: www.fema.gov/NIMS.

xx. National Institute for Occupational Safety and Health Pocket Guide to Chemical Hazards: http://www.cdc.gov/niosh/npg/pdfs/2005-149.pdf.

yy. US Department of Transportation's Emergency Response Guidebook: http://hazmat.dot.gov/pubs/erg/guidebook.htm.

zz. FEMA "Are You Ready Guides": http://www.fema.gov/areyouready/terrorism.shtm.

aaa. INDRAC: https://indrac.dtra.mil/Pages/default.aspx.

bbb. National Disaster Recovery Framework: http://www.fema.gov/pdf/recoveryframework/ndrf.pdf.

2. Department of Defense

a. UCP.

b. GEF.

c. 2010 Quadrennial Defense Review.

d. UJTL.

e. NDS.

f. NMS.

g. Strategy for Homeland Defense and Civil Support.

h. The National Military Strategy for Combating Terrorism.

i. The National Military Strategy (NMS) to Combat Weapons of Mass Destruction.

j. DOD Global Concept Plan.

k. DTRA *Foreign Consequence Management Legal Deskbook.*

l. DOD 3150.8-M, *Nuclear Weapon Accident Response Procedures (NARP).*

m. DOD 5200.1-R, *Information Security Program.*

n. DOD 5240.1-R, *Procedures Governing the Activities of DOD Intelligence Components that Affect United States Persons.*

o. DODD 2000.12, *DOD Antiterrorism Program.*

p. DODD 2000.15, *Support to Special Events.*

q. DODD 2060.02, *Department of Defense (DOD) Combating WMD Policy.*

r. DODD 3025.12, *Military Assistance for Civil Disturbances.*

s. DODD 3025.18, *Defense Support of Civil Authorities.*

t. DODD 3150.08, *DOD Response to Nuclear and Radiological Incidents.*

u. DODD 5100.46, *Foreign Disaster Relief.*

v. DODD 5200.27, *Acquisition of Information Concerning Persons and Organizations not Affiliated with the Department of Defense.*

w. DODD 5240.01, *DOD Intelligence Activities.*

x. DODD 5525.5, *DOD Cooperation with Civilian Law Enforcement Officials.*

y. DODI 2000.18, *DOD Installation Chemical, Biological, Radiological, Nuclear, and High-Yield Explosive Emergency Response Guidelines.*

z. DODI 2000.21, *Foreign Consequence Management.*

aa. DODI 3150.09, *The Chemical, Biological, Radiological, and Nuclear (CBRN) Survivability Policy.*

bb. DODI 3150.10, *DOD Response to US Nuclear Weapon Incidents.*

cc. DODI 6055.17, *DOD Installation Emergency Management (IEM) Program.*

dd. DODI 6200.03, *Public Health Emergency Management Within the Department of Defense.*

ee. Medical Management of Radiological Casualties Handbook, Armed Forces Radiobiology Research Institute: http://www.afrri.usuhs.mil.

3. Chairman of the Joint Chiefs of Staff

a. CJCSI 3110.01H, *Joint Strategic Capabilities Plan (JSCP).*

b. CJCSI 3121.01B, *Standing Rules of Engagement/Standing Rules for the Use of Force for US Forces (U)*.

c. CJCSI 3125.01B, *Defense Support of Civil Authorities (DSCA) for Domestic Consequence Management Operations in Response to a Chemical, Biological, Radiological, Nuclear, or High-Yield Explosive Incident*.

d. CJCSI 3214.01D, *Defense Support for Chemical, Biological, Radiological, and Nuclear Incidents on Foreign Territory*.

e. CJCSM 3122 Series, *Joint Operation Planning and Execution System (JOPES)*.

f. CJCSM 3150.13C, *Joint Reporting Structure–Personnel Manual*.

4. Joint Publications

a. JP 1-0, *Personnel Support to Joint Operations*.

b. JP 1-04, *Legal Support to Military Operations*.

c. JP 1-05, *Religious Affairs in Joint Operations*.

d. JP 2-01, *Joint and National Intelligence Support to Military Operations*.

e. JP 3-06, *Joint Urban Operations*.

f. JP 3-08, *Interorganizational Coordination During Joint Operations*.

g. JP 3-11, *Operations in Chemical, Biological, Radiological, and Nuclear (CBRN) Environments*.

h. JP 3-16, *Multinational Operations*.

i. JP 3-27, *Homeland Defense*.

j. JP 3-28, *Defense Support of Civil Authorities*.

k. JP 3-29, *Foreign Humanitarian Assistance*.

l. JP 3-30, *Command and Control for Joint Air Operations*.

m. JP 3-33, *Joint Task Force Headquarters*.

n. JP 3-35, *Deployment and Redeployment Operations*.

o. JP 3-40, *Combating Weapons of Mass Destruction*.

p. JP 3-57, *Civil-Military Operations*.

q. JP 3-61, *Public Affairs.*

r. JP 4-0, *Joint Logistics.*

s. JP 4-02, *Health Service Support.*

t. JP 4-05 *Joint Mobilization Planning.*

u. JP 4-06, *Mortuary Affairs.*

5. Multi-Service Publications

a. MCBRNCM 0026-02, Chemical Warfare (CW) Agent Exposure Planning Guidance.

b. FM 3-11.21/MCRP 3-37.2C/NTTP 3-11.24/AFTTP(I) 3-2.37, *Multi-Service Tactics, Techniques, and Procedures for Chemical, Biological, Radiological, and Nuclear Consequence Management Operations.*

c. FM 3-11.5/MCWP 3-37.3/NTTP 3-11.26/AFTTP(I) 3-2.60, *Multi-Service Tactics, Techniques, and Procedures for Chemical, Biological, Radiological, and Nuclear Decontamination.*

d. USTRANSCOM policy document: Policy for Patient Movement of Contaminated Contagious or Potentially Exposed Casualties.

6. Army

FM 5-19, Composite Risk Management.

7. Air Force

a. AFI 10-2603, *Emergency Health Powers on Air Force Installations.*

b. AFI 10-2604, *Disease Containment Planning.*

c. AFI 41-307 (Attachment 12), *Aeromedical Evacuation Patient Considerations and Standards of Care.*

8. International Documents

a. **Canadian Legislation**

(1) Emergencies Act (Revised Statutes of Canada: 1985 c.22 4th Supplement).

(2) Emergency Preparedness Act (Revised Statutes of Canada: 1985 c.6 4th Supplement).

b. **CANUS Agreements**

(1) Canada–United States Integrated Lines of Communications (ILOCs) Agreement.

(2) Canada–US Agreement for Enhanced Military Cooperation.

(3) Temporary Cross-Border Movement of Land Forces Between the United States and Canada Agreement.

(4) Canadian–United States Regional Emergency Management Agreements.

(5) Canadian–United States Joint Radiological Emergency Response Plan.

(6) Inland Pollution Contingency Plan.

c. Canada–US Civil Assistance Plan.

d. Security and Prosperity Partnership of North America.

e. NATO Article 5.

f. Chemical Weapons Convention Article X.

g. SPP.

Intentionally Blank

APPENDIX E
ADMINISTRATIVE INSTRUCTIONS

1. User Comments

Users in the field are highly encouraged to submit comments on this publication to: Joint Staff J-7, Deputy Director, Joint and Coalition Warfighting, Joint and Coalition Warfighting Center, ATTN: Joint Doctrine Support Division, 116 Lake View Parkway, Suffolk, VA 23435-2697. These comments should address content (accuracy, usefulness, consistency, and organization), writing, and appearance.

2. Authorship

The lead agent for this publication is the US Northern Command. The Joint Staff doctrine sponsor for this publication is the Director, Strategic Plans and Policy (J-5).

3. Supersession

This publication supersedes JP 3-41, Chemical, Biological, Radiological, Nuclear, and High-Yield Explosives Consequence Management, 2 October 2006.

4. Change Recommendations

a. Recommendations for urgent changes to this publication should be submitted:

TO: JOINT STAFF WASHINGTON DC//J7-JEDD//

b. Routine changes should be submitted electronically to the Deputy Director, Joint and Coalition Warfighting, Joint and Coalition Warfighting Center, Joint Doctrine Support Division and info the lead agent and the Director for Joint Force Development, J-7/JEDD.

c. When a Joint Staff directorate submits a proposal to the CJCS that would change source document information reflected in this publication, that directorate will include a proposed change to this publication as an enclosure to its proposal. The Services and other organizations are requested to notify the Joint Staff J-7 when changes to source documents reflected in this publication are initiated.

5. Distribution of Publications

Local reproduction is authorized, and access to unclassified publications is unrestricted. However, access to and reproduction authorization for classified JPs must be IAW DOD Manual 5200.01, *DOD Information Security Program: Overview, Classification, and Declassification.*

6. Distribution of Electronic Publications

a. Joint Staff J-7 will not print copies of JPs for distribution. Electronic versions are available on JDEIS at https://jdeis.js.mil (NIPRNET) and https://jdeis.js.smil.mil (SIPRNET) and on the JEL at http://www.dtic.mil/doctrine (NIPRNET).

b. Only approved JPs and joint test publications are releasable outside the combatant commands, Services, and Joint Staff. Release of any classified JP to foreign governments or foreign nationals must be requested through the local embassy (Defense Attaché Office) to DIA, Defense Foreign Liaison Office/IE-3, 200 MacDill Blvd., Joint Base Anacostia-Bolling, Washington, DC 20340-5100.

c. JEL CD-ROM. Upon request of a joint doctrine development community member, the Joint Staff J-7 will produce and deliver one CD-ROM with current JPs. This JEL CD-ROM will be updated not less than semi-annually and when received can be locally reproduced for use within the combatant commands and Services.

GLOSSARY
PART I—ABBREVIATIONS AND ACRONYMS

AC	Active Component
AFI	Air Force instruction
AFMAN	Air Force manual
AFRAT	Air Force Radiation Assessment Team
AFRRI	Armed Forces Radiobiology Research Institute
AFTTP(I)	Air Force tactics, techniques, and procedures (instruction)
ALARA	as low as reasonably achievable
ANG	Air National Guard
AOR	area of responsibility
APOD	aerial port of debarkation
ARNG	Army National Guard
ARS	acute radiation syndrome
ASCC	Army Service component command
ASD(GSA)	Assistant Secretary of Defense for Global Strategic Affairs
ASD(HA)	Assistant Secretary of Defense (Health Affairs)
ASD(HD&ASA)	Assistant Secretary of Defense (Homeland Defense and Americas' Security Affairs)
ASD(RA)	Assistant Secretary of Defense (Reserve Affairs)
AT	antiterrorism
ATTP	Army tactics, techniques, and procedures
BSI	base support installation
C2	command and control
C2CRE	command and control chemical, biological, radiological, and nuclear response element
CANUS	Canada-United States
CAP	crisis action planning
CBIRF	Chemical-Biological Incident Response Force
CBRN	chemical, biological, radiological, and nuclear
CBRN CM	chemical, biological, radiological, and nuclear consequence management
CBRNE	chemical, biological, radiological, nuclear, and high-yield explosives
CCDR	combatant commander
CDC	Centers for Disease Control and Prevention
CDRUSARNORTH	Commander, United States Army Forces North
CDRUSNORTHCOM	Commander, United States Northern Command
CDRUSPACOM	Commander, United States Pacific Command
CDRUSSOCOM	Commander, United States Special Operations Command
CDRUSSTRATCOM	Commander, United States Strategic Command

CERFP	chemical, biological, radiological, nuclear, and high-yield explosives enhanced response force package
CJCS	Chairman of the Joint Chiefs of Staff
CJCSI	Chairman of the Joint Chiefs of Staff instruction
CJTF	commander, joint task force
CMAT	consequence management advisory team
CMOC	civil–military operations center
CMST	consequence management support team
CNGB	Chief, National Guard Bureau
COA	course of action
COM	chief of mission
CONUS	continental United States
CS	civil support
CSA	combat support agency
CW	chemical warfare
CWMD	combating weapons of mass destruction
DCE	defense coordinating element
DCO	defense coordinating officer
DCRF	defense chemical, biological, radiological, and nuclear response force
DEPORD	deployment order
DHS	Department of Homeland Security
DLA	Defense Logistics Agency
DOD	Department of Defense
DODD	Department of Defense directive
DODI	Department of Defense instruction
DOS	Department of State
DR	disaster relief
DSCA	defense support of civil authorities
DTRA	Defense Threat Reduction Agency
EMAC	emergency management assistance compact
EMP	electromagnetic pulse
EO	executive order
EOC	emergency operations center
EOD	explosive ordnance disposal
EP	emergency preparedness
EPA	Environmental Protection Agency
ESF	emergency support function
EXORD	execute order
FAA	Foreign Assistance Act
FBI	Federal Bureau of Investigation
FCM	foreign consequence management
FCO	federal coordinating officer

FEMA	Federal Emergency Management Agency
FEST	foreign emergency support team
FM	field manual (Army)
FOB	forward operating base
FORSCOM	United States Army Forces Command
FPCON	force protection condition
GCC	geographic combatant commander
GEF	Guidance for Employment of the Force
HA	humanitarian assistance
HAZMAT	hazardous materials
HD	homeland defense
HE	high explosives
HN	host nation
HRF	homeland response force
HS	homeland security
HSPD	homeland security Presidential directive
HSS	health service support
IAP	incident action plan
IAW	in accordance with
ICS	incident command system
IEM	installation emergency management
IGO	intergovernmental organization
ILOC	integrated line of communications
INDRAC	Interagency Combating Weapons of Mass Destruction Database of Responsibilities, Authorities, and Capabilities
ITO	installation transportation officer
J-3	operations directorate of a joint staff
JCCSE	Joint Continental United States Communications Support Environment
JDOMS	Joint Director of Military Support
JFC	joint force commander
JFLCC	joint force land component commander
JFHQ-NCR	Joint Force Headquarters–National Capital Region
JFO	joint field office
JIEE	Joint Information Exchange Environment
JMC	joint movement center
JMETL	joint mission-essential task list
JOA	joint operations area
JOC	joint operations center
JP	joint publication
JPAC	joint planning augmentation cell

JRERP	Joint Radiological Emergency Response Plan
JRSOI	joint reception, staging, onward movement, and integration
JSCP	Joint Strategic Capabilities Plan
JTF	joint task force
JTF-AK	Joint Task Force - Alaska
JTF-CM	joint task force - consequence management
JTF-CS	Joint Task Force-Civil Support
JTF-HD	Joint Task Force-Homeland Defense
JTF-State	joint task force-state
kt	kiloton(s)
LE	low-order explosives
LFA	lead federal agency
LNO	liaison officer
MCRP	Marine Corps reference publication
MCWP	Marine Corps warfighting publication
ME/C	medical examiner and/or coroner
MHE	materials handling equipment
MOA	memorandum of agreement
MOU	memorandum of understanding
MRAT	medical radiobiology advisory team
MSR	main supply route
NARP	Nuclear Weapon Accident Response Procedures
NATO	North Atlantic Treaty Organization
NDP	national disclosure policy
NDS	National Defense Strategy
NGB	National Guard Bureau
NGCC	National Guard coordination center
NG JFHQ-State	National Guard joint force headquarters-state
NGO	nongovernmental organization
NIMS	National Incident Management System
NIPRNET	Nonsecure Internet Protocol Router Network
NMCC	National Military Command Center
NMS	National Military Strategy
NRF	National Response Framework
NSAT	United States Northern Command situational awareness team
NSF	National Strike Force (USCG)
NSPD	national security Presidential directive
NSPI	National Strategy for Pandemic Influenza
NSS	National Security Strategy
NTRP	Navy technical reference publication

NTTP	Navy tactics, techniques, and procedures
OEG	operational exposure guide
OPCON	operational control
OPORD	operation order
OSD	Office of the Secretary of Defense
PA	public affairs
PCA	Posse Comitatus Act
PFO	principal federal official
PI	pandemic influenza
POD	port of debarkation
PPD	Presidential policy directive
PPE	personal protective equipment
QSTAG	quadripartite standardization agreement
RC	Reserve Component
RDD	radiological dispersal device
RED	radiological exposure device
RFA	request for assistance
RFF	request for forces
ROE	rules of engagement
RS	religious support
RST	religious support team
RUF	rules for the use of force
SecDef	Secretary of Defense
SIPRNET	SECRET Internet Protocol Router Network
SJA	staff judge advocate
SMRC	Specialized Medical Response Capabilities
SOFA	status-of-forces agreement
SPOD	seaport of debarkation
SPP	Security and Prosperity Partnership of North America
SROE	standing rules of engagement
SRUF	standing rules for the use of force
STANAG	standardization agreement (NATO)
TACON	tactical control
TAG	the adjutant general
TF	task force
TIC	toxic industrial chemical
TIM	toxic industrial material
TRO	training and readiness oversight
UCP	Unified Command Plan

UJTL	Universal Joint Task List
UN	United Nations
USACE	United States Army Corps of Engineers
USAEDS	United States Atomic Energy Detection System
USAFR	United States Air Force Reserve
USAMRICD	United States Army Medical Research Institute of Chemical Defense
USAMRIID	United States Army Medical Research Institute of Infectious Diseases
USAR	United States Army Reserve
USARNORTH	United States Army Forces North
USC	United States Code
USCG	United States Coast Guard
USCGR	United States Coast Guard Reserve
USD(P)	Under Secretary of Defense for Policy
USG	United States Government
USMCR	United States Marine Corps Reserve
USNORTHCOM	United States Northern Command
USNR	United States Navy Reserve
USPACOM	United States Pacific Command
USTRANSCOM	United States Transportation Command
WMD	weapons of mass destruction
WMD CM	weapons of mass destruction consequence management
WMD-CST	weapons of mass destruction-civil support team

PART II—TERMS AND DEFINITIONS

active material. None. (Approved for removal from JP 1-02.)

actual ground zero. None. (Approved for removal from JP 1-02.)

background count. None. (Approved for removal from JP 1-02.)

base surge. None. (Approved for removal JP 1-02.)

blast effect. None. (Approved for removal from JP 1-02.)

blast wave. None. (Approved for removal from JP 1-02.)

chemical agent cumulative action. None. (Approved for removal from JP 1-02.)

chemical, biological, radiological, and nuclear consequence management. Actions taken to plan, prepare, respond to, and recover from chemical, biological, radiological, and nuclear incidents. Also called **CBRN CM.** (Approved for inclusion in JP 1-02.)

chemical, biological, radiological, nuclear, and high-yield explosives consequence management. None. (Approved for removal from JP 1-02.)

chemical dose. None. (Approved for removal from JP 1-02.)

chemical monitoring. None. (Approved for removal from JP 1-02.)

chemical survey. None. (Approved for removal from JP 1-02.)

chronic radiation dose. None. (Approved for removal from JP 1-02.)

civil nuclear power. None. (Approved for removal from JP 1-02.)

command assessment element. None. (Approved for removal from JP 1-02.)

consequence management. None. (Approved for removal from JP 1-02.)

conventional weapon. None. (Approved for removal from JP 1-02.)

critical mass. None. (Approved for removal from JP 1-02.)

decontamination station. None. (Approved for removal from JP 1-02.)

disaster control. None. (Approved for removal from JP 1-02.)

dispersion. 1. A scattered pattern of hits around the mean point of impact of bombs and projectiles dropped or fired under identical conditions. (JP 3-60) 2. The spreading or separating of troops, materiel, establishments, or activities, which are usually concentrated in limited areas to reduce vulnerability. (JP 5-0) 3. In chemical and biological operations, the dissemination of agents in liquid or aerosol form. (JP 3-41) 4. In airdrop operations, the scatter of personnel and/or cargo on the drop zone. (JP 3-17) 5. In naval control of shipping, the reberthing of a ship in the periphery of the port area or in the vicinity of the port for its own protection in order to minimize the risk of damage from attack. (JP 4-01.2) (Approved for inclusion in JP 1-02.)

emergency operations center. A temporary or permanent facility where the coordination of information and resources to support domestic incident management activities normally takes place. Also called **EOC.** (Approved for incorporation into JP 1-02.)

exposure dose. The amount of radiation, as measured in roentgen, at a given point in relation to its ability to produce ionization. (Approved for incorporation into JP 1-02.)

fallout prediction. None. (Approved for removal from JP 1-02.)

fallout safe height of burst. None. (Approved for removal from JP 1-02.)

fission products. None. (Approved for removal from JP 1-02.)

flash burn. A burn caused by excessive exposure (of bare skin) to thermal radiation. (Approved for incorporation into JP 1-02 with JP 3-41 as the source JP.)

foreign consequence management. United States Government activity that assists friends and allies in responding to the effects from an intentional or accidental chemical, biological, radiological, or nuclear incident on foreign territory in order to maximize preservation of life. Also called **FCM.** (Approved for incorporation into JP 1-02.)

ground zero. None. (Approved for removal from JP 1-02.)

height of burst. The vertical distance from the Earth's surface or target to the point of burst. Also called **HOB.** (Approved for incorporation into JP 1-02 with JP 3-41 as the source JP.)

incident of national significance. None. (Approved for removal from JP 1-02.)

induced radiation. None. (Approved for removal from JP 1-02.)

joint nuclear accident coordinating center. None. (Approved for removal from JP 1-02.)

joint operations center. A jointly manned facility of a joint force commander's headquarters established for planning, monitoring, and guiding the execution of the commander's decisions. Also called **JOC.** (Approved for incorporation into JP 1-02 with JP 3-41 as the source JP.)

Joint Task Force-Civil Support. A standing joint task force established to plan and integrate Department of Defense support to the designated lead federal agency for domestic chemical, biological, radiological, nuclear, and high-yield explosives consequence management operations. Also called **JTF-CS.** (JP 1-02. SOURCE: JP 3-41)

joint technical augmentation cell. None. (Approved for removal from JP 1-02.)

lead federal agency. The federal agency that leads and coordinates the overall federal response to an emergency. Also called **LFA.** (Approved for incorporation into JP 1-02.)

militarily significant fallout. None. (Approved for removal from JP 1-02.)

military posture. None. (Approved for removal from JP 1-02.)

national defense area. None. (Approved for removal from JP 1-02.)

National Disaster Medical System. A coordinated partnership between Departments of Homeland Security, Health and Human Services, Defense, and Veterans Affairs established for the purpose of responding to the needs of casualties of a public health emergency. Also called **NDMS.** (Approved for incorporation into JP 1-02.)

National Incident Management System. A national crisis response system that provides a consistent, nationwide approach for federal, state, local, and tribal governments; the private sector; and nongovernmental organizations to work effectively and efficiently together to prepare for, respond to, and recover from domestic incidents, regardless of cause, size, or complexity. Also called **NIMS.** (Approved for incorporation into JP 1-02.)

negligible risk (nuclear). None. (Approved for removal from JP 1-02.)

nonstrategic nuclear forces. None. (Approved for removal from JP 1-02.)

nuclear detonation detection and reporting system. None. (Approved for removal from JP 1-02.)

nuclear energy. None. (Approved for removal from JP 1-02.)

nuclear exoatmospheric burst. None. (Approved for removal from JP 1-02.)

nuclear incident. An unexpected incident involving a nuclear weapon, facility, or component, but not constituting a nuclear weapon(s) accident, resulting in any of the following: a. an increase in the possibility of explosion or radioactive contamination; b. errors committed in the assembly, testing, loading, or transportation of equipment, and/or the malfunctioning of equipment and materiel which could lead to an unintentional operation of all or part of the weapon arming and/or firing sequence, or which could lead to a substantial change in yield, or increased dud probability; and c. any act of God, unfavorable environment, or condition resulting in damage to the weapon, facility, or component. (Approved for incorporation into JP 1-02.)

nuclear proximity-surface burst. None. (Approved for removal from JP 1-02.)

nuclear warning message. None. (Approved for removal from JP 1-02.)

nuclear weapon(s) accident. An unexpected incident involving nuclear weapons or radiological nuclear weapon components that results in any of the following; a. accidental or unauthorized launching, firing, or use by United States forces or United States supported allied forces of a nuclear-capable weapon system that could create the risk of an outbreak of war; b. nuclear detonation; c. nonnuclear detonation or burning of a nuclear weapon or radiological nuclear weapon component; d. radioactive contamination; e. seizure, theft, loss, or destruction of a nuclear weapon or radiological nuclear weapon component, including jettisoning; and f. public hazard, actual or implied. (Approved for incorporation into JP 1-02.)

nuclear weapons surety. None. (Approved for removal from JP 1-02.)

peak overpressure. None. (Approved for removal from JP 1-02.)

permissive action link. None. (Approved for removal from JP 1-02.)

principal federal official. The federal official designated by the Secretary of Homeland Security to act as his/her representative locally to oversee, coordinate, and execute the Secretary's incident management responsibilities under Homeland Security Presidential Directive 5. Also called **PFO.** (Approved for incorporation into JP 1-02.)

radiant exposure. None. (Approved for removal from JP 1-02.)

radiation exposure state. None. (Approved for removal from JP 1-02.)

radiological accident. None. (Approved for removal from JP 1-02.)

radiological defense. None. (Approved for removal from JP 1-02.)

radiological environment. None. (Approved for removal from JP 1-02.)

residual capabilities assessment. None. (Approved for removal from JP 1-02.)

residual contamination. None. (Approved for removal from JP 1-02.)

surface zero. None. (Approved for removal from JP 1-02.)

technical nuclear forensics. The collection, analysis and evaluation of pre-detonation (intact) and post-detonation (exploded) radiological or nuclear materials, devices, and debris, as well as the immediate effects created by a nuclear detonation. (Approved for inclusion into JP 1-02.)

thermal energy. None. (Approved for removal from JP 1-02.)

thermal exposure. None. (Approved for removal from JP 1-02.)

thermal radiation. 1. The heat and light produced by a nuclear explosion. 2. Electromagnetic radiations emitted from a heat or light source as a consequence of its temperature. (Approved for incorporation into to JP 1-02.)

thermal X-rays. None. (Approved for removal from JP 1-02.)

toxic chemical, biological, or radiological attack. None. (Approved for removal from JP 1-02.)

types of burst. None. (Approved for removal from JP 1-02.)

Intentionally Blank

JOINT DOCTRINE PUBLICATIONS HIERARCHY

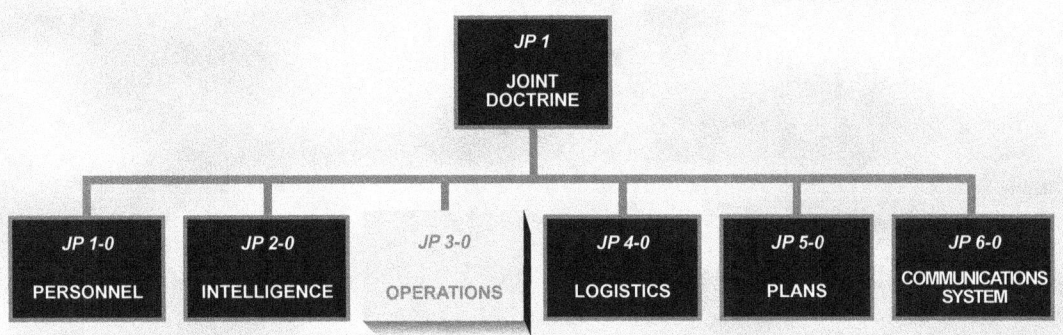

All joint publications are organized into a comprehensive hierarchy as shown in the chart above. **Joint Publication (JP) 3-41** is in the **Operations** series of joint doctrine publications. The diagram below illustrates an overview of the development process:

STEP #4 - Maintenance

- JP published and continuously assessed by users
- Formal assessment begins 24 27 months following publication
- Revision begins 3.5 years after publication
- Each JP revision is completed no later than 5 years after signature

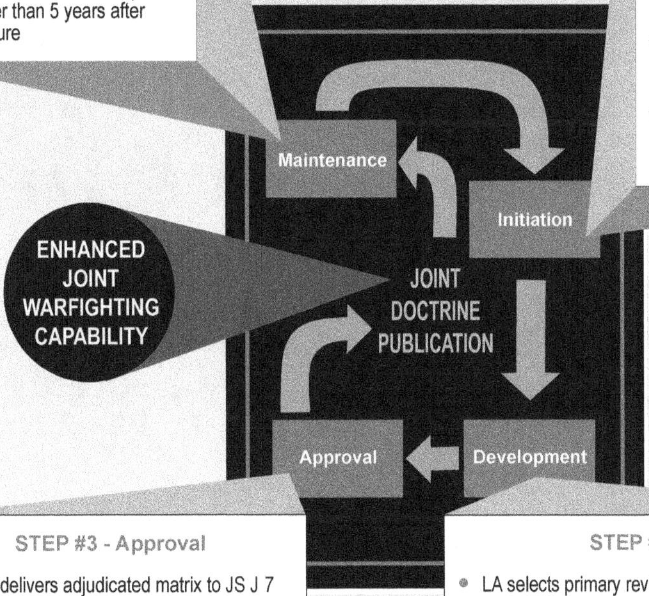

STEP #1 - Initiation

- Joint doctrine development community (JDDC) submission to fill extant operational void
- Joint Staff (JS) J 7 conducts front end analysis
- Joint Doctrine Planning Conference validation
- Program directive (PD) development and staffing/joint working group
- PD includes scope, references, outline, milestones, and draft authorship
- JS J 7 approves and releases PD to lead agent (LA) (Service, combatant command, JS directorate)

ENHANCED JOINT WARFIGHTING CAPABILITY

JOINT DOCTRINE PUBLICATION

Maintenance

Initiation

Approval

Development

STEP #3 - Approval

- JSDS delivers adjudicated matrix to JS J 7
- JS J 7 prepares publication for signature
- JSDS prepares JS staffing package
- JSDS staffs the publication via JSAP for signature

STEP #2 - Development

- LA selects primary review authority (PRA) to develop the first draft (FD)
- PRA develops FD for staffing with JDDC
- FD comment matrix adjudication
- JS J 7 produces the final coordination (FC) draft, staffs to JDDC and JS via Joint Staff Action Processing (JSAP) system
- Joint Staff doctrine sponsor (JSDS) adjudicates FC comment matrix
- FC joint working group